MW01171024

A Woman's Guide to Understanding Men

Decoding the Penis

How to Become the Woman No Man Can Ever Leave
and Create the Relationship You've Always Wanted

Marie Isabelle

DISCLAIMER AND/OR LEGAL NOTICES

The information presented herein represents the view of the author as of the date of publication. Due to the rate at which conditions change, the author reserves the right to alter and update her opinion based on such changes.

This material is general dating and relationship advice only and is not intended to be a substitute for professional medical or psychological advice. This book is for entertainment purposes only. This book contains sexually explicit material and is not intended for persons under the age of eighteen (18). This book also contains strong language and subject matter that may be offensive to some readers.

ISBN: 0692303219
ISBN 13: 9780692303214

Acknowledgements

This book is dedicated to the two men in my life, and the one who gave me life.

To my husband and best friend, the greatest man I have ever known and who's been my sole inspiration in writing this book. You are the wind at my back, the vessel that carries me through, and the ray of sunshine that guides me along the way. I am humbled by your love, and although words will never suffice in expressing my heart's gratitude, I will spend the rest of my days trying to show you how I love you "super much."

To my son, my little man, the one who stole my heart from the moment I laid eyes on him. You are my eyes, you light up my life and give it purposeful meaning. I am proud to call you my son and grateful that you call me mom. Like we always say every night: "You're the best… No, you're the bestest!"

And most importantly, to my father, the little Greek philosopher…The most dynamic and majestic man that ever was. The world was your classroom, you dreamed big, and lived even bigger. Thank you for teaching me how to bring imagination to life, showing me how to be a leader and to simply embrace the beauty of being different.

I wish to thank my dear friend, Marc Grobman, because without his assistance I wouldn't have had the motivation to finish this book. And for putting up with me on all those days I showed up at your office unannounced.

I also want to thank Cara Lockwood, who's not only a brilliant author, but also the very talented editor who worked her magic and helped me with this book. Thank you for being such an inspirational mentor and guiding me along the way.

And lastly, I'd like to thank my friends and all of those around me, who supported and encouraged me along the way. I also want to apologize for giving you all an earful on anything and everything relating to penis, and always having a mouthful to share. That didn't come out right, but you know what I mean. Okay, I'm done.

Introduction

Welcome to the *real* world of dating and relationships! Now, you may be wondering, "Why the emphasis on *real*? What other type of relationships *are* there besides real ones?" Obviously, it's *all* real. And when it comes to matters of the heart and it involves real, invested emotions, we mean business. The "real" part is emphasizing how we look at relationships, and there's a big difference between being realistic being a realist. The idea of being realistic is based on our own interpretation and personal perception of the realities we believe to be true. On the other hand, the realist mentality is based on scientific fact and the two are sort of like fact versus fiction. Now, I know that you may be thinking that you picked up a vagina science book by mistake, or that perhaps I'm off my vagina rocker. Albeit, I am guilty of having somewhat of a loopy vagina at times, I can assure you that this is definitely about relationships.

Truth be told, the common approach that people take in relationships is the realistic mindset, and it's only natural in relationships for our emotional investments to influence our mindset. Quite honestly, the thought of putting science and love together is a little unappealing. That is unless this science experiment promises to make love last, and add two inches to a partner's penis. In which case, we're all vagina ears… Okay, fine maybe not.

The reality is that when it comes to love, there really isn't an exact science, and we often go in with high hopes and do love the only way we know how. The only real knowledge and preparation we bring forth is the teachings from our upbringing and all the hoopla and societal standards that we collect along the way. And sometimes we find ever-lasting love, and sometimes we fall flat on our vagina faces. Our emotional investments cloud our mental clarity and our ability to acknowledge all the potential realities that we face in our relationships. We provide our bruised egos and hearts with nothing more than a little Band-Aid love, we scrape those deflated vaginas off the pavement and we're back in the game. We figure that at some point, the right shoe will come along and Cinderella will find her glass slipper.

I used to be one of those deflated vaginas, constantly throwing that hopeful love bitch into the game and trying my luck at making it last. I was that girl who wanted to get married and have kids. It finally happened at 29 years old, and within a couple of years I was married and had a newborn son. Similar to how we all do love, I took what I had accumulated from my upbringing and all the things that society teaches us about love and I trekked forward. Fast forward five years and I found myself divorced and once again discouraged. Quite honestly, if you asked me to define the exact cause of how and why my relationship failed, I'd say that it was an accumulation of many factors. Looking back now, many of these reasons are ones that are so common to many failed relationships. My ex-husband and I were never truly compatible and I was consumed with the idea of being in love, which often causes us to make hasty decisions. Truth be told, back then I saw no error in my ways, and like many people out there I thought that I had done all the right things. I mean, what could have gone wrong? I did love no differently than how everyone else does it. I followed the exact same recipe that society in general embraces. How are other people finding happily ever after and I'm finding failure after failure?

I was now a single mom who still wanted love, but now I was forced to change one important variable. I was no longer making choices that affected just me, I was making choices that would affect my son. This is the very thing that ignited a spark in my little vagina brain and it's what gave way to this entire journey. I started to question many of the practices that society preaches and thought to myself, surely there's got to be a better way. I have always been somewhat of a realist, but I realized that when it came to matters involving my heart, I didn't have the ability to apply the same realities to love. This is often the mentality that many people take in relationships and we have a tendency to follow the practices and standards that are put forth by society, because our very nature prompts us to want social acceptance. The idea that if everyone else is doing it this way, then I guess this is the way. Lacking that "realist" component, many of us don't realize that along with these standards and teachings, society also hands us the very grim statistics for relationship failure. Doing relationships as everyone else is does, puts us at a 50% chance for succeeding, or a 50% chance of it all falling to shit. This isn't something people think about when they're going into relationships, and they simply go in with great intentions and follow the social pack. Think about it: if you were told that a flight you were about to board on had a 50% chance of crashing and only half the passengers would make it out alive, would you still board on that plane? I don't know what everyone else's vagina plans on doing, but my vagina (and ass) would be headed straight to the nearest bus depot!

The reality is that when we have no emotional investments, we have clarity to make better judgments. No one wants to invest in a stock that has a 50/50 chance of crashing, and no one sure as heck wants to get on a plane that has a 50/50 chance of crashing, yet when it comes to emotional lack of clarity we don't see these things. No one ever goes into a relationship thinking that it's going to fail. We have faith and we follow our hearts. We like to believe that the love we have found is like no other, and that these shitty failure numbers are reflective of other people who don't have the same kind of special love that we've found. Ask any divorced vagina out there, and she will tell you that prior to wanting to strangle that annoying puny penis of his, she too had found that crazy magical love that we all talk about. Once upon a time, she was that determined bitch that was going to defy those odds and her vagina was going to walk on water and march on over to the promised land of Happily Ever After.

It was after my divorce that I became motivated and inspired to devote my study to relationships. Already having a psychology background, I invested my focus on behavioral psychology and the 'psyche of the sexes'. I was determined to find out two things: Why relationships fail, and what do men and women each look for in a relationship. My first finding was that relationships fail for a shit load of reasons… I know pretty helpful right? Actually the answer to both tie into one another and this is what I concluded:

It's our emotional investments that cause us to be guarded in relationships and assume a "self-serving" mentality in an effort to secure our own needs. People don't like to feel vulnerable, so it's a natural instinct to always place conditions on our love offerings and to ensure that we don't go without our own feedings. I found that because of this, it prevents us from having the ability to truly provide our partner with what they need for ultimate fulfillment and happiness. One other major factor is that both men and women base their offerings in the relationship, on their own mentality and needs. A woman naturally assumes that a man does love in the same way that our vagina does and we try to use our female formula to give him fulfillment. A man does the same thing and presents himself in the only way he knows how. While we're strumming our vagina strings, he's fiddling with his tool box and penis pliers and the two formulations never quite meet the unique needs of each partner. Sure, people find a way to make it happen and statistics say that 50% of us have nailed love on the mark. For the rest of us, we lack this valuable knowledge and we never see a need to do things any differently.

It's all of these experiences and knowledge that helped me change my outlook and become a realist on love. My philosophy for relationships is that there's two sides to every coin and one side is nothing like the other. If we want to change our chances at love we need to chance how we approach love...because when we remove ourselves from the societal common following, we also remove ourselves from the 50% failure statistics. Think about it, if you're forced to cheat on an exam from the person next to you who's only pulling a 50% in that class, it would be foolish to expect that you would Ace that exam. Right?

I'll bring you up to speed on my love story and journey... Having assumed a new mindset towards relationships I was damn ready for the next penis that came knocking on love's door. And one day, along came a guy who not only knocked on my door, but swept me off my feet and knocked me on my ass. I knew damn well that I found something good and I was determined to do all the right things and make this shit work. I was pulling out all the stops, and all the vagina tricks... okay, maybe not exactly that quick, because I held turning the tricks out as my secret weapon. The point is, that I vowed to myself that I would take all the mistakes I ever made and use those as a marker for what I didn't want to repeat. I also took all the studying and knowledge I had collected and I vowed to apply this new approach to this relationship. Trust me when I say that my vagina invested a great deal of time coming up with this formula and an approach that I knew would work. And I wasn't wrong, because this is the guy who I now call my wonderful and amazing, stupendous and stellar, magnificent and majestic husband. After seven fantabulous years my husband and I are happier today than the day we first met. We are best friends and sidekicks for life, and we are forever embarking on explorations and endless journeys. We have both been very dedicated to investing in this dynamic and have spent great efforts building what we have and we continue to invest equal efforts into maintaining it. Honestly, our relationship is like a dream come true and even up until this very day, I have to pinch my vagina-self just to make sure that it's all real.

Over the past seven years I have also been practicing my coaching on sex and relationships, because we know damn well those two go hand in hand and the penis wants to make sure we know this. I have worked with both couples and single individuals and I devote a great deal of time blogging about relationships online, providing a ton of advice and sharing the love secrets. When I first set out to write this book, I knew that I wanted it to be based on a combination of actual findings and studies on relationships, my personal views and interpretations and also real life feedback from men in the dating world. This book has been four years in the making, and I invested a great deal of time canvassing men from all walks of life. I really did my homework out in the field, and anywhere and anytime I could find myself a male source, be it online through dating sites, blogs and forums or even in person, I picked penis brains extensively and took detailed vagina notes. This is why I'm confident that this book brings a no holds barred, no bullshit, balanced and realistic take on the world of men and relationships. And this is where you and I come in, and our newly formed vagina sisterhood. Our mission is to become realist vaginas and as such we will look to dissect and question all the areas that people often ignore, to shed our old ineffective practices and replace them with new more effective ones that will also help us create a customized approach that is tailored specifically for a man's unique needs. We no longer have an interest to follow the common tide and do things the same way that best friend Becky and everyone else is doing love…because Becky may mean well, but she too is following all the same crap and plus that bitch is at the cougar singles club every weekend which is someplace our vaginas don't belong! We are no longer standard vaginas, and we are taking those bitches and turning them into epic vaginas!

I can assure you that the approach I've developed is a recipe for relationship success. How can I be so sure? I'm so sure that I will bet my vagina on it! The key is in the idea of *Decoding the Penis* and learning all there is to know about men and their unique needs. Using this knowledge we develop a unique recipe that will provide a man with ultimate fulfillment and happiness. Now, don't think that our vaginas are being neglected and it's all about the penis…HECK NO! Those bitches need to eat too, and we deserve to gain all the same benefits from the relationship. Rest assured that we will cover it all and learn how to communicate our needs and create the type of energy in our relationship that will motivate a man to rise to the occasion and invest his greatest efforts into the vagina's happiness! I know that I'm starting to sound like an infomercial here… "Not only do you get one, but two, two for the price of one." And no we all won't end up with two penis door prizes so calm those vaginas. Heck, we're still trying to unlock the one we have, who has time to fiddle with two?

Okay, let's focus here because we have work to do. As I said before, our mission is to embark on a journey of dissecting it all! Short of physically dissecting a penis, we will leave no stone (or testicle) left unturned. An epic vagina knows that sometimes the best way it may not be through the front door and we will do what it takes to unlock that code and influence the exact results we are seeking in our relationships. And the only promise you need to make is that you will come with an open mind, and a willingness to look at things from many different perspectives. Perhaps you embrace all it all, and maybe you take little bits and pieces that you find fitting to your vagina comforts. You have the freedom to pick and choose what makes sense to you… It's just like apple picking at the orchard. You pick and choose the apples that look the best to you, and you place them into your basket. Trust me, my vagina won't be offended if you turn down one of my advice apples, and I'm not one of those pushy vaginas that will try to sneak extra unwanted apples into your unsuspecting basket when you're not looking. Speaking of my vagina characteristics, I'm sure by now you've gotten a feel for my style and my personality. I will tell you now that I am not only a realist, I'm also someone who calls it like it is...I'm outspoken...to a fault and my humor is a mix between sarcastic and funny as shit. Hey what can I say, my vagina has stand up skills (yes in this story my vagina has legs) I also happen to rely on artistic articulation, which stands for sometimes cursing if it happens to be most effective...oh and I talk about penis a lot and I don't always call him by his first name and may use cock or dick interchangeably. After all, isn't this why we're all here? Hopefully I haven't lost you by now because my vagina ego hates hosting to crickets. So basically, you just gotta go with the flow and take me in stride. I'm a firm believer that if a woman takes no issue with handling a penis or putting it in her mouth, then she should be able to openly talk about it...but not at the same time and with a mouthful of penis, because that's bad vagina manners.

Alright, so who's ready to distance themselves from those crappy relationship failure statistics? Who's open to changing our common vagina approach, develop new and effective practices that are much more penile friendly and to up our successes and chances at love? I can't hear those vaginas?! WHO'S READY FOR A RELATIONSHIP REVOLUTION? WE ARE MOTIVATED VAGINAS...HEAR US ROAR! Now someone pass us a penis and let's get to work! Okay, maybe not so fast... Sorry, I always tend to get carried away during these vagina pep rallies... Put those penises down for now, because we've got real work to do. Let's get these fired up vaginas on the love bus, because we're taking ourselves a little unconventional field trip to the promised land of Happily Ever After (Hurry it up ladies... or we'll miss the penis exhibit)!

Contents

Appendix:

Chapter One

Decoding the Penis

Why a Book on Men? What about Our Needs as Women?

It's a well-known fact that in any relationship there needs to be a healthy balance where both partners equally find fulfillment and happiness. So if balance is the key, then what's the deal with placing all this emphasis on men, their needs and all their penile behaviors? After all, women have needs too! Here's the deal: we often don't recognize how we can be negatively influenced and impacted by certain factors in our environment. We may want to have a balanced relationship, but it's in our female nature to protect our emotional vulnerabilities, and we often don't recognize how this inadvertently causes us to place conditions on our love. To an extent, we all do it and it's only human nature. In any serious relationship, our behaviors are governed by three variables:

1. **Our Female Nature**: As women, we often follow our instincts, and we tend to lead with what we know and what is familiar to us.

2. **Our Social Environment**: Societal influence plays a huge role in our lives and accounts for many of our learned traits and behaviors. These are developed through our social teachings and our social environment.

3. **Fear**: As humans, in order to be survivalists, our brain is hard-wired to detect impending threats and this triggers an automatic fear response. This is what also controls our sense of comfort and security.

What ends up happening is that we go into relationships with our unique female perspective and way of doing things. Women place priority on love and security, and our "love offerings" are often limited to the level of comfort and security we find in the relationship. If a woman is unable to feel comfortable, she is less inclined to extend herself to accommodate her partner's needs. Emotional security in the relationship is a fundamental need for a woman and we often place precedence on fulfilling this need in the early stages of commitment. It's never a woman's intention to take a self- serving approach to love and unless she achieves ultimate security, her "unconditional love offerings" actually come with the condition that her offerings remain within her comfort zone. This is where many women miss out on the valuable opportunity to truly provide a man with ultimate happiness and while a woman is busy focusing on her needs, he is left feeling unsatisfied and unfulfilled. It's important to understand that men take the same approach, and if a man feels as though his immediate fundamental needs are not being met, he too is less inclined to fully accommodate his partner's needs. The best way to motivate a man is to ensure that his gas tank is filled up and he's fully equipped to endure the road trip and focus on fulfilling his partner's needs. People often don't realize what unconditional love really requires of them. Unconditional love means fulfilling your partner's needs. It means transitioning from a self-serving love approach into one that's selfless in nature. This is where we insert a bookmark, and make note of where we can benefit from taking on a different approach in our relationships. It doesn't happen overnight, and one vagina doesn't just come busting out with all these unconditional love offerings. These things take time to build, they require a couple to work together and help one another achieve this level in their union.

It's based on the notion "help me, so in turn I can help you. Help me develop the tools that are required to help me fulfill your needs so you can fulfill mine." This is exactly what we will look to accomplish throughout the book, and it's all about learning how to truly love a man unconditionally in the way he needs to be loved and teaching him how to return the love in the unique way we need to be loved. When you really think about it, doesn't this approach sound like it has better odds of success than just blasting him with female feedings? It's like tossing him a vagina and saying, "Here, try this on for size" and expecting him to be content with his newly customized mangina happiness.

Don't think that this misunderstood approach to unconditional love is exclusive to women, because men make the same mistakes. They sometimes act selfishly about love. There is one unique difference that sets men apart from women, and it's how they achieve fulfillment and happiness. Men prioritize love in their own unique way, and they place value on certain needs over others as having primary importance to their overall happiness.

Society, family and friends don't give us the insight we need about men. So, when we experience challenges in meeting a partner's needs, we're left feeling frustrated and not understanding why our efforts are not good enough…or why we're not good enough.

The common perception is that "if my partner really loves me, then my offerings should be good enough and he should be happy with what I bring to the relationship." But, the fact is, fulfilling your partner's needs has nothing to do with who YOU are, it has to do with what your partner wants. If you're trying to satisfy his needs and your approach is based on your own needs, then you're using the wrong ingredients in your relationship.

Think about it, banana bread requires bananas, and if we were to use oranges then it would be orange bread. No amount of oranges will turn that damn thing into a banana loaf. Like I said before, as women we are already well versed with our female needs, and this will come in handy when we are looking to educate the penis on the tools he requires to get the job done (in more ways than one). If we make our partners happy, they'll want to make us happy, it's as simple as that.

Love Barter Tripod: Change Your Approach & Change Your Odds

Here's the deal…In today's world, this common approach to love comes with 50/50 odds for success. I'm sure it's safe to say that you have no interest in such crappy odds, and it's not enough to believe that you will be the exception to these numbers, you must take a proactive approach and become that exception. The only way to make this happen is to find an alternate approach to negotiating love in the relationship, and developing a formula that will be serving to each partner's happiness. So how does one make this happen? It basically comes down to three Love Barter Principles:

- **Become An Expert On His/Her Needs**: You're already an expert on women, you've lived with your vagina an entire lifetime and you are well in tune with your female needs. What you need is to gain a better understanding and insight into what it takes to truly make your partner 100% happy.

- **Learn How To Love Unconditionally**: I'm not talking about unlimited love, because bountiful love that comes from a guarded heart is not unconditional. Unconditional love is based on a partner's needs and happiness and not on our own fears and comfort needs. We will develop the tools to make this happen, and learn how to lead with our strengths and not our fears, which often become our weaknesses.

- **Successfully Create A Unisex Friendly Relationship Environment**: By developing positive practices and focusing on each other's needs, no one person in a partnership takes priority over the other. Mutual happiness is achieved when each partner focuses on one another as a priority and not on themselves.

Think about it, if your partner invested even more efforts into the love and affections that he gives you, wouldn't this be a good thing? When has anyone ever complained about a spouse who was fully engaged and invested in their partner's happiness 100%? You'll never hear a man say, "Geez, I'm so sick and tired of all the blow jobs my wife keeps offering up." And just the same, you'll never hear a woman say, "Ew, I hate it when he treats me like a Queen." Trust me when I say that it's totally possible, and a very doable reality for us all.

So, the reason why we make it all about men and their needs is because for far too long we as women have unknowingly focused on what *we* want and have continuously missed the mark on cracking the code to a man's ultimate happiness. There's a big difference between being happy and that of ultimate happiness, which is what we're striving to achieve. We've congregated amongst ourselves and sought answers from our female peers. Best friend Becky may have some encouraging advice on love to share, and maybe even some tips on the stellar blow job skills that she's perfected... but unless she's recently been crowned Penis Ambassador Of The World, then, we need to stop taking her advice. It all starts by shedding the misguided idea that a "happy wife" means a "happy life" for the man and it's all about him catering exclusively to what we want. We've held men hostage too long when it comes to their happiness. The reality is that a man's happiness means just as much to him, he is equally put off when his happiness is not intact, and this in part is why many men decide to leave relationships.

It may seem like it's all about a guy and his needs, but believe it or not, you have the ability to influence the exact results you seek simply by the investments you make towards a man's happiness. The human brain is quite responsive to positive stimuli and being rewarded, and you can prompt positive behaviors from a spouse simply by the energy that you put forth. A truly content and happy man is a motivated man. He is inspired to return his gratitude to the one source that feeds his happiness, and he invests all of his efforts back into his partner. It basically becomes a mutual investment with each partner adhering to the Love Barter Tripod Principles, and a couple working as a team. Listen, the psychology behind it is pretty clear cut. This is how the human brain works, and the way to a man's heart is actually through his mind. I can tell you from first-hand experience, that this does work and it's the exact approach I took back when I first met my husband. I vowed to make his happiness my priority, and the contagious relationship energy prompted him to do the same. Seven magical years later, he has remained my priority, I have remained his and we have remained stupendously happy after all these years.

Now I know that for a clever vagina it doesn't take a whole day to recognize sunshine. If making it all about 'him' inspires him to make it all about you, then your epic vagina is making it happen! Am I right? EXACTLY! So let's get to cracking on this penile code, shall we?

The Penis Vs. Society: Ditch Everything You've Been Taught

Based on the Three Love Barter Principles we touched on earlier, this chapter focuses on the first principle of becoming an expert on a man's needs. Now, before we get started, there are a couple of things we need to discuss. For starters, because we are women, we obviously are impartial to seeing things through vagina specs. As such, we need to make an effort to remain open-minded, step out of our vaginas temporarily, so we can truly appreciate seeing things through a man's perspective. Obviously, we all bring our past and present experiences on men and relationships, along with a shitload of knowledge that we've acquired through our social environment. The problem with what society feeds us, is that a lot of it is misguided information. You and I are not trash collectors, so instead of weeding through all the BS, we are simply hitting the reset button and creating a new knowledge base on men, based on their views and not society's.

If we stuck with many of these misguided social theories we'd all still be trying to perfect our skills in the kitchen based on the notion of "the way to a man's heart is through his stomach." Um, no, it's not, and unless there's some sort of secret access tunnel between his stomach and his penis, then the key to a man's happiness is not best served on the kitchen table. Well, that is unless you're serving it up in heels, and you're the main course. The reality is that men place their primary needs at the top of the list, and baking skills don't make the top of the list…so for now, screw the muffin recipes! Sure any guy would be elated with this added perk, but if a man had to choose between amazing sex and home cooking? He'd happily settle for a burnt roast and lumpy mash potatoes any day of the week as long as it came with a side of stupendous vagina tricks in the bedroom. I'm not saying that these type of nurturing qualities, such as knowing how to cook, have no value. It all has value. It's just that society has a way of focusing in on just one acceptable variable, and overlooking many things that touch on the "taboo' topic of sex.

Men tend to gravitate to qualities in a mate that are supportive of their primary needs, and it's hardly news that sex sits at the top of their list. There's always been this notion that when a man looks to settle down, he seeks out a woman with wholesome "good girl" qualities, someone who would make a "good wife" by society's standards. If "good" is also in reference to the skills a woman possesses in the bedroom, then yes, every guy wants that. Sure, there's some justification to the "good girl" theory, and what guy wouldn't want a mature woman who was loyal and nurturing? However, in today's world, men have become more inclined to remain true to their needs, and the male version for an "ideal mate" is what coined the phrase "a lady in the street, and a freak in the sheets." It's not to imply that every man wants a 'freak' in his life and this quality is simply reflective of sexual confidence in a woman. Obviously, a man brings forth many needs and other than just sexual in nature. The ideal relationship quotient for a man is one that is supportive of ALL his needs combined. And a guy takes no issue with a woman who is sexually expressive, especially if it's something exclusive to the committed relationship. The fact that men strongly identify with their sexuality may not be news to any of us, but what may be news to many women is that men don't gravitate to sex entirely for the reasons that we often assume. Contrary to common belief, the penis is no shallow dude, nor does he have a one track mind. The relationship that a man has with sex and with his sexuality runs much deeper and beyond the head of his penis and it actually ties into his heart.

The Emotional Penis: Understanding the Relationship that Men Have with Sex

Now, I'll let that one sink in for a bit...I know that many of you may think that this was a typo, and instead of "heart," I meant to say that it ties into his testicles. It's no typo, sisters! And even though his testicles also play a role in all of this, sex for a man is not just a physical affair and it plays a big role in how a man achieves emotional fulfillment. There really exists an "emotional penis" and unlike Bigfoot, it is very real. For a man, all the physical and mental aspects that come along with sex do not solely serve his erection. Before we dive into all the needs and wants that men bring into the relationship, I want to first analyze what sex means to a man. So what exactly is this tale of the emotional penis?

Well, it's like this...As humans, men and women alike are heavily influenced and affected by physiological factors such as our hormones. They directly impact our sexual drive, our libido, and control our responsiveness to mental and physical stimuli and our behaviors. However, when comparing the two sexes, men have women beat by a far penis...I mean... mile. The reason being is that men have about seven to eight times more testosterone in their bodies than women do. This sex hormone influences everything from his penis to his brain, and all the behaviors in between.

For women, we have the unfortunate pleasures of a monthly menstrual cycle, which causes hormonal fluctuations throughout the month. This has a direct effect on our female sex drive and libido. Hence the reason why some days our horny little vaginas are seeking out that penis for play time, and other days the only penis we want is one coated in chocolate. Due to this hormonal roller coaster, our vaginas are up and down and all over the place like a faulty electrical circuit. And all the while a man who doesn't share in this unfortunate ride, is pretty much always up and erect and idling nearby, ready for action. This is why women are better suited as survivalists in the unfortunate circumstance of a sexual drought. We go into survival mode quite easily if we have to, and life resumes with little complications. The penis, on the other hand, doesn't fair quite as well, and in the wake of a sexual drought all the male hormones cause the penis to become delirious. Just ask any guy and he would tell you that in order to survive he requires air, food, water and a vagina. Actually, a desperate penis would easily give up any other lifeline, if it meant saving his sex resource. The overly dramatic penis will also tell you that he can die from one missed meal. You and I know that he's not gonna die, but try telling that to the hypochondriac penis who is already taking out an obituary and picking out a penis casket. If you think that this sounds funny, what's even more comical is that a guy's male ego would have him picking out a ten- inch casket when he probably only needs one half that size.

Okay, fun time is over, back to business…It's this very prominent level of testosterone that not only controls the male sex brain and a man's sexual behaviors, but it also impacts many of his other needs and behaviors. As women, we are able to separate many of our other needs from our sexual brain, but for a man it directly ties into how he achieves fulfillment in many different areas. Men rely on the sexual relationship as a way of expressing themselves emotionally, and achieving emotional fulfillment. Now this may sound like a load of doo doo that guys are trying to feed us, in an effort to squeeze in some extra blow jobs and pass them off as a gesture of love. However, this is very real to a man, as real as his male ego is to him as well. We often hear about this mystical "male ego," and all we envision is a bunch of guys standing around in some locker room all bragging about the size of their penises and their sexual conquests. However, the male ego is something very real to a man, and it's the very unique relationship that a man has with his male emotional identity. The male ego has a direct correlation with a man's hormones, and it feeds his emotional needs. This emotional element of male sexuality ties directly into a man's masculinity and male identity, and it creates a dependency for this element to be nurtured. This is not just reflective of a guy's male identity in the bedroom, but in the overall relationship. Men have an innate need to identify with their sexuality both as an individual and as a male spouse. A man needs to feel as though he is able to assert his masculinity and provide for his female spouse's needs. Not only sexually, but also as a protector and a sole provider to all of her needs. Men rely on sex and their sexuality to feed their emotional needs in the following ways:

It Feeds His Confidence:
Men have a need to have their male ego stroked, as this is the source that feeds his confidence and his self-esteem. Men require the ability to be emotionally expressive through the act of having sex. They also identify with their male presence in the relationship, through intimacy, and his ability to satisfy his female partner. A man's sexual offerings and the strong relationship he naturally has with sex, causes him to want to share his male offerings with a spouse, and for her to be accepting of the unique male relationship he has with his sexuality. A man's sexual prowess and his need to perform sexually *are* an emotional need. When he feels as though he has fulfilled his role as the male in the relationship, it grants him with a sense of accomplishment and it feeds his confidence. The fact that a man's sexuality ties into his emotional needs, exposes him to feeling vulnerable during the act of sexual intimacy. When he feels as though he has fulfilled his role and served his purpose as a "man," this makes a man feel empowered and that his partner has a 'need' for him in the relationship…A need that only he can fulfill.

It Makes Him Feel Desired and Accepted:
Men need to feel desired as much as women do. A man relies on sexual intimacy as a source for fulfillment and his need of feeling desired. When a man receives sexual affection, it gives him a great sense of desirability, and it's because of his strong inner relationship with his sexual identity. He feels as though he brings a very unique offering that only he can fulfill for his spouse, and the

need she has for him makes him feel special. Men are very sexually expressive, and rely on sexual affection in the relationship as their greatest source for fulfillment. When a man feels fully embraced by his partner and that she is accepting of his entire male identity, it grants him with a great sense of security in the relationship.

It's a Natural Way to Show Affection:

Men not only rely on sexual affection to feel desired, it's also a very natural way for a man to show his affections. It comes quite naturally to a man to express himself sexually, and to share his affections through sexual intimacy. Men may not always be well versed with their words and verbally expressing their emotions, but connecting on an intimate level is a natural way for a man to show his affections and devotions to his mate. During sexual intimacy, a man feels most connected to his spouse. He views his devotion to the exclusive sexual relationship as a sign of his affections and his commitment. Not all men know how to write love letters or poems, but they all know how to express themselves in the bedroom and to devote all of their focus on their partner during sexual intimacy. Men place a high value on this offering, and they feel most rewarded when their partner recognizes these efforts as a form of expressing their affections. Sometimes the grandest gestures are not the loudest, but they are always the most heartfelt and sincere.

Sexual Rejection Wounds More Than His Ego:

A man places a high value on the sexual relationship because he relies on it emotionally. This is why men don't take well to sexual rejection. It's not just his ego that takes a hit and makes him sulk, it also weighs heavily on his heart. If a man feels as though he's not fulfilling his role as a "man," he begins to feel unloved and unaccepted. The overall relationship may be in good standing, but if he's unable to express himself in the one area that means the most to him, he takes this personally and it has a big impact on him emotionally. Obviously, it's not to say that a woman can never decline a partner's sexual advances. Contrary to male belief, not every waking moment of the day is an opportune moment for sex. However, if the overall relationship environment prevents a man from freely expressing his sexuality and connecting on an intimate sexual level, this directly impacts his sense of security and his overall happiness. The male ego places a direct correlation between sexual rejection and a lack of emotional fulfillment for love in the union. This affects a man on every level: his confidence is compromised, his male ego and his manhood take a hit, he develops a sense of feeling undesired and that his spouse does not have a need for his unique male offerings in the relationship. This can make a man feel emotionally disconnected and unattached from his spouse emotionally. He takes all of these variables as a measurement for the love a woman has for him, and if it is lacking, then he does not feel loved in the relationship.

The male ego doesn't always know how to express these discontent emotions, and as women we simply view his sulky behaviors as a guy just being a baby because he didn't get sex. For a man, he often doesn't see it as just the sex being denied, he sees it as a personal rejection. The sulkiness comes from his ego and heart lashing out emotionally. Well that, and perhaps his backed up balls lashing out too, but it's important for us women to understand that it often runs beyond just his frustrated testicles. If a man feels as though the relationship is not supportive of the tight bond he shares with his sexuality, he interprets this as an overall rejection for what he truly represents. This is what often causes a man to become resentful and to pull away from the relationship. In order for a man to feel fully content in his heart, he must also feel as though the sexual relationship is in good. His overall happiness is dependent on him gaining fulfillment of both his sexual needs and emotional needs in unison. So there you have it, the untold story of the emotional penis. Pretty crazy stuff right? Who knew that there was so much psychology behind a simple erection?

What Men Need

So now that we have better insight into the unique emotional relationship men have with sex, it allows us to be a little more understanding and forgiving of a man's penile behaviors. Let's kick things up a notch and look at all the needs and wants that men bring into the relationship. A man will prioritize his needs and wants based on importance. His primary needs are what he deems as being fundamental to his happiness and he places these at the top of his priority list. Along with this list comes the "wants," which are representative of the qualities men seek out in a mate and the relationship characteristics that they commonly seek. The ultimate goal for a man is to find a relationship that is supportive of all their needs, and one that provides them with happiness. We often view men as being simple creatures and having simple needs. Men may take a very logical approach to love, but they still share many commonalities with women, even though women are often viewed as more complex. What separates men from women is that men have their own unique way of achieving fulfillment and happiness.

There's no denying that it takes a truly epic woman to embrace it all, cater to every element and to grant a man with true happiness. This is where you and I come in: we're going above and beyond and our epic vaginas are shooting for the stars! (yes in this story the vagina also flies.) Now, I know that it may seem like all the emphasis is being placed on the penis and our vaginas are taking second fiddle. I assure you, that this is not the case. Understand that sometimes the best way in is not through the front door (the vagina interprets this metaphorically versus the penis who may take it in literal context). And it may seem like it's all about men and their needs, but the approach of investing our primary efforts into a man's happiness has a way of paying itself forward, and it motivates a man to invest in his partner's happiness. You see? The epic vagina is always two steps ahead! So rest assured, the vagina does not go neglected…for now let's put those vaginas on ice and continue on cracking this penis code shall we? So what exactly is it that men need?

The Tripod Quotient

As humans we rely on a tripod quotient as a source of achieving fulfillment. For a man the tripod is comprised of his brain, his heart and his penis, and all three are interconnected with one another. A man relies on these three sources to provide him with fulfillment of his needs and to achieve happiness. Similar to women, men rely on all the same variables in a relationship, such as love, friendship, security, loyalty, respect, sex, and all the little added variables that feed into a man's overall happiness. Like I said before, it's just that men have their own unique way of achieving fulfillment, and there are certain variables that are characteristic and exclusive to their male primary needs. In order for a man to achieve and maintain fulfillment and happiness, he needs to have all three of these sources appealed to and kept in rotation. The most important source of them all is the brain. It's the brain that processes everything, through thought and stimuli the brain acts like a mission control centre to a man's overall operations. This is why appealing to the brain is most important, because when a woman knows how to penetrate a man's mind, she has the ability to override his entire operation. Like they say "perception is reality," and we as women have the ability to influence a man's perception, his sense of reality and his overall happiness.

We often focus on a man's heart and his penis when we look to fulfill his needs and feed his happiness. In reality, the male brain should be our primary focus. The heart and penis are simply passengers who are along for the ride, and it's the brain that actually steers and controls the entire male vessel. The perfect quotient is one that appeals to all three, but the brain must never be neglected.

He Needs Sex:

Well, this is hardly ground breaking news, so no need to alert the media. We already discussed the emotional elements of sex, and it's a big reason why men have such a strong association with sex. Obviously, the emotional aspects are not the only reason why men gravitate to sex with such propensity, and the physical and mental aspects of sex are of equal importance to the penis. When it comes to sex, men rely on many variables and forms of stimuli. The male sex brain is stimulated through thought, sight and touch. The perfect sex storm for a man is when all of these variables are appealed to in unison.

Stimulating His Sex Brain: Men Rely on Physical Attraction

We often view the penis as controlling the man, but it's the actual brain that has the ability to hijack his entire operations and to control his behaviors. Men happen to be very visual creatures and they rely heavily on visuals as a form of mental stimulation. The reason why men place so much emphasis on physical attraction is because their brain feeds off of the intense chemistry that is created by all the visuals. This is why men like the idea of having sex "with the lights on." In complete darkness the penis is left solely to his imagination, when the penis can see for himself all the virtual realities of a sexual encounter, it intensifies the experience to an all-time high. You see, the penis doesn't have eyes, so he relies on the brain as his source for sight. These visuals are processed by the brain, sending a message down to the sleeping penis, and waking him up with a clobber to the head...Presto! An erection is born! This is a foreplay appetizer for the male sex brain, and the visuals and mental stimuli are what create an anticipatory sequence that leads up to the main sex-course. This is why men need and rely on physical attraction, as it directly feeds into fulfilling their sexual needs.

DON'T: Miss out on appealing to a man's natural mental responders. Men need to feel sex, they need to see sex, and they want to enjoy all the mental highs and stimuli that is created in their sex brain.

DO: Keep this note handy as we will discuss it further in the sex chapter. Having the ability to penetrate a man's sex brain is one of the most effective tools for a woman, and an epic vagina never misses out on such an opportunity.

The Penis Explorer: The Need for Sexual Variety

When it comes to sex, the male brain enjoys the mental stimulation as much as the penis enjoys being physically stimulated. It goes without saying that every guy enjoys all the sexual chemistry that a new relationship brings to their life. Every relationship starts out like a rocket being launched into outer space, and the simple fact that it's new and unchartered territory is what makes the sex so great. Chemistry is flying in every direction, his pants are on fire, her panties are burning up and it's enough to have the fire department on stand-by. By nature men are natural hunters, they are a sexually exploring breed, and they have this innate need to achieve fulfillment through their sexual conquests.

Men have great comfort with their sexuality, and this allows them to explore their curious sexual nature. They have a natural tendency to want to explore their sexual desires and fantasies. For a man, the mental aspects of sex create an intense euphoric high, and he's always looking for new ways to replicate this sense of euphoria and maintain that high level. If the sex remains unchanged over a prolonged period of time, so does the mental stimuli and it starts to provide less of a gratifying dose to his sex brain. This is where the theory of "spicing up the sex and variety in the bedroom" comes from. By rotating sexual variety, it provides the male sex brain with a constant surge and high level of mental stimuli and sexual arousal.

This is where we sometimes misinterpret this unique male need as meaning a need for "promiscuity" and various sexual partners. The topic of sex is something I often write about in my blog, and I always receive tons of feedback and messages from both men and women on this very issue. I have spoken with women who struggled to understand their partner, when he expressed an interest to explore new ideas in the bedroom. Some women see this as a sign that he's no longer happy with the sexual relationship, or that he has grown bored of the sex. I often have men who also reach out to me online, sharing their stories and struggles in the sexual relationship. Men who have tried to express an interest in exploring new ideas, and not getting the reception they had hoped for from their spouse. One fella explained, "She's not really comfortable with the idea of trying new things and she's not open to my suggestion of trying sex toys." Another guy shared his situation by saying, "She thinks I'm not happy with our sex life because I'm asking for new stuff. I love my wife very much, and I don't want to be with any other woman, I only want her. I just want to try some different things, things that I'm kind of curious about."

Here's the deal on men and sexual exploration…The simple explanation that I always give women is that men just love sex! It's in a man's curious nature to be sexually exploring, and it's his excitement that makes him want to discover all the magical potentials and possibilities that the sexual relationship has to offer. Relationships don't stand still, they are constantly evolving and growing, and men look to also have the sexual relationship evolve and to continue to grow as well. Truth be told, there is actually great value that a monogamous relationship brings to a man's life. Many men will agree that the best sex is often found in a committed relationship, because it allows them to finally shed all their inhibitions and have the comfort to fully explore their sexual desires within the security of the relationship. A man can easily find fulfillment in a monogamous sexual relationship, when it provides him with the ability to explore his sexual desires and have sexual diversity.

My husband is always a great sounding board for me when it comes to providing male insight. During one of our discussions he summed it up the best, and this is how he explained it:

"The fact that it's something new, is what makes the sex so great in the beginning. The new sexual relationship comes with great ease, and it doesn't take much effort on a woman's part to meet a man's sexual needs. After the newness starts to transition and the relationship grows, that's when the sex needs to grow with the relationship, too. I mean, vanilla ice cream is a great treat and sure it tastes good, but after having it the same way for so long we're looking for something more...new ways to enjoy our vanilla ice cream and maybe even turn it into an ice cream sundae. We want to try some sprinkles on that ice cream, maybe some nuts, and even some whip cream—" (And perhaps even some whip cream on his nuts...sorry, I interjected with that one) ***"If it's the same thing over and over again, at some point it starts to lose its appeal. After so long, we're looking for new ways to enjoy our ice cream, and some new sex tricks in the bedroom. We're excited to explore all the possibilities, find new ways to have sex, and explore new ideas. Sexual variety creates unpredictability, and we like that because it makes it exciting. We're more than willing to be an active contributor and invest in whatever efforts are required, but it takes two in order to make it happen."***

And there we have it, straight from the penis source. And this sentiment echoes through much of the feedback I get from men when they write in and share their relationship stories. Sex is often viewed as a way to physically and emotionally connect with one another. People often equate the quality of a healthy sex life by measuring the sexual frequency. If we're having sex 3-5 times a week, then the relationship must be in good standing right? What many people often overlook is all the added little elements, the things that take vanilla ice cream and turn it into a supreme ice cream sundae. All the mental aspects of sex, the visuals and added stimulants, and the exploration and variety that men gravitate to. This is why men also gravitate to a woman who is confident, because confidence equates having the comfort to unleash her sexual persona and explore sexually. The perfect sexual relationship for a man is one that combines and balances all these variables, and keeps them on a healthy rotation. This to the penis is like having found heaven, and when a man finds this, happiness follows. Now I know this may seem like a shitload of content and discussion on sex, but if it's important to a man and it's fundamental to his happiness, then it's important to dissect every single variable inside and out.

DON'T: Fall into a sex cycle of unchanged repetition. This has negative effects on the vagina as well, and the less exciting sex becomes for the vagina, the less interested she is to have sex. Avoid becoming an uninterested vagina, and/or an un-interesting vagina. And DON'T, I repeat DON'T ever take a man's interest in trying new things in the bedroom as a bad thing. Change can be good, growth can be good, and when a couple changes and grows together it only strengthens their bond.

DO: Take Epic to a new frontier, and commit to always keeping the sex train in motion. And don't you fret sisters, we most definitely are coming back to this one (so highlight it!).

He Needs to Feel Embraced and Accepted Sexually:

One of the greatest qualities of a committed relationship is the comfort and security it brings to a man's life. In a world that's filled with judgments and criticism, it's no wonder that many men develop insecurities towards openly identifying with their sexuality and it often causes a man to mask much of himself from the outer world. Men rely on the comfort and security that a committed relationship provides them with, and they want nothing more than to feel embraced for all they represent, and finally unpack their sex suitcase. Every man comes into a relationship carrying his little sex suitcase, containing his sexual identity, his sexual desires and all of his sexual fantasies. A man comes with the hope of unpacking it all! A man needs to feel as though his relationship is supportive of his sexual identity, and that he will find acceptance from his partner. This is a huge source of security for a man, and when he finds a relationship that is fully accepting of his entire sexual identity he gains the greatest sense of security. And truth be told, this is also a great source of security for a woman, too, because when a man finds a home base that is accepting of him he becomes dependent on that source and locks in whole heartedly.

DON'T: Ever make a man feel as though he cannot express himself freely and openly in the relationship. We often don't realize that men are quite perceptive to our reactions and responsive behaviors. If a man feels as though the relationship environment is not fully accepting of his sexuality, he becomes guarded and only exposes the elements that he deems as "safe" and meets his partner's acceptance. We should never criticize a partner simply because they identify with certain interests, even if it's out of our comfort zone. No one says that we have to implement it all into the sexual relationship, but at the very least he must feel as though he can express himself without judgment. If a man feels as though he will be criticized or rejected for certain things that he identifies with sexually, he will suppress this part of his himself from the relationship. No man wants to feel as though he has to morph himself into two identities, and that he can't be himself towards the one person that he trusts the most. Let him openly speak his mind, and don't waste your time focusing on the areas where you two differ in interests and comforts. Instead, take that energy and invest it into focusing on the areas where you two do share similar interests and comforts and explore those things. With that being said, you should never ignore factors that could potentially cause you great discomfort or distress. If you and your partner have drastically different views on something, it should be discussed with an open mind but you should never feel pressured at any time.

DO: Create an inviting environment that provides him with the comfort to be candid and honest. Make him feel like he has nothing to fear and nothing to lose by being open and honest. When a man is met with positive reception and he feels embraced by his partner, he is more inclined to remain forthcoming with his disclosures and be honest. A man needs to feel accepted by his partner, in order for him to find the comfort and security he seeks in the relationship.

He Needs Emotional Security:

There's often this perception that men don't have the same emotional needs as women do, but this is totally not the case. Men have just as much emotional needs as women. Men may not like to admit it, as they battle the social perception that having emotional needs is a sign of weakness and not masculine in nature. The reality is that men rely on affection and everyday expressions of love, and also connecting emotionally through intimacy and sex. As women, it's easy for us to express our needs for emotional fulfillment, and if we ever feel that we're lacking in love we easily speak up and express our discontent. A man can easily be put off if he feels as though his emotional needs are not being fulfilled, and they don't always know how to come out and ask for what they want.

The funny thing is that despite my husband's perceptions, I can easily recognize when he's feeling put off emotionally or in need of some extra affections to fill him up. He often becomes cranky or pouty, and the moment that I tend to these signs with some extra love, all is restored in his happy world. I'm sure my husband would adamantly deny this, and it's his male ego that prevents him from seeing this. I hate to sell him out, and if he reads this he'll know that I'm on to his ways. Perhaps I should have titled this section "How to Knit Your Own Purse with Tampon Strings," because surely he would skim right over this section. Just like women, men like to be reminded of how much they are loved, desired and needed in the relationship. Becoming emotionally invested and dependent on an external source is something that men don't do often. When they do take the plunge and become emotionally reliant on a source, men don't like to feel emotionally vulnerable and they need to feel that this source is a secure one.

DON'T: Place your emotional needs before his, because he needs to feel equally validated in the relationship. His emotional expressiveness may differ, but it's not to imply that he doesn't ever feel hurt or vulnerable. Don't expect him to be a rough and rugged "man's man" all the time, and sometimes it takes an even bigger man to expose his vulnerabilities.

DO: Provide him with all the same emotional support that you expect from him. A man may not be quick to let on that he's feeling emotionally needy, and it's important to learn his queues and identify the behaviors that are sending this message. Rest assured that whatever you're serving up, his ego and his heart are eating it up. Let him know that it's okay to explore those emotions, and that you're a trust worthy source that he can depend on.

He Needs to Have His Masculine Presence Honored:

Now this is a big one, and it's something that we as women will never fully understand simply because we don't have a penis (or a set of testicles)...Thus, we don't have a male ego. Contrary to common belief, the male ego and "machismo' masculine factor is something very real and every guy has one. Men have a need to be recognized for their unique male offerings. I'm not talking about a woman being accepting of him owning the television remote, frequently scratching his balls in public (and without warning), or of his male tendency to never stop and ask for directions when he's lost... Those are all freebies that come along with the penis package! I'm actually talking about something more than that and it's embedded in their male species by nature. A man's need to be recognized for his masculinity has nothing to do with whether or not a couple has shared roles and responsibilities, or who's the bread winner and provider in the relationship. Regardless of what his role is, be it a stay at home dad, or the main bread winner, a man needs to feel as though his male offerings are honored and that the relationship is dependent on the unique presence he brings to the union. He needs to feel respected, and for a female spouse to acknowledge his masculinity, and for the things that define him as a man. This feeds a man's male ego, by making him feel needed and appreciated. He likes to feel as though he can please his spouse in the bedroom, and provide her with sexual pleasures. And he also needs to feel as though his male role is an important one in the overall relationship, and that he brings his female spouse great security with his male presence.

By nature, a man needs to have some form of dominance in the relationship. He may not dominate over every area of the relationship, but he feels the need to preserve his masculinity in one way or another. Men have a strong association with their male ego, and being celebrated for their manhood is a huge ego stroke for him. This feeds a man's self-esteem and also his confidence, and it provides him with a great sense of fulfillment in the relationship. The only way to explain it is that a man likes to feel that he's a great provider and protector of his woman, and if need be, he can save the day with his manly testicles. Okay, maybe not exactly like that, but you get the idea. Unfortunately, as I mentioned earlier this comes with some not so desirable added perks like a man's notion that he doesn't need a GPS because he has manly Penile-Navigation skills. The funny thing is, we often joke about men getting lost and not asking for directions, yet when he needs to get to the nearest vagina his penis is on that with impeccable navigational precision. It also gifts us with the jack-of-all trades and Mr. Fix-It that refuses to call a plumber, contractor, or any professional tradesperson. These manly dudes have flooded houses, taken out the power in entire neighborhoods, and even ended up in hospitals with severed toes and egos just from trying to remove a beehive from the garden in an effort to prove their manhood. Unfortunately, there's no convincing a man that the size of his penis is not determined by the size his screwdriver, and building an addition on the house does not add inches to his dick. However, it does feed into his emotional needs, so let him have his toolbox mentality and we will sing the praises of his penis as this also provides us with many benefits.

DO: Stroke his male ego, and often. He needs to feel recognized and honored as the man in the relationship. He wants praise and recognition for his male efforts, and it's important to never let his efforts go unrecognized. Whether it's commending his skills and efforts around the house, expressing appreciation for the great security he brings to your life, and even stroking his ego in the bedroom by complimenting the size of his penis. You think I'm kidding? It doesn't matter if he's bringing a mere five inches to the sex party or the whole nine yards, every guy likes to think he's packing a punch in his pants...Regardless of his actual size, just be sure to say it with a straight face or else it doesn't have the right effect. Men rely on praise both in the bedroom and in the overall relationship.

DON'T: Now, perhaps none of us have ever been guilty of this, but if it means something to a man and it has the ability to hurt his penis's feelings, we must discuss it. Don't ever find yourself doing the exact opposite of praising his manhood, and DON'T EVER TRY TO STEAL HIS BALLS! Such a practice deflates a man's self-esteem and it castrates his male ego. Men don't want a partner

who is critical of their ways or cynical of how they do things. Sometimes a woman may not recognize that she's doing this, and in the midst of a power struggle she goes for the gusto and what packs the biggest punch. I had a couple that I once worked with (we'll call them Larry and Becky), where Becky had a tendency to make passive aggressive comments or jokes, about Larry and his male like ways. She would say things like, "That joke was stupid, you've told it a million times, and you never tell it right." "That gym membership is a waste of money and you should just cancel it. Just face the fact that you will never be an Arnold Schwarzenegger, and having muscles doesn't exactly run in your family." The one that probably affected him the most, and that she would often joke about in front of their friends, "He has no idea what foreplay means, and even if he did it doesn't really matter because 'it's' usually over before it even begins." Becky may have seen this as no big deal, but to Larry it had very real and big implications on his male ego. Larry confessed that it made him feel like less of a man, and it made him feel ridiculed and really small when it was said in front of other people.

Imagine if the roles were reversed and Larry had the balls (assuming he still had them) to say to Becky, "You'd better slow down and not eat that whole slice of pie, Lord knows that fat gene runs in your family...just look at your mother's fat ass." Forget about asking for his balls back, he's better off taking what little he has left of his manhood and going into a penis protection program. There is no notoriety in a woman stealing a man's balls. For what? Just so she can proudly walk around with them in her purse and have them rolling around in there along with her lip gloss and tampons? Just so every time he pisses her off she can pull them out of her purse and smack him in the face with his own balls? Congratulations, yes, he feels like a pussy and now also has one to match hers. Balls don't make for a good trophy, and they look stupid up on the mantel or hanging from

the Christmas tree, so they should stay in his pants...plus they keep his penis company.

Straight to the penile point:

Men don't like to have their manhood knocked on, they don't like to be criticized for how they do things or why they do things, and they like to keep their balls and keep their sense of male-pride and manhood. This emasculating practice is major dick-repellant to a man, and this is not the type of relationship that any man sets out to be in. Not to mention that it totally kills the relationship in the bedroom by deflating his confidence and now you have two vaginas in bed. So just to recap: He brings the balls into the relationship and gets to keep them. And we ensure that the only practice we ever engage in is raising him up and celebrating his manhood.

He Needs to Feel that his Offerings are Adequate:

Men have their own unique way of expressing their love. A man's expressions of love may not always be grand in nature, but it's not to say that his emotional articulation isn't organic or sincere. As women, being emotionally expressive comes naturally to us, and we're naturally assuming that a man's expressions of love shouldn't differ from our own. We often equate the magnitude of a man's gestures as being reflective for the depth of his love. To love a man is to be accepting of his way of expressing his love. A man needs to feel as though his efforts and expressions are adequate and that his form of expression is "good enough." If it comes natural to him and he's being sincere, yet his spouse makes him feel as though this is not good enough, it causes him to become discouraged and to feel inadequate. It's important to keep in mind that men rely on many different forms of expressing their emotions. Through everyday gestures, and in the intimacy of the sexual relationship.

If a man does not feel rewarded for his love offerings, or he's made to feel like he falls short and that it's not enough, he will take it as an overall hit as him not doing enough in the relationship. Romance to a man may mean many different things, and even though these gestures may not always coincide with our female version of "romance," it's important to remain supportive of a man's unique way of doing things. Keep in mind, that anything is possible if we push for it, but a man's sole motivation to come home with Valentine's Day flowers, shouldn't be simply to avoid friction or a negative reaction. The gestures that a man brings forward are ones that he wishes to be rewarded for, and the simple fact that it comes from the heart is what matters most. My husband happens to have his own unique way of expressing his love, and even though I'm a grand gesture kind of gal, I make it a point to show my appreciation for his efforts. How does my husband show his love? When I'm craving a midnight snack and I have a serious need for ice cream, my husband will spring up off the couch, throw his shoes on and head to the store just so he can make it happen for me. His gesture may not involve twelve long stem roses, but his message is still loud and clear…"I love you so much that I will happily head to the store at midnight just to make my wife happy."

DON'T: Measure or compare his expressions of love to yours. When he does extend himself and makes an effort, don't analyze it and weigh its worth. The simple fact that it's his unique love language and it's sincere is worth its weight in gold. And don't ever let any effort go unrecognized, big or small.

DO: Take the time to express your appreciation and let him know that his efforts mean a lot. Positive reinforcement is rewarding and it motivates him to continue with his efforts and affections. Let him know that he is enough and his offerings are more than adequate.

He Needs to Have his "Special Spot" Preserved:

In any new relationship, both partners hold a valuable role. The new offerings a man brings to the union has him feeling valued and honored. As women, it's in our nature to be nurturing and we invest all of our efforts into our partner. Men like to feel that this new found role will be preserved, and regardless of what life brings into the relationship that he will never lose his special spot. The reality for many couples is that real life brings real responsibilities, and many relationships will evolve and also expand. What was once only two, now becomes three, four or even more as children come along and get added to the mix. Throw in a dog, cat and three goldfish and we now find ourselves attempting to juggle it all and spread ourselves in every direction. It's important for a couple to preserve the "twosome" dynamic, and to reserve a special part of themselves exclusively for one another.

I have coached many couples where this growing family dynamic starts to present challenges in the relationship, as they struggle to find time for one another. It goes without saying that as a woman, it's not an easy job being everything to everyone and all the time, and as a female spouse we're often the primary care giver to our children. Even though a big part of our emotional investments turn to focus on the kids, a male spouse does not want to part with the exclusive emotional feedings that he receives from his spouse and that he has come to rely on. We often view the responsibilities of being a parent as a mutually assumed sacrifice in the relationship. And a man is more than willing to make many concessions for his family, but not at the cost of losing his secured place and special spot with his partner. If a man starts to feel as though he's lost his place and he's been put aside, it can cause him to feel emotionally disconnected and abandoned in the relationship. A man needs to feel as though his place is secure, and that his female spouse has a need for him as a partner and not just as a co-parent. This is why it's important to nurture the intimate bond that we share with our mate, and remember that before there were three, four, five or six...There were only two. And it's the twosome that must remain unified as they are co-pilots in life.

DON'T: Ignore his ass after the baby comes. Okay, I'm joking.... Don't stop investing in the two of you, even after children come along...or anything else in life that complicates your situation. Regardless of how many variables get thrown into the pot, you must always remain mindful of the need to nurture the twosome and let a man know that he is very much needed in the relationship.

DO: Find ways to preserve solo couple time, even if it means locking yourselves in the bathroom and stealing time for a bubble bath. We will actually discuss all of this a little later on, and for now just know that the biggest baby you will ever have on your hands is your guy and his little emotional male ego. Show him that he will always have a special part of you that no one else will ever have, and that it's reserved exclusively for him.

Love & Happiness is Not Always a Package Deal

A man's happiness means everything to him. The funny thing is that when it comes to happiness, men and women see things much differently. You see, women often bundle love and happiness together, and where there is love there is also happiness for a woman. Men on the other hand, place love and happiness into two separate categories, and they don't always go hand in hand for a man. In order for a man to achieve true happiness, he needs to feel as though all his needs are being met and in all the areas that provide him with happiness. He also has a need to maintain his own unique identity and if this need for male independence is not being nurtured it can affect his sense of happiness. It's possible for a man to have great love in his relationship even when the relationship is not fully serving to his happiness. This goes back to the tripod quotient we talked about, and the need men have to fulfill their needs through the brain, heart and penis. A man can have great love, but if the sexual relationship is compromised and he is not finding fulfillment of his sexual needs, it can cause him an overall sense of unhappiness in the relationship. Just the same, if a man feels emotionally disconnected from his partner, he can easily still enjoy the sex as this is a primary need that he has. However, the emotional disconnection can create a sense of unhappiness in the overall relationship. Many times we often assume that when we find happiness, naturally our partner, too, is happy. However, perception is reality and if a partner feels as though certain areas of the relationship are lacking, their sense of happiness may not always coincide with their partner's perceptions. This is why it's important to foster the approach of placing a partner's needs as a primary focus in the relationship. When we invest ourselves into ensuring that our partner's needs are met and that they have achieved happiness, our perceptions become aligned with the reality of the relationship and with how our partner truly views the quality of the union.

What Men Want

Okay, so the areas that we just touched on tie into the primary needs that men bring into the relationship and that are fundamental to a man's happiness. It doesn't end there, and men may claim to be simple creatures, but there are many other variables men seek out in the relationship. So what exactly is it that men want in order to be truly happy?

He Wants More of the Same:

For a man, having an unpredictable dynamic in the sexual relationship is a good thing. However, when it comes to the overall relationship, and the offerings that a female partner brings, men want a predictable and reliable dynamic in the union. Men tend to take a logical approach towards relationships, and for a man he's "what you see, is what you get." When a man finds a mate and a relationship that provides him with happiness and fulfillment, his decision to "sign on the dotted line" and commit, is based on the initial relationship. Men make the logical assessment that history depicts the future. He expects that the relationship will continue to function and serve in the same way it always has. Obviously men are not stupid, and they know that every relationship will change to some extent. Maybe the romance changes a little and some date nights on the town are replaced with nights cuddled on the couch. Perhaps sex goes from three times a day and hanging from the chandelier to three times a week and hanging on to the bed posts. As long as this is still serving to his needs, he's a content fella.

However, what a man does not expect or accept, is a relationship that changes so dramatically, he doesn't recognize it any more. For example, if once upon a time Becky was putting out daily blow jobs like an iPhone assembly line, and now she's on blow job strike and Larry's penis hasn't seen a blow job since… well, since he can't remember it's been so long, and his penis is too depressed to think about it. Husband Larry is confused, and his penis is equally puzzled and perplexed. That's okay: word has it that Becky is gearing up for a birthday surprise, and Larry is getting a brand new shiny blow job for his big 4-0! Oh boy, Larry and his dick must be so excited! Only 126 more days to go!

The logical male mind may be accepting of many things, but a complete relationship renovation is not one of them. This doesn't apply to just sex, even though this is the one area that the penis worries about the most. It applies to the overall dynamic of the relationship. What men really want and what they come to expect is what they've come to know, what they now rely on and basically what they signed on for.

DON'T: Allow the comfort of a committed relationship to ever turn into complacency. It takes a lot of time and nurturing to build a solid relationship, and it's only through continued efforts that it remains solid and intact.

DO: This one is easy! The recipe to keeping a good relationship is found in all the ingredients that went into building it in the first place. The key to making a man happy? It's as simple as maintaining all the variables that helped him achieve that happiness in the first place. Find ways to preserve the "boyfriend/girlfriend" elements and all the fun and happy variables that were around back when you were dating.

He Wants to Keep his Male Identity:

When it comes to commitment, one thing that men are often weary of is losing their male identity and individuality in the union. When a man commits himself to a relationship, it's with the hopes that he can still preserve his male identity and his male rituals. Obviously, when two people come together, they form a new unified identity as a couple. However, even with this new coupledom dynamic, a healthy relationship is one where each spouse maintains their unique identity as an individual. A man wants to preserve his individuality, and to maintain his interests and male rituals. Men are willing to make many sacrifices for a relationship, but sacrificing themselves or the things that make them happy is something that men don't want. Men like to have their "dude" time, whether it's enjoying their interests in solitude, or to surround themselves with their own kind and peers as they engage in dude-like activities. I know that we as women may not always understand this about men, but it's because we don't have testicles. It is what it is, and a man simply has a need to be one with his penis, and sometimes hang out with a bunch of other penises as they all poke fun at one another over a round of golf or even some nachos and beer.

When I first met my husband, and as we progressed towards a bonafide commitment, he was very forthcoming with his male needs. I'll never forget the discussion, because he was very serious with his approach. He started out by saying, "Listen, there's some things we need to discuss, and I need to put it out there before we move forward." Based on his tone alone, I was expecting a doozy of a disclosure, something like "I need you to know that I like to dress up in woman's panties while I eat Twinkies and watch my pet turtles have sex." What he actually said was, "Listen, you know that I am willing to give you the world, and make many concessions in many areas in order to make you happy. There are only two needs I have, and that I want to preserve in order to be happy. I like to lay on the couch and watch the football game on Sunday afternoons, and I like to go to the gym right after work each and every day." Okay, so no Twinkies or turtle sex? And we're not having to share underwear? DEAL! Sure, I may have been giving up "together time" on certain Sundays, and for a couple of hours after work each day. However, what I was gaining was a happy husband, one who was appreciative of my understanding for his male needs and who was highly motivated to express his gratitude with even greater efforts.

Whether a guy finds solace by sitting on the couch and catching a football game, spending the afternoon waxing his coveted car or heading out for a round of golf with his buddies, he simply needs his guy time. Just like women like to have their girly time, some dudes like to partake in their dude-like rituals, while they engage in shop talk and simply scratch their balls. The way men see it, wives are not invited because for one, they don't have a set of balls. And while they are all sitting around scratching them, she'll have nothing to scratch. Now, I know that not all men engage in such rituals, but most do.

Men actually take this pretty seriously, and no guy likes to feel as though he's "not allowed to come out and play ball" with his friends, or that he has to trade his balls in for a brand new shiny mangina. Being ousted from his testosterone pack, he now has all the time in the world to join his wife's knitting circle, and how exciting that today he's learning how to crochet reusable organic tampons!

Okay, I'm done poking fun...And the penile point I'm making here is that men like to know that they can preserve their male rituals should they so desire. Whether their enjoyment involves hanging with the guys to discuss stocks and trading, sitting around and just being one with their testicles, or even sitting in solitude and all alone to meditate with his penis...It is what it is and men want to preserve their male identity.

DON'T: View his need for "guy time" as him trying to escape you or the relationship, because that's not where this need stems from. Don't expect him to completely banish his interests and male rituals. This is unhealthy and a man will only end up resenting the things he lost rather than appreciating the things he has gained in the relationship. If his interests bring him enjoyment and he has fun doing them, trying to eliminate them from his life only makes a woman the "Unfun Police."

DO: Support his male interests and encourage him to have his guy time, or even solo dude time. As women, we need this too. It's healthy to maintain our individuality and our own personal interests. As they say, "absence makes the heart grow fonder," and it will only enrich the time you two do spend together. A man is very appreciative of a woman who supports his need for male rituals, and he will return his gratitude with great efforts.

He Wants a Woman Who is Accepting of his World:

Men not only desire to hold onto their male identity, they also want their spouse to be accepting of their world. A man wants for a woman to be supportive of his hobbies, whether it be golfing, fishing, or even his hobby of obsessing over his Star Trek collectibles. If it means something to him, he wants it to mean something to his mate.

Men also want their friends to be accepted. A guy doesn't want to give up his friendships, even if she thinks his buddy is a goober and a low life. He wants a mate who is accepting of his family, and for the people who mean something to him. I know that this can be tough, and perhaps sometimes it's more of a "tolerance" and not a full acceptance. A man doesn't want to feel as though he needs to ditch these people and friends for his relationship. When a man is forced to abandon the things that bring him happiness, it only makes him resentful in the long run. Men don't want to have to choose between two worlds, and wish for there to be a happy medium. This is why men often seek out that "cool chick" quality in a woman. They want someone who is able to hang out with him and his friends and just have fun. The funny thing is that many times when my husband has an opportunity to go out with his friends, he says "I want you to come, too! It's more fun when you come." It's nice to know that he feels that way, and even though I encourage him to have his guy time, I'm always happy to join in on his world and for us to share in fun times together.

DON'T: Make him feel as though you are not accepting of his interests, or the things that bring him happiness. When a man feels as though his partner is accepting of the things that bring him happiness, he appreciates her even more.

DO: Support him in his interests and hobbies, and encourage him to partake in the activities that support his happiness.

Remain engaged, and make an effort to partake in the activities that he enjoys. Even if it means attending a family function filled with people you really are not crazy about. You're not there for them, you're there for him and he will appreciate that the most.

He Wants Romance:

Yes, you read that right, and, no, I didn't mix up my penis and vagina notes. The penis wants romance just as much as our vaginas do. This stems back to what we touched on earlier, and how men sign on for more of the same. A new relationship brings romance, excitement and intense chemistry. Men like to keep this lust infused spark alive, and by keeping the romance it keeps the fire burning… in his mind, heart and in his pants. This type of fire and heat the penis is okay with. Keeping the romance allows a man to see the woman he fell in love with, and it nurtures his soul. It makes him feel loved, desired and connected.

DON'T: Ever let the fire burn out! Don't think for one second that he doesn't appreciate the romance as much as you and your vagina do.

DO: Keep the spark alive by romancing him in the same way that you like to be romanced. The penis and male ego eat this shit up!

He Wants to Have Fun:

As the song goes, "Girls just wanna have fun!" Well, guys are no different. Men are attracted to a woman who knows how to have fun and brings spontaneity to the relationship. Men see this as a desirable quality for the sexual relationship, too, and it feeds into their need for variety and diversity in the relationship and provides for their happiness. As I mentioned earlier on, when it comes to feeding a man's needs, consistency and predictability are desirable qualities in the relationship, but not in a mate. It's in their nature for men to pursue that sense of adventure and having that unpredictable quality in a woman is a rush for the adrenaline seeking male brain. A man wants to preserve that unknown excitement and elated "boyfriend/girlfriend" feeling that is found in any new relationship. Keeping the fun alive is what makes him happy.

DON'T: Allow yourself to become so consumed with life's responsibilities that you lose sight of the fun factor in the relationship. Don't allow yourselves to become that old miserable couple that doesn't do fun things anymore.

DO: Take the time to have fun! In bed, at lunch, on the couch...Whatever it takes, find time to make it happen. It's important to let that kid come out, and to support his desire to simply let go and do fun things.

He Wants to Feel Understood:

I know that as women we are the ones that often find ourselves feeling misunderstood, and that a guy is not listening to our needs. Men are no different, and they too want to feel understood in their own unique way. Whether it's the way he does things, or how he tries to express himself, he wants to feel as though his partner truly gets him. It's the male ego that has men wanting to feel as though they have the ability to make sound decisions, without the need to explain themselves. Men don't like to hear, "I told you so," even when they don't get it right. If he does it his way, and perhaps it's not the way we would do it, he simply wants to feel understood and supported, even if it doesn't turn out the way he wanted. He wants a woman who can admit when she's wrong, and take ownership for her contributions.... not someone who deflects everything onto his lap and sees no fault on their end. A man wants to feel that he's good enough, that his efforts are adequate and that his emotional investments hold equal value in the relationship. He doesn't want his words or actions to be analyzed or criticized, or used against him. What he really wants is forgiveness, for a woman to be compassionate to his ways and if he fucks up, he doesn't want reminders of his errors. He wants a woman that has a forgiving nature, the ability to overlook his mistakes and move past them and to work on solutions together.

DON'T: Try to read between the lines and put your own spin on what he's trying to say. Don't come in after him and undo his "male" touch by applying your female fixer upper.

DO: Allow him to be as he is, think as he does and support his ways. Be forgiving and compassionate to his needs and his approach on things.

He Wants a "Safe Haven":

Men are simple yet odd little creatures, and they want nothing more than peace and consistency in their lives. Men like to feel that no matter what the world throws at them and however many dragons they have to slay in the outside world that they can come home into the comforting arms of their relationship and find peace in their safe haven. A man likes to know that no matter what transpires in his daily dealings with the outside world, that the inside world of his relationship will always be a positive and inviting environment. He wants the type of relationship that he can "escape to," and not one that makes him feel like he wants to "escape from." For the most part, men want to have peace and a reliable home base that provides them with serenity and happiness. It's true when they say that a man's home is his castle, and he wants to feel that this safe haven is his happy sanctuary.

DON'T: Allow toxins from the outer world to penetrate the relationship and to dilute the happiness in the union. The time that a couple shares together should be filled with quality and substance.

DO: Make the effort to preserve the happiness by keeping the relationship environment supportive and positive. And don't worry, we will be discussing all the ways to make this happen!

He Wants to Feel Taken Care of & Fussed Over:

Okay, bring back the damn muffin recipes! The way to man's heart may not always be through his stomach, but it sure helps make a guy feel special. Men like to feel nurtured, taken care of and fussed over. Whether it's home cooked meals, running him a bubble bath or a simple foot rub, men appreciate all the little efforts that make them feel special. This one is easy, because these simple daily efforts don't require any elaborate planning, no extravagant vagina tricks in the bedroom, and there's no need to get all dolled up in heels and harnesses. No, ma'am! It's the simple little efforts that make a man feel loved. I try to find many different ways to let my husband know that he's loved each and every day. Anything and everything from him coming home to a massage, a simple little foot rub on the couch, running him a bath, and packing him little notes along with his lunches. A little goes a long way and my husband often tells his friends, "My wife takes good care of me." And I love doing it! My husband treats me like a Queen and in return

I'm happy to treat him like the King in my world. It's these types of efforts that feed into a guy's happiness, and where a man finds happiness he finds great motivation to return his gratitude and show his appreciation by investing back into his partner and her happiness. See?! It's a win/win all around and everybody is happy! All hail Queen Vagina and King Penis! It may sound corny, but aren't all romance novels filled with this fluffy stuff?

He Wants a Partner Not a Parent:

One thing that is most important to men is that they not only want to be accepted for who they are and what they represent... They most definitely don't want to be changed. As women, we often have this little innate need to always perfect everything, and even when it's good we look to make it even better...new and improved. Some things don't need fixing in life, and men most definitely don't want to be "fixed." Change for a man is something that comes naturally, and it must come from within. Sometimes people have this need to hold on really tightly to the things that matter most to them, and an overbearing type of love can feel suffocating to a man. They don't like to be managed or controlled, and this is how overbearing love comes across sometimes. Men are not very receptive to a forceful hand, and they often repel with great resistance. A man does not want a mother figure or a smothering figure. What a man wants is a partner, not a parent. They want to keep their freedom and not feel restricted. I'm not talking about freedom to act single, I'm talking about the freedom to make their own choices and decisions, be in control of their own identity and not feel as though they have rules or restrictions that make them feel suffocated. He wants the type of partner that enhances and enriches his life and not one that takes things away or enforces limitations and restrictions. The reality is that if a woman feels that she has no choice but to police a man's poor behaviors, then she didn't choose wisely in a mate. In a mature, committed relationship a man doesn't want someone who is always going to tell him what to do and how to do it and to feel as though he can't be trusted to make the right decisions. Simply put, men want a partner that stands by their side, and not over top of them. Keep in mind that even though he may at times have questionable male like behaviors, he is still a grown man and needs to feel like one in the relationship.

DON'T: Allow your nurturing nature to turn into a management role. Have faith in the person you have chosen as a mate, and his abilities to simply do things on his own and without criticism or too much input.

DO: Nurture him and support him in ways that make him feel competent and as being an equal counterpart in the relationship.

He Wants a Best Friend in his Mate:

One thing that men truly value is the friendship in a relationship. A man wants a woman that stands by his side, a partner in life and for life...A reliable sidekick that he can conquer the world with. Someone that he can laugh and cry with, act stupid with and have stupendous sex with. Men want a best friend who is their confidant, someone they can trust and depend on, someone to tell all their secrets to and who will embrace them unconditionally. What he truly needs is a woman who does not carry him to see him through, but a woman who acts as the wind on his back and that propels him forward. Not everyone finds this in their relationships, and many couples share as spouses but not always as best friends. This is a unique dynamic and when a man finds a best friend in their mate, this is something that he holds onto, that he cherishes and that grants him with a great sense of security.

The Greatest Security for a Man

As I've mentioned before, for women our greatest security is often found in the reliable love from a partner and someone that acts as the protector of our heart. For men, the greatest security is when they have found one source that fulfills all their needs. It's because sex ties into their emotional needs, as well as their male ego, that a man finds true security when one source is embracing of all his needs. As women, we have the unique ability to maintain multiple emotional bonds all at the same time and parallel to the relationship we share with our spouse. We find fulfillment from the various emotional relationships we share as sisters, daughters and as best friends with those around us. Men on the other hand, are not as liberal in their emotional nature. They choose to secure one reliable source that they can open up to emotionally and this becomes their security. This is why a man is extremely selective in his selection criteria, and it's the only source that he will rely on for all his emotional feedings and his overall happiness.

When it comes to the type of female characteristics that men are commonly attracted to, they tend to gravitate to qualities that are reflective of their needs and supportive of their happiness. This is why men are drawn to a multi-faceted woman, a dynamic woman who has the ability to transform herself and adapt to any type of situation and environment. Men want the type of woman who exudes confidence, someone who believes in herself and who's passionate about life. Intellect is also a very desirable quality for a man as it feeds into his need for mental stimulation. All of these elements are things that he translates into being valuable assets both to the sexual relationship and the overall union. They are also qualities that are representative of what allows a man to achieve security in the relationship, as they are providing for all his needs. The reality is that being all a man could ever want, are some pretty big vagina shoes to fill. In his world, we need to be a man's emotional caretaker and his sole source of feedings and security. We're also his fun and excitement committee, the adventurous ride in his sex life and a reliable friend and shoulder to lean on. Man, it's starting to sound like we inherited a newborn baby! Actually, it may sound like a tall bill to fill and the amazing thing is that when a woman has the ability to become all of this in a man's world, she also becomes her own greatest asset in the relationship.

The funny thing is that the greatest security a woman will ever find in a relationship is the security and dependency that her partner actually has for her and the relationship. You see, a woman's security is not based on what her partner can do for her and her needs, or the amount of security that he can grant her through his investments. A woman's greatest security is based on what she brings to a man's life, the investments she makes and the fulfillment and happiness that she bestows upon his world. A woman is her greatest asset when she commits to becoming that one sole source, a dynamic woman who brings it all and who becomes his everything. Are you starting to see how this works? This is where we say that sometimes, the best way in is not through the front door. An epic vagina knows how to recognize a good opportunity and secure her place by securing his happiness. You can see now where the "epic" part comes into play and it takes a truly open minded and selfless woman to make it happen. Lucky for us, this is exactly what we are striving to emulate. And when a man finds all of this in one woman, he has found heaven on earth...along with having found stupendous happiness. Hook line and sinker, this little (I mean big) penis fish has taken the bait and as long as the waters stay inviting and warm, his little (I mean big) fishy tail is staying put.

DO: Take the initiative to step out of your vagina box and allow yourself to reap the rewards of rewarding a man with what he truly needs to be happy. Learn to love a man in the way he needs to be loved. Honor his needs and go above and beyond to also honor his 'wants' as they too are serving to his ultimate happiness. Remember, in a man's world the sexual relationship is serving to so much more than just his penis and physical needs. Recognize the importance of accepting a man for who he is and how he expresses his love. When you make sex a priority in the relationship it makes a man feel as though he is the priority. Keep in mind that this is how he expresses himself emotionally and gains emotional fulfillment. The sexual relationship provides a man with the opportunity to feel valued, desired, doted on and appreciated for his unique male offerings. Men are most appreciative of a woman who allows them the freedom to preserve their male identity and to give and receive love in their own way. Most importantly a man doesn't want to be renovated, for his world to be reconstructed into a vagina mold, or for his partner

to govern the worth of his happiness. When a man finds a woman who understands all of this and provides such an environment in his world, it grants him with ultimate happiness and great motivation to return his gratitude onto his spouse.

DON'T: Miss out on the opportunity to make this happen! And lucky for us, this is exactly what this book is all about!

Alright ladies, there's no time to waste! Let's get these epic vaginas back on that bus. We're heading into the next chapter and towards greatness!

Chapter Two

The Inside Out Vagina

I know that you're probably thinking *what the heck is up with the vagina chapter?* We just agreed that we're focusing on men and their penile ways. Here's the deal: you know and I know that you and I are perfect, but somehow that message doesn't transmit well in relationships involving those penis types. And perhaps "perfect" may be a strong word or a bit of a stretch. Maybe more along the lines of.... Ah fuck, who are we kidding?! Listen, let's just be real here. We always have the best intentions, but we're not always received in the way we intended... We mean well and we love hard. Sometimes, we get it right, and sometimes despite our best intentions, we simply fuck up. The truth is that no one likes self-reflection that paints them in a negative light. However, you and I, sister, are on a different trajectory. We are not here to smile at each other reassuringly as we say "Oh no, your ass looks great in those pants," as we both head out on the town with our hideous assess bouncing about.

Remember, we are keeping it real, and as realists the reality is that our female contributions in relationships have a huge impact on the course of the relationship. Good or bad, our behaviors and interactions directly influence how a partner achieves happiness and how we achieve our own happiness. The idea is simple, and if we expect to create greatness in our relationships we need to ensure that every single variable and ingredient we put in is of the finest quality and of equal greatness. Every gal can benefit from a little self-evaluation. And because we are keeping it real, we want to identify the areas where we can improve and rehab poor practices into positive ones. One thing that every woman must know is that from the moment you walk into a relationship, the fate of that union is already sealed and it's determined solely by the relationship you have with yourself. This is something that we as women don't often recognize, because we simply see love as a solution to everything and if we can find great love, it will conquer all.

This is a false perception, and the single most important relationship you will ever have in life, is with yourself. This chapter is a DOOZY and I can't stress it enough, but don't fret sister…we have each other and we will fly through it and come out on the other end with brand new shiny epic vaginas! Okay, let's keep it simple and to the point. Working on ourselves and ensuring self-love and our own sense of security is what will allow us to achieve the second principle in the Love Barter Tripod. Being able to truly love unconditionally, without the potential of any static interference from internal struggles we may be facing. Keep in mind that our behaviors and interactions in the relationship have a way of setting the tone in the relationship, and the energy we put forth directly impacts a partner's behaviors. In simple terms, we need to make sure that we are bringing our best vagina foot forward (yes, in this story our vagina have feet…so hush), as this will ensure that we are creating the best possible relationship environment that will grant us with happiness and success. It's not only important to ensure that we are entering into relationships with the best possible version of ourselves, but that we do regular vagina tune ups and maintenance to ensure that we never lose ourselves along the way. Okay, so what's involved and what do our vagina's need to know?

1. Stop Following Societal Standards:

The greatest lessons I have ever learned in life came from my father. He was such a philosophical man with such wisdom. He felt very passionately about the structure of society and the standards that are pushed on us and on our personal loves. One of the greatest things he ever taught me was this: *Never fear the thought of being different, and don't follow everyone else.* Those actually weren't his exact words, mainly because he had a heavy Greek accent and he cursed a lot…his version started out (insert Greek accent) "Maria (my name in Greek), don't follow the stupid assholes, they find you trouble!"

His reference to "assholes" pertained to the pressure that society puts on us to follow their standards and the things that they classify as being acceptable. The key point here is that the societal standards which are pushed upon us by our friends and acquaintances, is actually a woman's worst enemy when it comes to relationships. Think about it: if you're lost and looking for directions, do you stop and ask someone who's holding a map and who looks equally lost?

The reality is this: that mainstream relationships abiding by all the social norms come with a 50% failure rate. Not to mention what's deemed as "acceptable" is based on the comforts and insecurities of everyone around us. So why do we often feel compelled to follow these social norms?

It's basically like a throw-back to high school and the peer pressure to fit in. It's human nature to seek out and gain social acceptance from our peers. The reason why we are heavily swayed by social influence is because no one wants to be viewed as an outcast. We just want to fit in, we want to blend in and we want to be embraced by the scrutinizing arms of society. So we naturally try to emulate the ideals that society sets forth for what a wife should look like and how she should act. Here's the problem...When it comes to relationships, the ideals that society pushes on women drastically differs from the image that men gravitate to and the expectations that they bring into relationships. Furthermore, society has thrust explicit sexuality into our mainstream world, yet they maintain a "hush hush: taboo notion on sex in committed relationships. Society celebrates us for our professional accomplishments, our baking skills and our roles as nurturing mothers. Society takes no issue in openly discussing all sorts of explicit sexual positions when it comes to trying to conceive a baby, but heaven forbid anyone ever openly talks about having wild sex with their husband ...AND JUST FOR FUN! Who does that? Who has sex for fun?

Seriously speaking, the unfortunate part about it all is that even in today's day and age, this is still pretty much the general mindset in society. I'm not sure how a female spouse having sex in a committed relationship somehow falls into the same classification as "hooker sex"...but somehow, somewhere, society has taken one brush and with one stroke paints unconventional sex as taboo. According to society, "Committal Hookering" is when we're having too much 'fun sex' that involves experimentation into the 'taboo' world of sex. So we can have fun, but not too much fun. What? What's even funnier, is that all over the Internet there's mainstream publications and social media sites where people share recipes for baking penis cupcakes, and cock-cakes (yes it's a real thing) yet the moment a woman openly proclaims "I love cock!" everyone has this perplexed disapproving look on their face (the same look that people make when they inhale someone else's fart.) Okay, just so we're clear…it's okay to publicly post recipes for the kind of cock you bake, but the moment we talk about the real one we've got cooking at home, everyone looks at us like we just farted. Seriously? When a man speaks candidly about sex, he's just being a man and when a woman does the same, she's being unladylike and should stick to baking dick dumplings (or whatever they're called.)

Okay, fun time is over… Let's reel those vagina's back in and get back to work. The reality is that men place sex at the top of their happy list. And, by the way, WOMEN LOVE SEX TOO! And if we can't openly identify with sex, then we're not openly discussing, and we're missing out on some damn stellar orgasms.

Enter The Epic Vagina Approach

Grab those Epic little vagina super hero capes, because we are changing the tide. If we expect to create greatness in our relationships and appeal to a man's needs, we need to distance ourselves from these social views and it will also distance us from the grim statistics. They can keep their crappy cock-cakes and their crumby failing relationship recipes! We have the freedom to be equally celebrated for our intelligence, our beauty and the natural essence of our female sexuality. We're not looking for any public recognition, and you have the freedom to remain as private as you wish within the comforts of your own relationship. There is no need to have a huge penis trophy publicly displayed next to your employee of the month plaques on your desk at work… One that proudly boasts the title of "Number One Hooker Wife: East Coast Division 2013-2014."

The notion I'm pushing here is simple: Never change how you are, who you are, or alter the way you dress, speak or act just to avoid being criticized by others. There will always be those who will pass judgments, and who will have something to say. Understand that their reactions, thoughts, words and criticisms, are about them and not about you. These are people who are forced to face their own inadequacies and the things they dislike about themselves, simply by your presence. It's not your job to change, alter or suppress anything about yourself, in an effort to accommodate those around you and provide them with the comforts they seek. Never feel shameful for what you identify with, and don't ever feel the need to suppress your sexuality simply to please your external world. If you allow your focus to be on making your external world happy, you will never find true happiness in our inner world, nor will you ever be in a position to make your partner truly happy. Your happiness is job one, and you must never be apologetic simply for being true to yourself and being happy.

Understand that in a committed relationship, one where there is great love and respect, a woman is not sexually objectifying herself simply by unleashing her sexual inhibitions in the privacy and comfort of her personal relationship. There are only two people who need to be approving of your relationship, and that's you and your partner. What women wouldn't want the opportunity to play right into all the things that her partner is most responsive to? And if she's happy to do so and they're both happier because of all this, then that's all that matters. Society is not going to tell you what makes your partner happy, your partner has the answers on what makes him happy. As long as you two have comfort with your dynamic, then society and their views can go suck on hairy cow balls (and no, this is not a new recipe.) I'm not exactly sure if it's cows or bulls that have balls…Whatever, that's not the point because you only have one set of balls to concern yourself with and that's the set belonging to the guy you're trying to appeal to and who loves you very much. End of story, let's move on!

2. *Invest in Yourself and the Rest Will Come:*
This is one that I've learned in the not so easy way throughout my adult years, and it's a life-long project that never ends. I coach

many women who are all in the same stilettos as myself and as many of you out there. The reality is this: If you expect someone to invest in you, you must first invest in yourself. Want someone to love you unconditionally? Learn how to love yourself, as this will make you lovable. Looking for respect in a relationship? Know what it means to respect yourself, treat yourself with respect and hold those around you to the same standards. I love watching me some Dr. Phil, and he says it best… "We teach people how to treat us" (maybe not in those exact words, but along those lines.) People don't hear your words as much as they see how you treat yourself, and this is what sets the standard for how people treat us. If it's your desire to have your partner believe in you and see certain things in you, you must first believe in yourself and see it in yourself.

Here's the deal: the relationship we have with ourselves pretty much seals the fate of our personal relationships from the very moment that we walk through love's door. Understand that the relationship you have with yourself is something that will influence every single behavior, interaction and expectation you have in your relationship. Let me explain the importance of this by painting two thoughts: one being a lack of self-investment and the other being enriched with self-fulfillment.

Avoid the Vagina Void

If we neglect to invest in ourselves, our self-love and our self-worth, our sense of security becomes compromised. It disables our ability to love freely, and it really becomes a cycle of 'conditional' love based on the things that feed our own insecurities with comfort. No woman willingly sets out with a self-serving mentality, but the lack of self-love forces this cycle on the relationship. It causes a woman to have inflated and unrealistic expectations of her partner, because she needs him to fill her inner void. This becomes exhausting and burdensome to the relationship, because no matter how hard he tries, a man *cannot* fill this void.

Only *you* can fill this void for yourself. Many years ago, I struggled with this type of emotional void and it heavily impacted my relationships. At the time I didn't realize that it caused me have such unrealistic expectations from the relationship and anytime my insecurities acted up, I made it my boyfriend's problem to fix. This is exhausting for someone on the receiving end and he quickly began to realize that no matter what he did, he could never get ahead or make me happy for very long. I always felt that my relationships were failing, when the reality was that I had failed myself. It wasn't easy and all I wanted to do was just throw myself in the comforting arms of the next relationship and forego the ugly inner reflection shit. However, I knew in my heart that unless I took a time out to work on myself, I would only find myself in this same exact place over and over again and I was getting too old for the nonsense so I sent my vagina to boot camp. Well not exactly, but I gave myself some tough love and finally found some self-love, which by the way is a lifelong project and something that I try to work on as often as I can.

If a woman doesn't know how to find happiness within herself, then no efforts on a man's part will ever be good enough to make her happy. It becomes disabling in every aspect of the relationship. Sexually, it causes a woman to become reserved. Understand that a woman will never be in a position to fully accept a man for all that he represents, until she has found this within herself. And this is super-duper important because a man's truest wishes are to be fully accepted.

Lead by Example: Being Your Own Vagina's Biggest Fan!

Alright, this is where we pull out those epic vagina capes. It's so true when they say that positive energy is contagious, and the most reassurance a woman will ever have when it comes to a man loving her, is when she is loving herself from the inside-out! There's a reason why men are attracted to confidence in a woman, and it's because this quality is convincing and it influences how a man sees a woman. You need to have some serious love for your own ass, and believe in your worth. When a man says "I love you," it shouldn't prompt the thoughts of "Really? How do you love me? Or why do you love me?" It should prompt the thoughts, "Damn, straight, who wouldn't love all of this… I'm all sorts of awesome!" As women, we often don't realize the impact of our words and how the perceptions we have of ourselves affect our relationships. The reality is that we all have our little insecurities and sometimes it's comforting to get some reassurance from our partner, but the underlying fact is that we won't be able to accept a partner's love until we love ourselves.

I had a discussion with my husband many years ago and it drastically changed my outlook. My husband explained, "Men don't see the things that women often see in themselves." He gave the example of when a woman stands in front of the mirror and says, "Ew, I hate my thighs: look at these lumps." He went on to say that "when we love a woman, we see everything through our love goggles, and we see nothing but beauty and perfection. We don't see the lumps that she sees, especially when we're both naked in the bedroom and hormones are raging. This is when we not only have love goggles on, but also our trusty penis binoculars, and all we see is a sex goddess with no imperfections whatsoever. A woman's confidence is what makes all of her imperfections disappear."

"It doesn't even matter if she doesn't fit the social standard for beauty, when a man chooses to commit to a woman, he takes and loves it all. If she does not make an issue of it, and instead embraces it with confidence and rocks it out in the bedroom, those extra few pounds, those lumps, or whatever she sees, are none existent in our eyes. However, if a woman constantly sits and bashes herself and always focuses on herself in a negative light, then her negativity becomes contagious and we, too, start to take on her mindset. She creates beliefs in our minds that were never there to begin with, and if you hear something often enough it starts to become convincing. We feel as though it's not even worth the effort to try and convince her otherwise, because our true words will never be acknowledged."

What he said made so much sense. Picture going to a restaurant and saying to the waitress "I think I'll have the chicken wrap, is it good?" Imagine if her response was "Ew, you don't want to eat the chicken wrap! I don't even think it's real chicken!" How inclined would you be to ignore her words and still order the chicken-less surprise? This is why it's important to understand that 'one's perception is their reality.' If we perceive things to be a certain way, it becomes our reality, and also the reality that others see in us as well. Our self-worth should never be dependent on those around us, and every woman should truly be her biggest fan club of all time. One of the greatest aspects of having great love in a relationship, is that by default it makes you a goddess in his eyes.

So here's the deal. It's not only important to make sure we are a whole lotta woman when we are going into relationships, it's important to keep things in check and make sure that we never lose touch with ourselves. Sometimes life changes, work, stress, having kids, blah, blah, blah, and we find ourselves in a place that we're not happy with. Your happiness is job one! We always need to be content and happy with ourselves inside and out. If you lose touch with yourself, you also lose touch with the happy woman you once were and the woman that your partner fell in love with. Never stop investing in yourself, working on yourself, growing and enriching your life.

The Self Evaluating and Self Validating Vagina

I know that for many women we often put everyone else before ourselves and our own needs. However, this is the one time that it's acceptable to have a selfish mentality and you need to maintain your mind, body and soul if you expect to fulfill all the roles in your life. If we ignore this, it will surely come back and find us one day. It's just like a car with a flat tire: it can only drive a certain distance before the other three tires begin to wear from picking up the slack. Eventually, the car will become unreliable and not drive the same. Keeping yourself tuned up will ensure that you never end up with a flat vagina...because they don't make vagina spares like they do tires.

Our goal is to be self-sustained vaginas. To be able to validate ourselves and feed our own sense of happiness and security. We must always look within to help ourselves, and make sure that we don't place unhealthy expectations on a partner to pick up the slack. Sometimes when we become frustrated with the things we cannot do for ourselves, we mistakenly place unrealistic expectations on a mate. "You're not being supportive...If you loved me it shouldn't matter..." It's totally healthy to lean on a partner for support and encouragement, but not to place the brunt and burden of what we are unable to do for ourselves and put it on them. The greatest gift a woman can ever receive is one she can only give herself and that's self-love. So this is what we need to do:

- **Do Frequent Self-Assessments.** Am I happy? What makes me unhappy? What's causing me distress? Make a list of the things you love about yourself and ones you'd like to improve on.

- **How Can I Help Myself?** Take the first step to help your situation and help yourself. Do I want to lose weight? Take up yoga? Find ways to relax more? Take up hobbies? Eat better? Identify the things you can do to directly help yourself.

- **Implement an Action Plan**. Start today, not tomorrow, not next week! START TODAY! We want to eat better? Then our next meal will be better. Want to work-out? Find the time tomorrow even if it's sit-ups before bed.

- **Reach Out And Get Help**. If it's something bigger than you can handle, if it involves feeling depressed for a long time or unresolved issues from your childhood or past, then reach out, go to your doctor, and ask for help. Build a support group with your spouse and close friends. They can become that extra bit of wind in your sail and help see you through. Anything you need to do, stop at nothing to make it happen and find happiness.

Investing in yourself involves everything from simply eating better and even working to seeing a therapist for self-improvement. It can also mean coloring your hair or getting your nails done, and even taking up hobbies like reading, writing or drawing and painting. Understand that you need to have the ability to sustain your own happiness. The positive energy you create is contagious and it promotes more positive energy in the relationship. Happy vibes give way to more happy vibes, and people naturally gravitate to this type of environment. Whatever it takes, make a pact with yourself to make it happen and become the advocate of your personal happiness.

3. Embrace Your Vagina & Find Comfort in Yourself:

The idea is simple: Think for yourself, decide for yourself and find comfort within yourself and with the decisions you make. Don't seek validation from the world or those around you, because the way the world sees it is not always in line with how a man sees things. Society may have their version of an "ideal wife," but a man's version includes the quality of having great sex appeal and sexual confidence. If you find comfort with something and you and your partner are on the same page, then it's the only page that matters. Define your own identity and enjoy the comforts that your relationship brings to your life. Men find it attractive when a woman can own who she is and not feel the need to hide certain parts of herself. So many women struggle with being true to themselves. We're distracted with stupid standards like, ladies don't curse, they don't belch, they don't pee, they tinkle and they definitely do not take number two's in the bathroom. Like seriously? First off, you and I both know that plenty of us like to not only say 'fuck' but do it, too. I have frequented enough 'powder rooms' in my time to attest to the fact that women definitely burp, they fart (and sometimes both at the same time), they piss like horses, and many clogged toilets out there say that women do a shitload more than we let on. Yet, our need to appease our social audience and appear as though we defy the laws of nature, have us driving to the freaking corner gas station just to take a shit in peace and not stink up the house. Obviously, logic applies here and there does exist a happy medium: a place between pretending that you haven't shit since your days in diapers, and accidentally shitting yourself during a farting competition with your boyfriend.

Listen, obviously this doesn't have to do with bathroom activities and speaks to something bigger. It's about having comfort in your own skin, and comfort with all you represent. Keep in mind that even our little imperfections and quirks are what make us unique, and in part it's what a man falls in love with. This comfort is something that affects all aspects of the relationship. It affects your ability to let yourself go, to be silly and simply have fun. It also plays out in the bedroom with the comfort to let it all hang out and to hum the star spangled banner with your vagina lips. How's a woman supposed to relax and enjoy the experience of being orally serviced by her partner, when she's too busy obsessing over the thought that her vagina must look like a corned beef sandwich from his angle and view.

Seriously? In a loving and committed relationship he doesn't care what type of deli meats her vagina resembles and as long as she's not a vegetarian and likes to eat hotdogs, he's totally kosher and happy with it.

'The Power of the Pussy'

Speaking of vagina lips... One of the greatest gifts that has ever been bestowed upon women is the essence of our female sexuality. Now, I know that it's often hard to see the positive benefits of vagina ownership, especially when that bitch is acting up once a month and the only remedy in the moment is an ice cream sundaes topped with chocolate sauce and 150,000 calories of vagina guilt. Are we having fun yet? You know, the kind of fun that all those frolicking and giggling chicks are having in those tampon commercials? Dolling themselves up in satin white dresses, smiling, dancing, and meeting cute boys out on the town. LIARS! They're all liars! I must be one of the unfortunate ones who ended up with a defective vagina model...because that bitch doesn't do any of the things that those other commercial vaginas claim to do. When I'm toppled over with period cramps (and feel like I'm about to birth a mini refrigerator) the last thing I'm thinking is "oh, let me slip into some heels and crisp white pants and hit the club with my girls!" Bitch, please! I can't squeeze this bloated ass into anything that doesn't have an elastic waist, and the last place I want to be is the club! Especially when I feel like I'm in labor and about to deliver a damn mini-fridge that better have some chocolate in it.

Okay, sorry...rants and jokes aside, if we can actually look beyond all of this there's no denying that women bring something truly valuable to the world. ENTER THE POWER OF THE PUSSY! It's true, and whether it's viewed as a good or bad thing, the reality is that men happen to have a serious weakness when it comes to their sexual needs. Our female representation (AKA our sexuality, AKA our vagina, AKA the power of the pussy), has an influence over men similar to that of what kryptonite is to Superman. It can weaken a man's mental capacity, and bring him to his knees. This vagina bitch is like a freaking super hero! It kind of makes you wanna throw on that little vagina super cape and run out into the streets shooting laser beams out of your crotch and blowing shit up doesn't it?! Okay, maybe not...That would be kind of awkward.

Now, we may not be looking to use this powerful tool for evil purposes, but in a committed relationship it surely has its benefits. The presence of our female sexuality and how we assert ourselves in the relationship is a universal language that all men speak and that all men gravitate to. So of course, a smart epic vagina is one that will embrace this wonderful quality and unleash it for all it's worth! Hang on to those vagina super hero capes, they will come in handy!

4. Empower Yourself by Vowing to be Proactive Instead of Reactive:

This concept is really important, and as humans it's something that many of us are not aware of. It basically involves the psychology behind the approach that people take in life, and how they navigate their existence. People fall into one of two categories of either being a Primary Proactive Force or a Secondary Reactive Force.

A Primary Proactive person is someone who makes realistic assessments, and considers all the potential variables and outcomes before they take place. They focus on what their desired goal is and they identify the areas where they do have control and where they can help influence their desired outcome. They commit to proactively invest their efforts into the areas they can control. This approach has positive benefits because it allows us to avoid potential undesirable outcomes from transpiring. This type of person basically uses their positive force and energy to strategically place themselves out into the universe and greatly influence their desired destiny.

A Secondary Reactive type is someone who takes a passive stance and waits for the universe to gravitate to them and to deliver their outcomes. This is the role that most people take, and they have no idea that they are doing so. It's based on the notion that you really don't know what's going to happen in life until it happens, so you might as well deal with it when the time comes. Only when they are met with an undesirable outcome, do they then try to assert their efforts into navigating out of it successfully. The problem is that this is like trying to undo a car accident right after it happens. What they don't realize is that when we proactively take advantage of the areas we can control, we eliminate many crappy outcomes.

People don't come along and determine your happiness, and your entire existence should never wager on external forces. This mentality applies to the relationship as well, and if it's happily ever after that you seek, you need to proactively invest in the efforts that will make this happen because this outcome is promised to no one...It does not transpire on its own, and no piece of paper or marriage certificate grants us with the false sense of invincibility that people often assume. We do not wait for the relationship to deliver us to destination unknown and only then do we spring into action. Proactively remaining in action will keep the relationship on track and our happiness intact. Remember, the type of "everlasting love" found in storybooks doesn't just fall in our laps. It takes a great amount of work and effort to achieve that fantasy type of relationship.

So moral of the story, an epic vagina is a primary proactive force. We will secure our destiny and our happiness through proactive investments in ourselves and in our relationships. An epic vagina is always two steps ahead (Yes, she also walks in this story...Oh just amuse me and play along!).

5. Staying Connected with Yourself is a Life Long Commitment: Investing in yourself is the best gift you can ever give yourself, because it's something that no one can ever take away from you. And it puts you in the best position to be able to truly fulfill your partner's needs. It really takes a truly dynamic woman to bring it all, and when we do find this within ourselves, success is ours for the taking. With that being said, I have included a Toolbox section at the end of this book where you will find exercises and helpful tools. I've included a helpful Vagina Checklist, which is something that should become your vagina's bible. Stick it to your fridge, tape it to the toilet, sing it in the shower...whatever it takes... read it, reread it and let it become your daily vagina affirmations. Actually, you may want to avoid reading it while you drive and be a prudent hands-free vagina. I'm telling you, it has a way of gifting you with a contagious vagina. Like not the bad kind of contagious that people avoid from catching... but the good kind of contagious that men want! ... Kinda of like a Spidey Vagina with those sticky webs that pulls people in. Wait... maybe not, sticky webs and a vagina combo because they don't sound good together ... okay, forget Spidey Vagina... We were good at Epic...

The overall idea is that it's important for us to create positive energy and influence the destiny that we seek. It's important for us to nurture ourselves and to fulfill our own fundamental need for self-love and self-worth. We must create a self-identity that we are content with and have a great sense of self-confidence. We must not allow the outer world to suppress our inner greatness or negatively impact the richness we build within ourselves. Remember, nothing is ever forced upon us or taken away from us. It's only when we allow those toxins into our world that we readily hand our existence and fate over to an unknown destiny.

You must make a pact with yourself to always be a proactive force in your life and the sole owner of your personal happiness. This will ensure that you are always the narrator and author of your story and not simply someone who is reading along. A proactive, self-sustained vagina is one that will never be caught in a rainstorm without an umbrella (yes, in this story vaginas have their own umbrellas). Alright ladies, now that our epic vaginas are empowered and rearing to go… let's take these bitches on over to the relationship section and let us start redefining greatness!

Chapter Three

Penis and Vagina Negotiations

Now that we have thoroughly discussed a man's needs and touched on the importance of readying ourselves for a relationship through self-fulfillment, it's now time to bring it all together and look at the overall relationship dynamic between a man and a woman. When two people come together they each negotiate their roles and form a newly defined coupledom identity. The art of negotiation is something that many people don't focus on and where they also have the most misconceptions in their relationships. Unaware of what "compromise" and "negotiation" truly means in relationships, people often lack full insight into the expectations they have of a spouse and of their own role in the union. People often think that if you simply grab a book on relationship advice and follow all the steps, then magically everything will become exactly as the book coaches. However, relationships are like a cooking recipe, and the greatness of a final product is in the ingredients that actually went into making it. I always say, that even one bad ingredient can spoil the entire batch and never produce greatness. This is why it's important to identify that both ingredients and partners are of sound quality, and each person is bringing an equal amount of great investment in order to make it happen. So before we get into building greatness, we need to touch on some of the challenges and not so great realities couples may face in relationships. We need to ensure that we have the right approach and that we are indeed with a quality mate who is also in it to win it.

Negotiables Vs. Non-Negotiables

Anyone who's ever been in a relationship knows that love requires compromise. There will always come a time for making concessions, compromise and also sacrifice for the sake of the relationship. Negotiation comes with the territory of love and in every healthy relationship it's all about balance. It really comes down to understanding what negotiating truly means in a relationship. When and where we should be making sacrifices for love, and when we inadvertently end up sacrificing ourselves in the process of making concessions in the wrong areas. For many people, they don't understand what is considered healthy negotiations and unhealthy negotiations. There are small and big negotiables in a the relationship: Small negotiables are things like who gets to sleep on what side of the bed, or choosing to bite your tongue about his constant habit of leaving the toilet seat up.

In the grand scheme of things, these are pretty insignificant factors. I mean, sure it takes two seconds to put the toilet seat down...and it sure would eliminate the fucking heart attack of falling in and baptizing your ass with toilet water at three am and in complete darkness...but in his defense, and according to the penis handbook, the "up" position is the natural position for the toilet seat and he wouldn't miss the toilet when peeing if the vagina simply followed this logical rule. And does it really matter if he leaves globs of toothpaste in the sink, or speckled all over the mirror? True love means wiping it up and choosing not to say anything. Same goes with him forgetting to close the garage door and leaving it open all night (so the raccoons can have a buffet feast out of your trash can), or forgetting to take off his shoes and trekking mud on the carpet…I mean it was only mentioned to him like a million times…plus, it's not as bad as him trying to make a sandwich and leaving the kitchen looking like a bunch of preschoolers just had a freaking bake off!. Like seriously!? What fucking pack of wild sasquatches raised his ass?! Okay…Breathe… let's put down the stiletto and think about the love… In all seriousness, when you love somebody you learn to let go of the little things that are far less significant than the overall picture perfect happiness we look to maintain.

Even though relationships are all about compromise, there are certain factors that are not up for negotiation…EVER. I'm talking about something called Non-Negotiables, and every single person needs to have them. Non-negotiables are the standards and values we set for ourselves and what we expect from the relationship and a spouse. These standards involve the big ticket items that affect you as a person: your values and your worth, and are etched in stone. Anyone coming into your life must meet these standards, honor them, and they must never be broken or compromised at any cost. Non-negotiables are deal breakers, and when they do become compromised, so does the relationship.

Three Non-Negotiable Must-Haves for Every Relationship:

Even though no two relationships are alike, every relationship must have three fundamental elements (aside from love of course) in order to succeed:

- **Respect:** Respect requires each partner to be considerate of one another's needs, emotional investments and vulnerabilities and place them equal to our own. Having mutual respect for one another provides a balance of importance for each individual and shows them that they are valuable to the union. Love and respect go hand in hand, and true love means to never disrespect or dishonor the one we love. This rule applies at all times, and even during heated arguments there must never be hurtful words or behaviors that stand to leave lasting effects on the union. Even before there is love, there must always be respect, and without respect there really is nothing.

- **Loyalty:** Each partner needs to honor the relationship and their behaviors must be reflective of their commitment. Loyalty is expressed through the exclusive investments we make towards a partner, and through our willingness to remain invested and committed at all times.

- **Trust:** In order for the trust to be solid in the relationship, each partner needs to bring the trustworthy and loyal behaviors we just discussed. This element is a little tricky, because it's not just based on what a partner is willing to bring. There's an equal requirement on our part to have a healthy inner relationship with ourselves and a good sense of security. Otherwise, it won't matter how loyal a partner is because where there are unhealthy insecurities, there will always be a lack of trust.

It's these three elements of respect, loyalty and trust that act as the foundation to the relationship. If even one of these elements is compromised, it affects the entire union. People often think that love is the most important element in a relationship. It's not love that's most important, it's respect. Respect is the most fundamental element for humanity let alone relationships, and before love even flourishes, respect must already be in place. Love is nothing without respect. When it comes to these three elements, the rules are simple. One can only expect to receive if they too are prepared to give in return. If it's respect you want, you need to show respect to your partner. If you want to trust your mate and for them to be loyal, then you too must be trustworthy and you must be just as loyal in return.

Remember, it's not about demanding respect, it's about commanding respect through our own investments and behaviors. It's important to understand that these fundamental elements are critical factors in determining whether or not a relationship will succeed. The quality and richness of a relationship is based on the ingredients that go into it. If both partners are not equally invested in honoring these rules, then a book such as this one will be of little value and benefit to the relationship. The best way to preserve greatness in the relationship is to always honor these 3 elements and ensure that they are maintained as a constant throughout the entire union.

Respecting Each Other's Personal Non-Negotiables:

Aside from these three fundamental elements, each partner also brings their own unique non-negotiables into the relationship. This includes both personal values and standards, and also non-negotiable elements that are exclusive to each partner's sex. Again, a "non-negotiable" standard is a term or expectation based on one's needs and their personal values. Many people base their non-negotiable deal breakers on their beliefs, and are unwilling to compromise on finding a mate who shares the same faith or ideals in raising children. Things like wanting to have children, or a desire to get married, or even to never get married. These are all personal non-negotiables that people bring into relationships and are not willing to bend on under any circumstance. This makes perfectly good sense, and it's important for people to identify these non-negotiables prior to embarking into any relationship.

It helps us navigate more precisely in finding a compatible mate, and by communicating these factors a couple is able to determine whether or not they are a good fit for one another. It' also is a crucial variable when it comes to identifying whether or not a relationship will have lasting power and be successful. One of the reasons why relationships fail is because people fail to clearly identify their non-negotiables when entering into a relationship. And once in a relationship, many people allow their non-negotiables to become compromised. They continue to stay on in the union long after it is no longer serving their needs, which eventually leads to unhappiness and failure.

When you make the choice to commit to someone, you also commit to honoring their personal non-negotiable standards. It's a package deal and there's no trying to alter or redefine their standards to suit your needs or comforts. This is where many women have a misconception about relationships, and it's our emotionally intuitive nature that makes many women think that the "power of love" can conquer all. This perception is the reason why so many women experience struggles in their relationships, and instead of seeing things for what they truly are, they see things for what they have the potential of becoming. Many women naturally assume that as long as the love is grand, and almost everything matches up, that they will somehow arrive at their intended destination. The problem is that what's not included in "almost everything" can be pretty big deal breakers that people choose to ignore. They figure that because there's potential, they can somehow influence change and they'll deal with it at a later time. When it comes to a man's non-negotiables, this is something that shouldn't be ignored, because they are not negotiable. Women often have this perception that somehow the love will change him, and she will eventually have her own non-negotiables met. This is the reason why many relationships fail, and it's due to that "things will work themselves out" mentality. The reality is that things do work themselves out, and it's called divorce.

The reality is that we're quite expectant for a man to honor our non-negotiables in a relationship, and in turn he expects the same and it's just as important to honor a man's non-negotiables. All too often women see these things as being negotiable, that they can somehow influence a man to have a change of heart, and when it becomes a struggle they blame their partner for not being open to compromise. My husband and I have a friend who was dating someone for over 4 years. He was married once before, for over 20 years and after his divorce he decided that he had no intentions of ever getting married again. He loved his girlfriend very much and committed to the relationship wholeheartedly, he just didn't see the need for that title. They were both in their 40s and from the very onset of the relationship he was very candid and honest about his wishes and intentions. In the beginning she was accepting of this and about a year into their relationship she decided that she did want to get married. She was rightfully entitled to her change of heart and her changing needs, but she did not recognize the fact that she was now pushing for something that did not meet his needs. The relationship became a tug of war and filled with endless quarrels, break-ups and make-ups and just an overall strained dynamic. They both deserved to be happy and have their needs honored, but neither of them would achieve this in the relationship they shared. It's important for couples to share similar views in the relationship and to have likeminded expectations for what they hope to achieve.

Sex is a Non-Negotiable for the Penis:

People often view sex as a physical affair and don't recognize the importance of what it truly means to the relationship. Now, I know that sex means just as much to the vagina, but we're focusing on the penis right now…so hush those horny gals for a moment. Women rely on the sexual relationship as much as men do, but we have the ability to achieve the same fulfillment from other areas of the relationship. Men too achieve the fulfillment from other areas, but the physical sexual relationship is something they heavily rely on and that they are not willing to part with. Men don't need every single day to be a booty shaking sex fest in the bedroom, but they do require some form of constant feedings on a regular basis. Whether it involves connecting intimately through touch, kissing, cuddling, light foreplay, sensual massage, and various other forms of affectionate expressions. As long as it's something that stimulates his sex brain and gets his bodies juices flowing, he's a content and happy guy.

This is a definite non-negotiable for men, and something they are not willing to part with or greatly compromise on in their relationships. We already discussed the fact that women are natural-born survivalists, and even though it may not be by choice or our desire to, we would be able to part with all the pussy and penis Olympics if it became absolutely necessary. For the penis, on the other hand, well, it's like taking a goldfish out of water and expecting it to live. Oh sorry, for the male egos we just offended... It's like taking a killer whale out of the water and expecting this massive beast to survive. Women can easily gain emotional fulfillment through many other areas of the relationship, as can men. However, by default it's those abundant male hormones that cause men to gravitate to sex as their most prominent form of emotional expression and fulfillment. Also, when this intense male hormone builds up it creates impulsive behaviors and causes a man to seek physical gratification to resolve the pent up sexual tension in his system. I know this sounds like some sort of farce that a bunch of desperate penises came up with, but it's true. Women can't appreciate the intensity of what the penis experiences because we simply don't have one. Hey it is what it is, and it just so happens that guys take diesel fuel and gals take a more refined unleaded fuel when filling up their love tanks.

I've coached couples in the past, where the sexual relationship was non-existent. This is not as uncommon as many people think and some studies show that one out of every five long-term relationships, are sexless unions. This can create a disconnection in the union and create unhappiness. Now understand that we are not speaking about exceptions to the rule, and relationships where couples endure extraordinary circumstances such as pregnancy, illness, medical reasons etc...because when a partner's health and welfare is in question, both men and women alike go into nurture mode and sex is the furthest from their mind. I'm talking about relationships where for no valid reason, the sex somehow falls to the wayside. There's only one thing that our epic vagina's need to know about this. A man is unwilling to part with sex, and when a relationship becomes sexless, it is not by a man's own free choice.

People often don't realize how crucial the sexual relationship is to the overall relationship. The sexual relationship provides for emotional, physical and mental fulfillment and this is why in order for the overall relationship to thrive, the sexual relationship must always remain in good standing. When the sexual relationship suffers and stops providing for fulfillment, it creates a huge void both emotionally and mentally. It also affects a person's desire to continue investing good efforts into a union that no longer provides them with happiness. When someone experiences a void in any capacity and in an area that they deem fundamental to their needs and happiness, it's human nature for them to try and find some source of fulfillment. Anything, even tiny feedings will suffice. A sexless union is no different than a starving person and a vagina may not see it this way, but a famished penis does and it's foolish to think that anyone in a deprived state of starvation wouldn't instinctually look for food out of desperation. It's this sexual starvation that causes people, specifically men in this case, to start making stupid decisions out of desperation. Feeling disconnected and neglected, it starts to make everyone else's grass start to appear a lot brighter and greener. The reality is that the grass isn't always greener on the other side, it's greener where you water it. And when the grass isn't being watered or nurtured, it has a way of making the other side look a lot greener. Oddly enough, you would think that any man would be the first to pipe up the second his feedings have been taken away from him…but such is not the case. I have coached many men who confide that their sexual relationship is lacking, yet they don't have it in them to come out and say something. The reasoning is often because they love their partner very much and they don't want to hurt their partner's feelings in the event it's taken personally.

When the sexual relationship, or any other area in the relationship is not being nurtured, we shouldn't assume that a partner's happiness is unaffected simply because they haven't said anything. One cannot assume that the grass will remain green and continue to thrive when it's being neglected and it's a lot easier to maintain a healthy lawn then it is to try and save a dead one and bring it back to life. I know that this seems like a somber discussion, but we vowed to keep it real and as realists we need to acknowledge the common areas where people make mistakes in relationships. Women often don't place the same non-negotiable expectation on sex as they do on love, but men do. A man places equal importance on both love and sex and it's because he relies on the sexual relationship as a way of expressing his love and gaining emotional fulfillment.

Expectations and Offerings in the Relationship

When we enter into a new relationship, and as it progresses into a more bonafide level of commitment, this is when we look to communicate and establish our non-negotiables and the parameters of the relationship. Two people coming together must negotiate their newly defined roles, their expectations and create a unified identity for the relationship. Negotiations take place in relationships all the time, and it's not only found in the form of verbal communication. Any time a couple interacts with one another, negotiations take place through their behaviors, their actions, and reactions towards one another.

Everyone goes into a relationship with both expectations and offerings. Our expectations are based on what we want and need from our partner in order to achieve fulfillment and happiness. We, in turn, offer up what we're willing to do to fulfill a partner's needs. This is what I call the "Love Barter," and it's basically a bartering and exchange of offerings with the intentions of mutual fulfillment and happiness. Once this is established, we believe the relationship will continue on in this way indefinitely. The reality is that throughout our lives and the course of our relationships, we evolve, we change and we grow. This is very much expected and even with a continuously evolving dynamic in the relationship, the only goal is for a couple to stay connected and to grow together. Change can be good, as long as the union continues to serve each partner. But change can be bad if we get sidelined by these common mistakes and often overlooked factors:

1. We Lose Momentum and Get Lazy:

It's a very expected reality that as a relationship progresses, the honeymoon stage transitions into a deeper bond and a new found embracing comfort is born. Many of the couples I speak with share a similar struggle in their relationships and find it challenging to manage new variables along while keeping the excitement of the honeymoon phase alive. For many people, the wonderful comfort that commitment brings to their lives inadvertently becomes complacency. And instead of working to find solutions in maintaining the most important variables in the union, they simply start investing less and less effort in certain areas. The reality is that this is simply real life. However, this is also the very factor that distinguishes successful relationships from the one's that end up failing. Losing momentum and allowing certain aspects of the relationship to fade is a choice, and those who choose to invest great efforts to prevent this from happening are the ones who persevere and succeed. It's no easy feat, especially when we are trying to manage it all. This is when they say 'relationships are hard work'. Actually, it should be worded 'successful relationships require a lot of work'. When there's a will there's always a way to make it happen.

Quite often the reason why people begin to invest less into the relationship is because they stopped investing in themselves. This causes an inner sense of unhappiness, and it depletes their motivation to invest in the relationship. Let's use good old Becky as an example... Becky used to take pride in how she looked. She was all about eating healthy, working out, and she loved to get dolled up every day when she first met Larry. Putting on cute and sexy outfits, and doing her hair and make-up used to make Becky feel beautiful inside and out. Nowadays between work, carpooling the kids around and all the other million tasks on her daily list, Becky has little desire to invest the time and energy in things like hair and make-up. Her workout regimen used to be a great way to relieve her stress and it made her feel energetic and positive about herself. Nowadays, she simply can't find the time or energy to walk to the mailbox let alone workout. Not only has Becky lost touch with herself, she has lost touch with Larry and especially Larry's balls (which happen to be very blue and backed up, and attached to the penis who is also not feeling the love).

Self admittedly, Becky's only look these days is "Death Becomes Her" and at any given hour it's hard to tell if she's just getting up or perhaps headed to bed? Poor Larry (and his backed up balls). He wonders what ever happened to happy and fun Becky...Where is she these days? She must be around here somewhere (turns corner)... HOLY CRAP WHAT IS THAT?! GRAB YOUR BACKED UP BALLS AND RUN LARRY!!! IT'S A ZOMBIE APOCALYPSE!!! Oh Wait... Phew! False alarm, it's only Becky with no make-up on and sporting an oversized mumu... Larry loves his wife very much and he's quite compassionate for how she must be feeling.... But Larry's balls on the other hand are a tad puzzled and wondering WHAT THE FUCK HAPPENED TO BECKY? (speaking of hand, this is the only love his balls are getting).

And don't think that it's always going be Becky, because Larry could easily be the one who checks out. Once upon a time, hot and buff Larry used to work out six days a week, and had three promising career projects on the go. He was a go-getter and somehow, somewhere, he's now a go nowhere sort of guy and his full time job consists of sitting on the couch and shouting dollar amounts at the TV during the Price Is Right. His only workout involves holding the TV remote in one hand and his penis in the other. Just when it appears that Larry may have died on the couch 'cause he hasn't moved in three days, he surprises Becky by putting the remote down. Holy shit, is Larry getting up off the couch? Nope, no such chance...Larry just needed a free hand to pick his nose. Surely he'll have to get up now to fetch a tissue... aaaaand nope... Larry just launched a boogie across the room and it landed on the dog. That's great, Lar, real great, you sexy beast... Okay, funny time is over, we'll let Larry get back to his season finale of Naked and Couponing. Perhaps this sounds over the top, but sadly it's not that far-fetched for many struggling couples. This may not be descriptive of you and I, but let's make a pact that neither of us will end up this way (and we'll never own a mumu, or at least until the age of sixty-five, when we'll need something to drape over those elasticized boobs that are bobbling down past our knees.)

2. *Expectations and Offerings Must be an Equal Exchange:* It makes sense that one's expectations and offerings will always remain balanced and that the two way street will continue to flow both ways. However, there are times where people don't recognize the fact that they have stopped investing in certain parts of the relationship and that their offerings have drastically declined. I have dealt with many couples where they still share love for one another, but where the sexual relationship is suffering and has become disconnected....Or where they no longer share a connection and they have stopped investing in the romance. A couple that now has "good love" for one another but is no longer "in love' with one another. Here's the thing: when we stop investing our offerings in certain areas of the relationship it affects the overall union. Many people have this misguided notion that even though their offerings change, they still maintain the same level of expectations. If one partner starts to slack and they're no longer going out of their way to ensure their spouses needs are being met, then they mustn't expect for their spouse to keep up all the work on their end. It's that simple. And if the sexual relationship becomes compromised and these needs are not being met, then it would be foolish to expect the relationship to continue to provide for one's security.

3. You Cannot Allow Certain Offerings to Fade (Or How Men See It):

Here's the harsh reality for us women. Many of us will hear about relationships where the love is still intact, but for one reason or another, a couple is barely having sex or not having sex at all. Just as damaging as a sexless union, is a relationship that's based on 'maintenance sex' and when a couple's sole motivation for having sex is just so that they can say "Hey, look we're fulfilling our dutiful obligations as husband and wife and we're maintaining the sexual relationship in good standing."

That's not a real sex life and having unfulfilling sex leads to feeling unfulfilled in the overall relationship and unhappiness. The reality is that many couples struggle to find time to juggle it all and all the added stress and distractions ends up killing the sexual chemistry in their relationship. A fire doesn't keep itself burning and it takes work to maintain it.

We often hear about a marriage that still has love despite the sex void, but how often do you hear of a committed union where the love is gone and it's only sex. See, for women as long as we still have love and security, the missing link of sex is not always life-altering for us. However, it is to a man. Imagine if it was the other way around and we had only sex to rely on but no emotional security? The International Vagina Union would start a movement and go on strike, until that shit got resolved! I know that we're placing a great deal of emphasis on sex and the risks of sexless unions. We get it! A man wants sex, it's good for the relationship and without it things will fall to shit. Unfortunately, many women don't get it and it's the one definitive factor that divides men and women in relationships and that leads to failure. Remember, it may seem one-sided and that the vagina is getting a bum deal. And yes, many women need sex just as much as the next penis, but we're here to learn about men and that's what this book is about, so let's put those girls on ice and keep on moving.

Women often have a sense of invincibility in a committed union, and a perception that the relationship can survive on sexless auto-pilot. Men don't see it this way, and for a man to consider the union in good standing, he's expectant for the sex to remain just as plentiful as the love is. The reality is that men look to preserve the same variables that they have come to know. The logical male brain operates on 'what you see is what you get'. It's no different than going to the car lot and buying a brand new sports car. The logical male brain understands that overtime and in years to come, perhaps the car won't shine or run like it used to. What he doesn't expect is to walk into the garage one day and find that the sports car turned into a station wagon (Now I know the vagina/car comparison was somewhat insulting, but we're trying to get into the mind of the penis, and well need I say more?) Men rely on physical and mental attraction to stimulate their sex brain and remaining emotionally connected. Men are very expectant of change, to a certain degree. Obviously after twenty years of marriage and a couple of kids, not everyone is going to look the way they did on their wedding day. Women see things no differently, and we're quite accepting of certain marginal fluctuations over the years, but not for a stallion horse to turn into a warthog. Embracing life and these changes and taking care of ourselves the best way we can is all that we can do. However, if someone simply loses touch and stops investing in themselves, and they no longer resemble the person they once were (be it lifestyle, 100lbs weight gain/loss etc…) it's unrealistic to expect that such a change would not affect a spouse. A man may still have great love for his wife, but the physical and sexual attraction may not be the same.

This is simply a reality, and commitment does not imply that regardless of what we are not willing to do for ourselves, that a partner must be accepting of it all. The physical aspects are a small part of a much larger picture, and such lifestyle changes create a disconnection in the commonalities that a couple once shared. If a couple used to share a common interest for biking, hiking and the outdoors, and one of them is now putting in marathon hours on the couch while the other is still enjoying those outdoor hobbies they no longer connect in that part of the relationship and foster two different lifestyle values. Small to moderate changes can be good, even large leaps that are taken in unison can be just as good, but a complete lifestyle renovation that's one-sided is unexpected and often difficult to become fully embracing of.

4. Understanding How the 'Exchange' Process Works:

When it comes to our offerings in a relationship, they must be based on a partner's wants and needs and not on our own needs and wants. Quite often we go into relationships with our own needs in mind, and this becomes our sole motivation. It's based on the self-serving mentality of "What will I get out of this, and what's in it for me?" Quite often people are of the mindset "This is all I'm willing to give, this is how I will give it, and only after

I get mine." Imagine being in a restaurant that operated this way. You place your order for a chicken salad, and out comes the chef totting 3 measly leafs of lettuce, no chicken because he wasn't feeling very generous today, and he asks you to first pay the full priced tab before he releases the wilted lettuce. Man, this place must get all the best reviews online! Most people aren't even aware of the fact that they take this approach, and it's our need for security and the fear that stems from not having it that causes us to often be like this by default. It's this exact self-serving approach that holds many women back from achieving greatness in their relationships. It's that disabling security factor that causes women to place conditions on their love offerings.

The approach that produces far greater results is when we customize our offerings to suit a partner's needs, and their happiness is our sole motivation. It's based on the notion that "because I love you, I am giving you this to make you happy, with no conditions or expectations in return." This rare approach would cause most men to be skeptical, because it sounds too good to be true, so there must be a catch. There is a catch, but a good one…and in a man's eyes, this type of woman is a great catch and a dream come true. The idea of forsaking our own immediate needs can be an intimidating one to commit to, but there must be faith in the fact that we have chosen a mate who will be motivated to do the same. Think about it, if we have to worry about securing our own needs first, in fear that we will invest in him and that he won't do the same…then we haven't chosen wisely in a mate. And truth be told, women are quick to point it out when a man appears to have self-serving motives. Like when a man is being too sweet, and extra helpful around the house we often joke that his penis is bobbing for vagina apples. In his defense, it's those damn male hormones that often cause his penis to hijack his brain. Ultimately, when two people are invested and committed to one another's happiness then their offerings should come easily… and their expectations should never exceed their offerings, or come with strings attached. Tampons come with strings attached, not truly epic relationships.

5. Shake the Invincible Mindset (Reality Check Please!): The reality is this... The very reason people end up unhappy or disconnected in relationships is because they feel as though the union is no longer serving their needs. When someone feels unfulfilled, they begin to lose motivation to continue investing in the relationship. The basic psychology behind human behaviors is no different than most trainable animals, and I know that it's odd to compare humans to dogs but it is what it is. Humans are motivated by positive reinforcement and rewards. When we feel rewarded for our efforts and our happiness is being provided for, it motivates us to continue investing into the positive rewards cycle and relationship. If the relationship ceases to put out rewards, the momentum and motivation begins to fade.

They say that hindsight is 20/20, and if the very people who find themselves in unhappy relationships understood the repercussions of unhappiness and even divorce prior to all of it taking place...I assure you more couples would work harder. My father always used to say that as humans our greatest motivator is fear. It's not to say that we should live in fear and not enjoy the comforts that commitment brings us. However, many people live with a sense of invincibility. They view marriage and commitment as an iron clad fortress one that is bullet proof. They do not see the delicacy in relationships, and they do not see the risks and potentials of becoming complacent and losing momentum.

If relationships were similar to annual renewable leases, and couples had to renew their commitment every single year based on the quality of the past year, I assure you that a lot more people would be hustling in relationships. Think about it, when we're locked into a cellular contract and it comes up for renewal, how inclined are you to renew if the service was no good, and you could never catch a darn signal to make a call? We wouldn't, and we would take our business elsewhere. The only time we stay and complain about crappy phone reception is when we are locked in a contract and there's a penalty to break out of it. I'm sure we can both agree, that we'd want our partner to want to be in a relationship with us, and not because he's feeling trapped or that he's avoiding the high cost of leaving. It may seem like I'm comparing apples to oranges here, but I assure you that if a marriage contract worked in the same way that many other contracts do in the business world, people would make a relationship their number one job. Couples would have far greater reception in their relationships than on their cell phones, and they'd be serving their relationships better than any business out there. Way more kinky sex would be had, Hallmark stocks would be soaring, hair salons would have lines out the door, and there wouldn't be a vacant treadmill to be found at any gym around.

Commitment and marriage are privileges that grace our lives and not entitlements. Not many people see it this way. This is the exact approach I encourage people to take towards their relationships, and it's the mindset I foster in my own relationship. The investments I make each and every day are with the notion that each year on our anniversary my husband and I sign on for another year based on the one that we just had. This has a way of keeping us on our toes, it keeps us invested and greatly motivated. Anyone who has ever endured divorce and found themselves back out in the dating world for a second go round, will tell you that it is no fun out there! For every one decent person you will potentially find, you will likely encounter a thousand losers. Trust me when I say that knowing what's out there and what's not out there, is what has become my greatest motivator.

An Epic Vagina Holds Herself to a Higher Standard

The most important factor is this: If we expect the relationship to continue to provide for us in the same way it always has, then we must be committed to continually provide for the relationship in every area and not just where we deem as most important. Remember, perception is reality... And one partner may perceive happiness as focusing solely on love, where a spouse may find this dynamic an unhappy one because their hopes are focused elsewhere in the relationship. Remember, we shouldn't simply rely on the notion that if a man is unhappy, he would say so. If he's not griping then he must be content. The reality is that it's not always in someone's nature to be forthcoming with how they feel, especially if they feel as though it will hurt their partner's feelings or be interpreted in the wrong way. The real way of knowing that everything is truly in check and the only time we should ever feel a great sense of security in the relationship is when we are invested and providing for every area of the relationship, especially in the areas that matter most to a spouse. And it's not just about investing in a spouse, because when we invest in ourselves it creates contagious positive energy. It prompts us to continue to invest in ourselves and our mate, and it motivates our mate to do the same in this positive environment. As women, it's very possible for us to have our expectations met in a relationship, and for a partner to invest their greatest efforts into making this happen. It all starts when you take the first step to invest your efforts and your offerings towards the areas that matter the most to your partner, and in turn he will do the same.

The key is to never lose momentum, and as long as you continue to fully invest in his happiness, you can continue to enjoy the comforts and security of him being fully invested in you as the primary source of his happiness. Remember, the best way to keep a man is to keep him happy. And a happy man is a motivated man, one who will reciprocate his happiness by investing in yours.

Chapter Four

The Love Barter: Changing the Way We Love

FINALLY! (Insert a round of vagina-flap applause) This is where all the magic begins! Now, before we start casting fairy dust vagina spells, there are two major factors that are required in order to make this work. Since our vaginas already have a great rapport, I am keeping it simple, straight to the point and REAL! So the two major requirements are:

1. Open Yourself Up to Understanding The True Definition of 'Unconditional Love':

We often reference the ultimate form of committed love as unconditional love. However, people often confuse "unlimited love" and having a lot of love to give, as being "unconditional." In relationships we are guided by our comforts, and our love offerings are limited to the level of comfort and security we find. So even though we say "unconditional," the common practice is "plenty of conditional love." Obviously, the reason why we have conditions on our love makes total sense, because who would want to push themselves out of their comfort zone and cause themselves distress just to accommodate a partner? However, using that "comfort crutch" simply because we don't want to face change can often act as a blinder and we end up missing out on achieving better results. Be open to compromise and making concessions where you can, just as long as it doesn't come at the cost of losing your own identity in the relationship.

Now, I know that many of you may be thinking that we are totally re-designing love and remodeling our approach entirely. Actually, it's much simpler than that, and even though there is a lot of change it has more to do with our mindset and our focus. It's about learning where to invest our efforts and how, and teaching ourselves to love more freely by focusing on our strengths.

2. Teamwork is The Only Way it will Work:

Going back to my dad and his always profound philosophies on life, he had once shared a story that explained the type of teamwork that a marriage requires (I'll spare you the heavy Greek accent)....

There are two pirates sitting on a ship (Ahoy, Mate!) Their pirate ship sits far off the coast of an island where they cannot pull into the shallow waters, but they are desperately trying to get onto the island and get their little hands on a treasure chest filled with loot (loot equals happiness in this story). The chest is locked away in a cave, and only one of the pirates has the map and key to the loot. However, the waters are infested with sharks and it's the other pirate who has the dingy boat. They each have a need for one another because if the key-holder swims he will become a shark snack and the dingy boat pirate has nothing to gain when he reaches the locked cave. They each have a need for one another, and if they join forces they can use the boat, unlock the cave and bring the loot back to the pirate ship.

Now, I know you may be thinking that you can simply throw that fucker overboard and steal his dingy boat. Don't ruin my story! Throwing him overboard, means his penis goes with him, and the goal is to keep him and his penis in the relationship boat! As a side note, using the pirate idea in the bedroom as role play is always a great way to spice things up.... (Except you may want to forego the wooden peg-leg and parrot... that would be a little odd and distracting). Essentially, the only way this approach will truly work is if both sides commit to implementing it and both are willing to invest good efforts towards keeping it up.

Love That Fits Like a Glove: Creating a Customized Formula

In Chapter One, I introduced the 'The Love Barter Tripod', and the three principles that it was based on. This is where the second principle comes into play, 'Learning How to Love Unconditionally'. As I mentioned earlier, our female viewpoint assumes that men achieve fulfillment in the exact same way as we do. However, this approach does not guarantee a man's happiness because it is not based on his male needs. Thus, the reason why a customized approach, one that takes a partner's unique needs into consideration, is far more effective and has the ability to grant true happiness in the relationship.

Unconditional (Selfless) Love Cycle:

Based on this theory, I have developed the concept of the Unconditional Love Cycle (aka. Selfless Love Cycle). It involves a practice which helps shift the focus from "loving with restrictions" and navigating with fears, to developing the confidence to love freely and focus on creating a more positive relationship environment. It's about learning how to invest in the right areas, utilizing your strengths and working as a team to strengthen the areas where comforts differ. Doing this aligns a couple's individual comforts with one another's needs and this creates a much higher rate of compatibility across all areas of the relationship. It increases the fulfillment they each receive, thus also increasing each partner's sense of happiness and ultimately increasing their chances at success. There are essentially five parts to developing this approach:

1. Assume a Selfless Role, Not a Self-Serving One.

The Unconditional Love Cycle is an approach to love where each partner assumes a selfless role, instead of a self-serving role. The common approach that we often take is to place emphasis on our own needs and look to secure the things that feed our own comforts and our security. Instead, place your focus 100% on your partner's needs, and make his happiness your number one priority in the relationship. This may seem one-sided and it may make you feel vulnerable to expose yourself to such uncertainty of whether or not your desires will be met. However, you must have faith in the person you have chosen for a mate. Trust that your partner's love for you will act as his motivation to ensure that the same is being met for you and your needs. The very purpose of seeking out companionship and the reason why this guy is in your life is because he brings unique offerings. So why would you interfere with that process? If our focus is on having our needs met, and we expect his focus to be on meeting our needs, then who's focusing exclusively on his needs? If you lead with insecurities and caution it prevents you from granting your partner true fulfillment and achieving your own ultimate security. Have faith to lead with your strengths, as this will not on grant him happiness, but also provide you with the ultimate sense of security by having taken this approach. Let your happiness be his job and his happiness remain as your number one job.

Each partner must be willing to invest all of their efforts into their spouse's needs. Catering to his happiness becomes your primary focus, investing in anything and everything that provides him with fulfillment. The cycle takes place when this approach starts to pay itself forward. This goes back to the concept of positive rewards influencing desirable human behaviors. The brain is quite responsive to a positive reward system, and the positive stimuli creates a contagious cycle. It prompts a person to want to share this elated happiness by giving back into the source that has made it all possible. It's kind of like honoring the hand that feeds you, and people are greatly motivated to express their gratitude and loyalty by investing back into this source and securing that the cycle will continue. All you need to do is concern yourself with what he requires in order to be happy, and by doing so his happy ass will come back at you with the greatest motivation and investments.

2. Know Where to Place Your Investments.

Men and women prioritize their needs differently, and just like every lock having its own unique key, the key and formula to unlocking a man's happiness is going to differ from what it takes to unlock your fullest happiness potential. There is no standard to how we prioritize love, and if it's important to him and it sits at the top of his happy list then this is his reality and how he sees happiness. Understand that "love" is not going to be at the top of everyone's list, and if sex or friendship is something that someone heavily relies on for emotional fulfillment then it will rightfully be at the top of their list.

Identifying the needs that each partner deems most important to their happiness is a very crucial step and this is why couples must be willing to be open and honest. You want to know, what are the things he gravitates to the most? What makes him happy? What is most important to him? Remember it's important to remain supportive of a partner regardless of how they prioritize their needs or view happiness. This is his reality and what provides him with happiness. There are no rights or wrongs, and if sex happens to be at the top of his list, in bold print and highlighted... understand that this is how he sees happiness and it's equally valid to a woman placing love or security at the top of the list. Maintaining a positive and receptive environment promotes candidness and honesty and this is the goal. A man is going to be the only person in the world that will ever give you the best relationship secrets and advice, because it comes straight from the source and it's exclusive to his happiness.

3. Honor Each Other's Comforts.

It's important for a couple to not only identify one another's unique needs, but to also identify their individual comforts. Having our comfort zone honored is something that we all require in order to maintain a comfortable sense of security in a relationship. It's important for each partner to clearly communicate their comfort boundaries, and openly discuss the areas where they share similar comforts and where their comforts may differ. There are no wrongs or rights when it comes to comfort level, and the ultimate goal for a couple is for them to share similar comforts in as many areas of the relationship as possible. This is where good negotiating comes into play, and a couple will lay out both of their needs and their comforts. The goal is to identify the areas where comforts and needs complement one another and where a partner has the comfort to fulfill their spouse's needs.

Now, here is where you need to take yourself to task. You need to have a balance between having your true comforts honored and respected by a mate, but not allowing yourself to hide behind your comforts and use this as a crutch simply because you want to avoid the unknown. In relationships, people are often uneasy about stepping out of their known comforts. Thus causing them to remain closed off to a partner's needs by placing their needs first. There must be a happy medium, where at the very least you are open to considering what a partner is asking of you. Sometimes if we allow ourselves to venture out of our little comfort box, we are surprised with how we grow and we create new comforts for new things. Obviously, pushing yourself out of your comfort zone should never come at the cost of placing distress on yourself or compromising your standards and values. I'm simply talking about opening yourself up to unknowns that you may have never tried and cannot judge or determine until you fully explore it. If you entertain the idea of something and decide that it does not meet your comforts, then you have at least honored your partner. Nothing should ever be forced or be distressful to the relationship, and each partner deserves to have their feelings honored.

Take for example a partner expressing an interest to explore sexually with the introduction of sex toys. This may be something that his partner never considered before, yet she's open to exploring the idea and stepping outside of her normal comforts. Ultimately if they both find enjoyment in this new venture, and she has embraced her newly defined comfort in the union, then this growth will only act as a positive contribution to their mutual happiness. Understand that it's not all about matching up in every area and this is not a compatibility race. It's about balance, and focusing on your strengths and on the areas where you and your mate share commonalities. Expanding our boundaries can be healthy, and it helps a couple grow together.

You want to focus on the areas where you share common ground with your partner and where you can find comfort in meeting his needs. Don't allow yourself to exude wasted efforts thinking about the areas where you differ or where you lack comfort. Sometimes women become consumed with focusing on the areas that make themselves feel inadequate and insecure. It has nothing to do with being inadequate and different people have different ways of finding enjoyment and happiness. When you focus on your strong suits and the areas where you can deliver, you create a much more positive environment. Remember, where there is love and honor there will always be a man that respects this differential and sees no significance in it. You don't have to try and be a Super Woman and a man is much more appreciative of a woman who gives as best she can, yet still remains true to herself. So instead of harping on weakness, negativity and short comings, take that energy and invest it in the areas that you can fulfill and where you share a mutual comfort. I assure you that this will create a much more positive relationship environment and make the areas that differ less significant. So the goal is to invite growth and change into our lives, push our comfort boundaries where we can but not to the point where it causes distress because then it's no longer meeting your own needs let alone his.

4. Communicate, Negotiate and Educate.

Working as a team and having good communication is what will make this successful. You need to help yourself by teaching your partner what you require in order to be in a position to fully meet his needs. Think about it: if a man places sex at the top of his happy list and a woman has a great need for love and security before she can have the comfort to fully unleash her sexuality in the relationship, then these two factors need to become job one. You need to communicate to your partner exactly what it is you're looking for and what you rely on. Men are not mind readers and they won't always know exactly what a woman is looking for or what it takes to meet her security needs. You need to help put yourself in the best position possible to make this happen, because this is what you will rely on in order to meet his needs. Trust me when I say that if a man knew that the investments he makes into a woman's security and the love offerings he brings, have a direct impact on the kink factor and sex play he gets in the bedroom... He will happily throw himself into this venture.

It's your job to teach him what you need and how he can help you achieve fulfillment, so you can then help him achieve fulfillment in the areas that matter to him. It becomes a process of helping each other develop the tools to in turn help one another achieve fulfillment. It's your job to educate him on your female needs, what is required and how it's required in order to make it happen. He too will do the same and educate you on everything he relies on and needs. It becomes a negotiation of identifying the primary areas that will unleash all the other areas, and this is where you two will invest your efforts. Basically, you are helping one another each gain a full gas tank, so that you will have enough fuel to make the trip all the way to happily ever after.

Women often assume this passive role and want a man to magically fulfill all her needs without her ever defining them. They have this perception that if they have to ask for something than it is not organic in nature and not sincere on his part. This is totally not true, and a man's sincerity is found in his willingness to commit and continue to invest the necessary efforts to make it work. This communication process is crucial, and you must also invite your partner to do the same and to let you know exactly what he needs and how he needs it delivered in order to be happy. Essentially, you are teaching and learning each other's love language and sharing all the tips on how to make it happen for one another. This process is so valuable and it basically grants you the key to his happiness.

5. Keep The Cycle in Motion. Commit 100% and Re-Evaluate Often.

It's important to stay invested and to keep the momentum going. My husband and I made this pact since day one, and for the past several years we have never lost our momentum. I start each and every day by asking myself, "What can I do today to make my husband happy, and to show my appreciation?" Every single day we both make the effort to do something for one another that will provide us each with happiness. It's also important to stay connected and frequently evaluate each other's happiness. As the relationship grows and evolves, so do our needs, our desires and the things that we rely on for happiness can change too. It's almost like doing a satisfaction survey that companies do…and they do it for good reason too! They want to know if their customers are satisfied and if there's anything they can improve.

Survey your partner and ask him:

- *Are you happy?*

- *Am I doing enough?*

- *What can I do more of?*

- *What can I do differently?*

These frequent evaluations helps keep things on track, and doesn't allow things to reach a point of becoming bigger, deal-breaking problems. This allows us to be proactive and implement growth and change, rather than wait for complaints and only to react after the relationship is off course. This helps us remain connected, to keep up with the growing dynamic in the relationship and to help refresh our focus on each other's happiness.

One Stop Love Shop

Everyone comes into relationships with a basket that they hope to fill. Ultimate fulfillment and happiness fills that basket to the top. The common approach that people often take is one where they pick and choose the things that suit their comforts and most end up with half-filled baskets. The selfless love cycle runs on the notion of "Tell me how you need to be loved" versus "Let me tell you how you will be loved," and it's based on exactly what a partner needs to be happy and what it takes to fill their basket. It's just like going to the hair salon and expecting to get exactly what we asked for without saying a word. Imagine if François "The Hair Guru" wasn't having a good day because his boyfriend just broke up with him…So instead of the gold highlights and 1 inch cut, he gives you fire engine red hair with a 6 inch cut… VIOLA! WHAT THE FUCK, FRANCIOS?! Chances are his chair and your ass will never see one another ever again. When you find that one place that just totally gets your needs and nails your hair vision spot on, that hairdresser wins you for life!

Anytime we ever find something in life that totally meets our needs, what do we do? We become loyal to that source. Just like grocery shopping and having a grocery list. Who likes to run around to three different places just to cross everything off their list? Imagine having one mega super store that had it all, a one-stop shop where you could go and find everything you're looking for and cross it all off your list. This is the place that becomes your source, because they have everything that you need. It's this very idea that supports the unconditional love cycle approach and provides the ultimate security. Creating a relationship that acts as a one- stop shop and provides for all of a partners needs and their happiness.

It's important to embrace a way of loving freely, and allowing a partner to achieve happiness without condition or restrictions. Providing bountiful free love grants a greater security than that of guarded love. When you have it in you to place his happiness first and freely love him the way he needs to be loved, he finds ultimate happiness. What man would want to fuck up a relationship that allowed him to be himself, accepted him as he was, provided for all his needs in the very unique way that he needs to be loved and granted him with stupendous happiness? NO MAN WOULD RISK HEAVEN ON EARTH! These are the types of relationships that men try to hold onto and do everything in their power to secure the source that feeds their happiness.

Chapter Five

Transforming "The Misbehaved Vagina" into a "Miss. Behaved" Vagina

Alright, ladies, we're shifting gears here for a bit, and discussing what is arguably the single most important element in a relationship…Communication. Anybody will agree that having effective communication in a relationship is of utmost importance. However, what many people don't realize is that a couple's interactions, reactions, behaviors and responsiveness to one another are what set the tone for the "relationship environment." People communicate through various forms, be it verbal, or non-verbal and through body language, and every single interaction that a couple shares directly impacts the relationship environment. We have the ability to either create positive or negative energy in the relationship based on our communications and interactions. Obviously, when times are good, it's easy to maintain the positive efforts and energy. However, when we are heavily invested in something emotionally, it's hard to avoid being emotionally reactive during challenging moments. As women, when we feel emotionally distressed, it's easy for us to resort to common female behaviors that come quite naturally to our nature. However, this doesn't always translate well to the penis and these are the things that cause further friction in a relationship.

I'll be the first to admit, trying to bring male/female behaviors together in harmony is no easy task. The biggest challenge is that as humans we are viewed as having superior intelligence to other species and we're held to a higher standard. Life would be so much easier if we could simply hash it out like the monkeys do. If a guy started acting up and pissed you off, you simply fling a pile of pooh at him. He's not listening to your needs? Fling pooh at him. He's acting like a jerk? Fling pooh at him. He didn't pick up milk on the way home, put the toilet seat down, pick up the kids like he was supposed to, or last more than three minutes in bed? Just keep flinging heaps of pooh until he gets the idea. Yup, life as a monkey would rock…with the minor exception of probably needing to pooh on command, because what happens if he goes and pisses you off and you're constipated that day? I guess since poohing on command, or carrying around travel-size back up pooh in your purse are not options, then this monkey business may not be for us.

I'm sure if we left it up to men to come up with a better solution to solve the battle of the sexes, they'd have us convinced that their penis has better hearing than their ears. And if we really want to be heard, using his penis as a megaphone mic would be much more effective. Surely there are better alternatives other than pooh flinging, or enduring endless hours on the "cockaraoke" penis mic. The reality is that it is very possible for a couple to distance themselves from the common "battle of the sexes'" tango, and it's our job to proactively do our part in the areas we can control. It's all about learning how to create a more unisex-friendly environment, and avoiding the common go-to female behaviors that get us in trouble. Keep in mind that something that makes sense to the female brain is often lost in translation for the male brain. As women, there are certain female behaviors that we don't even acknowledge that we do, but that have negative effects on the relationship. Even though we always have the best intentions, we don't always exhibit the best behaviors at all times, especially when we feel emotionally put off. Going back to the 'Love Barter Tripod' theory, this chapter encompasses tools to implement the third principle of 'Creating a Unisex Friendly Environment' and one that a man will be more receptive to. It's important to understand that there are some undesirable behaviors that not only don't translate well to a man, but that act as major penis-repellant and produce the opposite results to what we are seeking. So what vagina behaviors are we looking to avoid?

1. There's No Room for Self-Righteousness, or Self-Serving Egos in a Relationship

Basically, don't take the stance that your shit doesn't stink or that you're never wrong. I mean we all know that as women we are always right, and that men, well, they are pretty much of the "less-right variety" and all we're doing is simply bringing this to their attention. Okay, fine…maybe not exactly as so, but truth be told if we keep this mentality up we'd likely spend the rest of our days with our trusty vibrator and our sixteen cats (Think 'Cat Lady'). The reality is that for most of us, none of these characteristics are reflective of what we really believe, and contrary to the stigma of women always needing to be right…such is not the case. However, the funny thing is that as humans when we are in a neutral environment it's easier for us to be self-reflective and objective of our behaviors be they good or bad. It's not so easy in the heat of the moment when we feel put off, and it's often a challenge for us to view things objectively, see any wrong in our ways, or take ownership for any negative contributions.

As humans when the emotional investment stakes are high, we tend to communicate in a style that serves our own needs and comforts. Obviously, we mean well and it's not as though we're purposefully trying to ignore the immediate needs of our partner. The problem is that when two people are both looking to secure their own needs in the moment, it becomes counterproductive for both parties. I always coach couples who are struggling to communicate with one another, to look beyond the moment. There is no room in a relationship for self-serving egos. Being right may seem like the most important thing in the moment, but there's no notoriety in a one-sided win especially if it dismisses a partner's feelings. Like Dr. Phil always says, "Do you want to be right, or do you want to be happy?" Remember, we're not looking for a win in the moment, we're looking for an overall win in the relationship.

It's all about tapping into your emotional intelligence and emotional maturity, having the ability to identify and control your emotions and view things with better clarity. You must always be of the mindset that there are two perspectives in a relationship, and two invested emotions. Just because he's of the male species variety, does not make him any less important emotionally. By design, humans are protective of their emotional vulnerabilities, and this causes us to go into defensive mode when we feel emotionally threatened or put off.

I can't even begin to explain how long it took me to master this one. I can seriously be a stubborn "right fighter" (as Dr. Phil calls 'em), and it took a lot of work on my part to change my ways. Admittedly, I would often resort to deflecting and trying to place blame on anyone or anything around me. It took a long time to find my emotional maturity and change my perspective and allow myself to grow in my relationships. It's about knowing how to take ownership and being accountable for our contributions towards our circumstances. Being blinded by our own perceptions causes us to repeat poor toxic cycles and it prevents us from growing. If a partner is constantly made to feel as though their side is invalid, they become discouraged and less invested. It actually takes a conscious and willing effort to change our behaviors, and even though in the moment we feel compelled to say and do otherwise, in the long run it will benefit the relationship. It's about learning how to take ownership for our contributions, and understanding that both sides hold equal relevance… keeping your eye on the prize and the bigger picture of having a win in the relationship.

2. Forego the Dramatics: Turning Up the Heat Only Chases Him Away

I don't know about all the other vaginas out there, but I sure as hell have been guilty of starting penis fires and then running for cover. You know, the ever so common female act of turning up the heat but then not liking the fire that results. Unfortunately, I had to learn the hard way that attempting to turn up the heat and opting for Oscar-worthy dramatics comes with a high probability of it back-firing on the vagina. Case in point, once upon a time I did what many people often do, unknowingly cycle bad behaviors and poor practices simply because it's the only thing we know. That was until one day, I had a huge wake-up call and a good dose of reality.

I had been dating a guy for a couple months whom I really, REALLY liked….like, uber much! And rightfully so, as he was an amazing guy. It was a long distance relationship, and I had gone down to see him for the weekend. We had gotten into a stupid argument (I can't even tell you what it was about, as is often the case) and resorting to what I knew: I became extremely emotional and when I was in that zone I also felt the need to raise the stakes in an effort to send the most impactful message (Hi, my name is emotionally immature and I am a drama queen) The argument reached a climax with my classic, "FINE! I'M LEAVING!" (STOMP, STOMP, STOMP…Insert overly-animated marching out of the room). My naive perception was that by threatening the extreme, he'd respond immediately for fear of losing me, and that I would gain validation by him chasing after me (sounds like a reasonable analogy, no?). As I put on my overly-animated production of starting to throw all of my belongings into my suitcase and prepare to (actually, pretend) leave, he looked at me and asked, "Is that what you want? You're leaving?" I thought in my head, No *you dumb ass, I want you to be the one to give in and stop me from leaving.* Yet, out of my mouth came out an emotional "YES! I'M GOING HOME!"

Now crying hysterically, I thought that at this point, surely he would stop me from leaving, or chase me down in the process of… You know, like in the movies where the guy runs in the rain for miles, and when he gets to her house he's standing outside of her window shouting, "Baby, don't go, I can't live without you!" I had it all planned out in my head, and I even had a theme song picked out, you know Player's "BABY COME BACK! YOU CAN BLAME IT ALL ON ME" as he professes his love for me. Anyway, back at the reality ranch it sort of played out like that… minus the music and the part about him running in the rain… oh yeah, and minus the fact that it didn't play out like that at all! (Insert a HUGE ASS RECORD SCRATCH HERE) And the next thing I heard was "YOU WANNA LEAVE? LET ME HELP YOU PACK!" And just like that in two minutes flat he had my car packed up, running and ready to go (what a gentlemen)

At that point I was in disbelief, because this shit used to work with every other ex-boyfriend I ever had (insert the fact that this may have been the very reason why these guys ended up becoming exes) THE NERVE! Like, seriously how far did this threat have to go?...because this crazy bitch was prepared to (pretend) drive home all of 500 miles (800km's because it was back to Canada, eh?) just to prove a point. The truth is that there comes a humbling point when admitted defeat kicks in, and we realize that the added dramatics and over-the-top escalated emotions has put us in a place that is furthest from where we intended to be. As I sat in my car I knew in my heart that this guy was well worth the effort, and that my uncontrolled emotions were working against me. I also knew that I was the one being an irrational jerk, and it was up to me to take the initiative and attempt to make good. I ended up apologizing and we made up. His reasoning behind his reaction actually made a lot of sense. He basically told me that he was committed to trying to make the relationship work, and that he'd be more than willing to hear me out and even try to work towards a resolution...as long as I was not being emotionally irrational and I genuinely yet effectively communicated what I was expecting of him and what I needed in the moment.

That was a defining moment for me in my life and I realized that when I allowed my emotions to escape me and I lost my shit, I inadvertently would lose any control I had over the situation. I also realized that if I expected to get better results I needed to find more effective and level headed ways to articulate my feelings. You may be wondering what ever became of the long distance dude that taught me about emotional maturity... I MARRIED HIM! He is the very loving, mature and reasonable man I now call my husband. And I can tell you that since the day we had this argument (several years ago), I vowed to reconstruct how I did relationships, discontinue my ineffective toxic cycles and replace them with more effective practices that were supportive of both our needs and not just mine.

The biggest difference between men and women is that women are often more well-versed in emotional articulation. We look to explore all the emotions attached to what we are experiencing, and we want to not only be heard but to also be understood and to feel validated in the moment. Men on the other hand are "fixers" and have a solutions-based mentality. They take a logical approach of assessing the issue, and it's in their nature to attempt to fix the problem and find a solution. This is why men and women don't always come together in harmony, because while we're turning up the volume in an attempt to be heard, he's fiddling with his little tool box approach trying to get that shit fixed with his trusty penis-pliers. It may not be our most desirable quality, but as women we often have a way of being relentless when we are seeking emotional resolution in the moment and looking to deliver our message. When a woman has an "emotional package" to deliver, we're not leaving that shit at the front door...We want confirmation and we want in! If we encounter resistance and the front door is locked, we are far from done or giving up (Like seriously, UPS could so benefit from our resourceful delivery skills). Who needs keys?! We are checking the garage, the back door, any open windows, and even the chimney! Shit, if Santa fits through there, then surely Hell on Heels is making it down that chimney.

The problem is that by a man's perception, where there is smoke, there is always fire and he's running in the opposite direction. Raising the heat makes a man feel apprehensive and attacked, so he naturally repels from the heat source and threat (not to mention that the penis is not flame retardant). The louder a woman gets, the harder of hearing a man becomes. So unless you purposefully want to produce exactly the opposite results of what you likely intended, then understand that raising the heat and all the added dramatics only works against you. These efforts are better spent on make-up sex after you have effectively communicated your needs...at which time, turning up the heat is totally acceptable and all the added dramatics only make it better.

3. Never Resort to Bitch Mode or Silent Treatment as a Form of Communication

Alright, ladies, we may not be the first to admit it, but there's a reason why there are stereotypes about what women say and what they really mean when they are mad. There may be times when we are pushed to the point that we feel extremely emotionally put off. At times like this, it's easy to find ourselves converting the feeling of being hurt into anger. Sometimes, we have this expectation that a partner needs to deliver what we need in the moment and that we shouldn't have to ask for it. The perception is that if we actually have to ask for it, then it's not sincere or genuine on his part. The reality is that as humans, we are not mind readers, and a guy does not have the ability to determine exactly what it is you want in the moment.

Everyone is entitled to feeling mad or hurt, and no one is expected to simply snap out of a funk just like that. However, shutting down and resorting to bitch mode as the only form of communicating, is never effective and only creates further toxins in the relationship. Relying on indirect communications such as "I'M FINE!" when you're anything but fine serves no purpose. Especially when it really means, "You didn't do anything for Valentine's Day you puny pecker ass wipe!" (Because we all know that a man's penis size is always ample when times are good, but when times are bad or things are over…all of a sudden his dick shrinks to microscopic proportions).

The point is that simply going into bitch mode resolves nothing, and it only hurts you in the long run. It takes a lot of emotional investment to harbor all those negative feelings, and it robs you of your own happiness. The same goes with giving your man the silent treatment, as this is totally ineffective and never cool. Attempting to send the loudest message and "fuck you" by shutting down and going silent does nothing but damage the relationship. No one likes to have to guess at what they did wrong, and women especially hate the guessing games! If you ever need a reminder for what it feels like to be on the receiving end of all the guessing and having no clue... think back to your days of immature puppy love. Waiting to hear back from that heartthrob boy, and wondering why he hadn't called you yet? As the guessing insanity ensued...Maybe the phone is broken and not working? (Picks up phone to test dial tone...Repeats process six more times just to be sure). Maybe it's not the phone company, and it's just his phone that's broken? Or worse yet, maybe he's broken? Maybe something happened to him? What if he was trying to cross the road to get to a pay phone to call you, got hit by a car and now his ass is in the hospital and in 3 different pieces?! OMG! That must be it! He was trying to call you right before he died...OMG YOU KILLED CHAD RICHARDS! Who's only the hottest guy in school, and he died for your love. Just to be sure that your guess is correct, you go to the funeral to pay your respects to his inconsolable mother and as you give your condolences you slip in... "I'm so sorry for your loss...so, do you know if he was trying to call me?"

Seriously, though, do you see what I mean about not having any answers? And, never truly knowing if Chad was the love of your teenage life, or simply a small dick wanker who never called you back? The point is that if it's a committed relationship you'd like to keep for infinity and beyond, then you must never resort to emotional immaturity or treat your partner any differently than you expect to be treated. Think about it, no woman would be okay if a man simply decided to become an asshole every time he was mad. HELL, NO! That dude would have to put out a "Missing Testicles Report" with the local authorities. Just the same, bitchy behaviors are major dick repellant and a total turn off for the penis. Not to mention that allowing such negative energy to linger within yourself takes away from your happiness. Neither partner should ever rely on poor behaviors, or poor treatment of one another as a form of communicating because this will only deliver the exact opposite results than what you intended. So remember, the motto is "what's good for you, is good for two," and you should never resort to indirect communications because they only take away from the quality of the relationship. Shutting down only creates negative energy in the relationship and leaves both sides feeling resentful. So look to the bigger picture and always look to more positive and effective ways of communicating your emotions.

4. BANG BANG! The Pussy Pistol: Never Use Your Offerings as a Weapon

Now this is a tricky area for women, because our emotional well-being is tied into our libido. When a woman is emotionally put off or feels as though the relationship is off, or that her emotional needs are not being nurtured...she often doesn't feel like having sex. The reality is that when we are pissed off and put off, who's thinking "man, I could so go for a cock right now"? Perhaps there are those who can turn that rage into angry make-up sex, but for most of us when we are put off emotionally, we become the proud owners of the desert vagina. That bitch is AWOL!... dried up, put away and any sight of her is merely a mirage to his delirious penile state of mind.

Obviously, it's unrealistic to think that the sex won't be temporarily affected during times of static friction (like the unsexual kind of friction). Women have a direct correlation between their overall security in the relationship and their desire to want sex. If a woman feels as though her security is somewhat compromised, then she will likely become reserved and guarded in the bedroom. Until her security is restored, she will struggle to find the comfort to let herself fully go in the bedroom. This is understandable, which is why I say that it's important to keep the lines of communication open with your mate and work together to ensure that you always have a good sense of comfort in the relationship. And it's because sex and security go hand in hand, and it involves two things that mean the most to both a man and a woman.

That being said, it's actually unhealthy to ignore underlying issues and allow them to fester into bigger issues so they affect the sexual relationship. It's no ground-breaking revelation that sex means a lot to a guy and that it is a common male weakness. Using sex as leverage with men is never cool. Holding out on sex until a man starts to display the desirable behaviors you want …is never cool. Using sex as a bargaining tool, by holding it over his head in exchange for something else…is never cool.

This type of treatment is no different than how a badly behaved child gets grounded or punished, and loses their toys and privileges. In parenting, this may be an effective tool, but not in a marriage and men are not receptive to such treatment. A young child may lack the mental maturity to outgrow such a practice, but a man is smart enough to eventually become immune to the vagina hostage negotiations. If a man is exposed to this cycle long enough he will go from "Oh, how I would do anything and everything just to be reunited with my coveted cupcake," to "Oh hell, enough with the vagina hostage negotiations…just shoot the bitch already and let's be done with it!" Men take their sex seriously, and they don't like to feel as though they are being punished or controlled with sex as an incentive. Men are well aware that women are privy to their weakness towards sex, and when a man senses that this is being used against him it prompts him to resist even more and show her that he has no need for her goods. A man is very understanding of the fact that in distressed times the sex will naturally be affected, and most guys feel equally put off at times like this and their libido is also affected. However, if a man feels as though he has to beg for sex, earn his way in or that it is being used as leverage and dangled over his head… He becomes resentful and eventually turned off by the idea that he has to earn his feedings with good behavior. It's extremely damaging to man's ego and self-esteem. At some point, a man becomes discouraged and unmotivated to continue the pursuit, and starts to view the reward of sex as a lot less desirable and not worth the effort.

The best way to truly understand the impact, is to look at it from a man's perspective. Women might be able to make do without sex, but what if the man withheld all affection and told us he wouldn't love us until we put out?

Once again, there'd be a missing testicles report filed with local authorities. This is why sex should never be used as a bargaining tool or intentionally withheld as a motivator. Such a practice can also fracture the trust in the relationship. A man becomes untrusting of his spouse if she withholds sex whenever she feels like drawing that weapon. One thing the penis doesn't take kindly to is being deceived, or hit with unwelcome surprises. This is unhealthy for the relationship and every effort should always be taken to restore the happy environment in the relationship and also restore the intimacy in the union. Again, this may not be a practice that any of us rely on, but it's always important to remain mindful of the mile markers on the road and know the signs for what to avoid. Always keep in mind the motto, "what's good for you is good for two" and exactly what we expect for ourselves is exactly what we should be putting out.

5. Always Go Straight to the Source and Avoid Outside Interference

Every time I think about this concept, I find it amusing that as humans we're not always quick to jump on this one. Men and women have struggled to understand one another for eons, and for some odd reason whenever we encounter a glitch with the opposite sex we turn to our own kind. I'm sure this sounds all too familiar, and anytime we experience pains and strains in our personal relationships, we turn to our trusty girlfriends for their comforting support. Something about hearing, "Girl, you shouldn't have to put up with that! I'd be mad, too!" feels so therapeutic in the moment. Listen, you and I totally get it, and unless you've lived a day in the life of vagina ownership, no guy can ever truly relate to us like another woman can. This is totally understandable and it's great to have that external support system when needed. However, nothing can ever replace going straight to the source when it comes to getting all the answers on making your relationship work.

I recently had a discussion with a 42-year-old male friend, who had been dating a divorced mom of two for the past year and a half. He explained that they both wanted a long term commitment, but couldn't quite get there because every time they had a disagreement or when an issue arose in the relationship, she would turn to her sister for advice. He said that this wore on the relationship because the sister was recently divorced herself and was going through a tough time, and he felt as though the sister's perception was jaded due to her own circumstance (often known as temporary man-hating and cock-blocking) He was frustrated that his ex-girlfriend would allow the sister into the relationship instead of them dealing with one another one on one and resolving their own issues. He eventually reached a breaking point and they broke up because he felt that there were always three people in the relationship. His ex-girlfriend was saddened by the break up, but she didn't understand or see the severity of the dynamic she was cycling in the relationship.

Keep in mind that the opinions of others are often based on their personal experiences, and their advice can be more harmful than helpful. Especially when you put two skeptical vaginas together because that's a recipe for a dick disaster. It may be comforting to call best friend Becky to bitch about your husband Tom's new job...how his new schedule is putting a strain on your relationship and once again he's running late for dinner. No harm done, until you mention the fact that his new job came with a new secretary named Ashley…Aaaand off Becky goes on a rant about how the exact thing happened to her hairdresser's, best friend's boyfriend's sister (You get that?) How the husband worked long hours and was always late getting home from work, and how he was really having a secret affair with his new secretary…blah, blah, blah…Before you know it your ass is on fire, and Becky's ass is on her way over.

Dinner isn't even done cooking and now your simmering ass and her ill-advising ass are both decked out in camouflage gear, and hiding in the bushes outside of his 'new secretary's' apartment so you can bust Tom in the act.

While you two concoct an attack plan and carefully study blue prints of 'Ashley's' apartment complex (AKA. The apartment belonging to the bitch who stole your man), Tom is now at home and wondering where the heck you are? Eager to surprise you with the flowers and ice cream he stopped to grab from the store on his way home (part of the reason why he's late) While the ice cream melts back at the house, you're having a meltdown in the bushes at this other bitches house. Are you starting to see the problem here? And bird brained Becky's nonsense doesn't help. What have you become? Decked out in war paint, a carton of eggs in one hand and a bottle of mace in the other. Your vagina is dressed like Rambo and falling apart at the seams. Man, talk about feeling silly when you finally get home and come to find out that this was all a huge misunderstanding. Maybe you and Tom will even get a good chuckle out of it over dinner (tonight's special: the burnt roast you forgot in the oven and melted ice cream soup) Hopefully you'll still be laughing when you find out that 'Ashley' is a unisex name, and that 'she' is actually a 'he'…As in the guy who's your husband's new secretary (AKA the bitch…AKA man who stole your man?).

Oh well, the good news that there is some recovery from all of this and all is not lost. The Rambo gear from the surplus store can be put to good use in the bedroom with some commando role play! And you'll need to pull out all the vagina tricks if you hope to distract Tom for when he finds out that you "accidentally" may have slashed "Ashley's" tires. While this alone may not have directly incriminated you…Becky taking it upon herself to 'help you out' by spray painting "YOU CAN HAVE TOM! U HUSBNAD STEALING BITCHY ASSHOLE HOOKER TRAMP!" all over the car…will surely get you busted. And yet another good reason to not listen to Becky and her stupidity… That bitch can't spell under pressure, and her trash talk skills could use some work. Moral of the story, avoid becoming the owner of a delusional Rambo vagina and bringing outside interference into the relationship.

External interference dilutes the quality in the relationship and it's important to always go straight to the source. The only person who can provide you with the resolution you seek, is the partner with whom you share the relationship with. When you're feeling put off and need fulfillment, you should go straight to the source and communicate your needs. All the answers you will ever need lie right within the relationship itself. Want to know what it takes to make a man happy? How to become all a man will ever need? *Cosmo* doesn't have all the answers to your man and his penis, or for your relationship…and that's because *Cosmo* has never met him or his penis, or walked a day in your relationship. All the answers you will ever need are found right within your relationship and with100% accuracy. A man knows his needs best, and he's the one who can tell you what it takes to make him happy and what it takes to keep him from feeling sad. Too many people rely on looking outwards and seeking answers, and letting external factors infiltrate the relationship. External static interference is a major source and cause for many relationship struggles. The best thing you can ever do for yourself and your relationship is to preserve the bond by turning to your mate for solutions and resolutions. When a couple allows external sources into the relationship it starts to dilute the quality of the union and acts as a distracting force between them. When a couple strives to always keep the quotient 'one on one' they remain connected and unified.

Conflict Resolution: Learning How to Argue More Effectively

The reality is that even when we're on our best vagina behavior, we're not always going to see eye to eye with our ~~little~~ penis companion. Even the happiest couples in the healthiest relationships have arguments. We're only human, and anytime people come together there's bound to be a differing of opinions at some point or another. The stakes are even higher when two people are emotionally invested in one another and the deeply-rooted emotions are what cause us to feel passionately about anything and everything involving the relationship. Believe it or not, there is such a thing as "healthy conflict." There may be no way to avoid conflicts altogether, but there is a way to minimize the occurrence and effects of negative interactions. It's about learning how to become a better communicator and developing the skills to resolve conflict more effectively.

Ultimately, the goal is for a couple to successfully navigate through the encounter and to come out of it unscathed. We often have this perception that all arguments are negative experiences and that it's a sign of an unhealthy relationship. This is totally not true, and sometimes finding resolution can be a great growing experience for a couple and it can even strengthen the bond that a couple shares. When conflict arises and you are faced with the task of attempting to find a resolution, there are certain factors that can help guide the process. I have devised a series of "Effective Conflict Resolution" steps that can help guide the communication process more smoothly and assist a couple in achieving a mutually benefiting resolution. To do this you should:

1. Focus on the Issue at Hand.

Believe it or not, this is one of the most difficult things to do in the heat of the moment. When emotions are soaring and we feel the need to validate our position, it's easy to stray off track and bring in all these other unrelated variables in an effort to support our position. It's easy to lose focus and create a generalized distaste for your partner's behaviors and reactions. It's important to focus on the main issue at hand, and focus on the immediate behaviors and reactions that are tied into that specific issue. If you turn it into an overall generalization involving your partner's character, it only makes them feel attacked and it will cause them to retreat and shut down. Saying things like "You always do that, and I hate it!" or "YOU NEVER LISTEN AND YOU HAVE NEVER EVER HELPED ME!" do not help. Words like "always' and "never," are not realistic and this is usually an inflated exaggeration of the truth. If "always" and "never" *are* the truth, then the problems run deeper than this particular argument, and during a flare of temper is not the time to hash out these differences.

2. Make Realistic Assessments and be Realistic When Evaluating Your Needs.

During time of conflict when we feel emotionally displaced, it's easy to place blame on external sources and identify the negative contributions that your partner has made. You need to take a step back, and look within yourself first. Identify how you yourself contributed to the argument, and take ownership for your part. You must also explore the reasons behind why you are upset, and what you are trying to accomplish. You must remain realistic, and ask yourself:

* What is most important to me right now? How important is my need and is it a deal breaker for me? Be realistic, and don't place a high value on something that does not hold significance in the grand scheme of your overall needs or happiness. It's easy

to say that something is "do or die," when in reality we are not really going to die if we don't get what we seek in the moment (try convincing the drama queen vagina of that).

3. Take a Step Back & Evaluate Your Partner's Needs.

This is probably the most overlooked factor during an argument. Think about it, arguments are about two sides disagreeing, so who the hell wants to assume the opposing role when we're so sure *we're* right? However, learning how to place yourself in your partner's shoes, allows you to gain better understanding and have more compassion towards his feelings. You need to take a step back, and try to understand how your partner is feeling. Ask yourself:

- What are my partner's needs right now? What are they trying to gain in the moment, and what are they asking for? You need to weed through the behaviors that they are exhibiting, and look past the hurt and anger. What is it that they want and need from me right now?

- How have my behaviors in the moment affected my partner and his feelings? How can I alter my approach to ensure that I do not add further fuel to the fire? Remember, you are trying to defuse the situation (think sunshine not black clouds) It's very easy to continue down a destructive path when we are emotional. Your goal is to turn the situation around and find a resolution.

You must remain mindful of the behaviors and interactions that negatively impact the situation. You want to ensure that you are not being combative, competitive, or engaging in avoidance for all the factors involved. Understand that sometimes what we are looking for in the moment may not be what we truly need. Try to assume a more neutral role, focusing on being more collaborative with your partner, and open to compromise.

4. Don't Inflate or Over Exaggerate and Don't Deflate or Invalidate True & Real Emotions.

When we feel passionately about something, and we are deeply invested, it's easy to blow things out of proportion. We often see this as a form of delivering our message most effectively. Keep in mind that raising the volume and the stakes often produces the opposite results, and causes a partner on the receiving end to retreat away from the static. The level of invested emotions you articulate should be reflective of the situation at hand. If it's a squabble over him often leaving the bathroom a mess and not tidying up after himself, then you shouldn't be bouncing off the ceiling with fireballs shooting out of your ass (Now would be a great time to be a monkey and squash this tiff with one swift pooh fling). It is unhealthy to make mountains out of molehills and being emotionally over-reactive in the moment only works against you in the long run.

That being said, it's also unhealthy to downplay the severity of your emotions when it involves something very important to you and your needs. You should never suppress how you truly feel, or try and downplay the emotions you are experiencing simply because you are seeking a quick resolution or because you feel defeated. Don't allow your partner's differing views to convince you that your feelings don't hold validity or cause you to second-guess what is truly causing you distress. If it's real to you then it's real to the relationship, so don't ignore it. You must look to find a balance and if something has truly upset you, communicate how important is to you.

On the flip side, you want to make sure that you don't try to invalidate your partner's emotions, either. Remember, a partner feels no differently than you do in the moment, and they are experiencing all the same heated feelings. It should never become a battle between whose emotions are more hurt, who is more valid in how they feel or who wins the ultimate victim role. Remember, perception is everything, and two people can equally feel hurt and misunderstood. Taking the stance that your feelings always hold precedence over his simply because you're more emotionally vulnerable, or always playing the hurt and victimized role, serves no purpose and it will only cause your partner further frustration. Constantly playing victim and over dramatizing has a way of desensitizing a partner's responsiveness to your emotions (it's like the vagina who cried wolf) You need to remove yourself from your female shoes, and try to understand what your partner is feeling and what their needs are as well. Look past a partner's behaviors in the moment, because their interactions may not be reflective of how they truly feel.

5. Take the Initiative to Help Yourself.

Understand that we often have something that we are looking for in the moment. We have something in mind of what we need in that moment, a need to be filled and we most often look to our spouse as the source to fill it. Sometimes, when we feel flustered, we see our spouse as the one who put us in this place, and we have this expectation that it's up to them to fix it and restore us to our happy place. We also come with an expectation of what we hope to gain from the argument and set our sights on needing to achieve this in order to feel as though we have resolution. You need to identify:

- What response am I looking for from my spouse? And what is it that I'm hoping to gain? This should include things like: you want him to hear you out, or perhaps your need for affection in the moment.

Understand that sometimes what we need in the moment is only something that we can give ourselves. And sometimes what we need from a spouse is something that they may or may not be able to deliver. This is something I have learned all too well in my relationship with my husband. I am of the mindset that regardless of who is wrong or right, everyone says they are sorry and we move on. Well, my husband happens to be a more logical being and he doesn't understand the concept of apologizing simply because we don't see eye to eye. I used to be of the mindset that unless I got an apology, I could not move forward. I realized that it had nothing to do with hearing him say 'I'm sorry', as much as I needed to feel as though he understood me. I learned to stop pushing for apologies and instead allow my husband to approach me in his own way. Eventually his 'I'm sorry' was in the affections he brought forth and the 'I love you and I don't want to fight'. In the moment I may not have received an apology, but I learned how to provide myself with comfort. And that was in the notion that I knew that somehow someway my husband always comes around in his own way and in his own words.

We won't always get what we are looking for from those around us, and we won't always be granted the resolutions we seek in the moment. Before you place your expectations on your spouse, look within yourself and identify how you can provide for your own needs. If you avoid the very necessary step of tending to your own needs and nurturing your own emotions, it can cause us to place an unhealthy level of expectations on our partner to bridge this gap and pick up all the slack of restoring your happy place. Sometimes we harbor internal guilt for what we did or didn't do, and this adds to the negative waves we send towards our partner. If we take the time to identify this within ourselves and find inner peace, it allows us to remove this variable and frustration from the mix and re-approach our partner in a better state of mind. Assess your expectations, and look at areas where you can provide yourself with validation. When we are faced with a disagreement, we often need our spouse to recognize our viewpoint and to agree with our opinions. Understand that this may not always come to fruition, and sometimes two people will stand firm in how they perceive a situation. You may not fully get what you hope to gain from your partner, but you should not allow this to invalidate how you feel. Don't allow a partner's differing views to put you in a position of questioning your needs. Remain realistic, and understand that even though he may never agree with your views, you two can still find resolution by coming to a middle ground by compromising. Remember, you are not looking for a win in the moment, but an overall win in the relationship.

6. Timing is Everything.

As women, it's in our nature to seek immediate resolution and restore our emotional balance. We not only want to be heard and understood, but we want it all to happen like NOW! Keep in mind that there are always two sets of needs in every situation, and sometimes a partner's communication style may not coincide with yours. Healthy communication is when both partner's needs are taken into consideration and it's not one-sided, with one partner having to overly compromise their comforts just to accommodate their spouse's needs in the moment. Case in point. I am an I-need-to-make-good-like-right-now person, and my husband is an I- need-time–to-defuse-and-come-back-level-headed person. Well, I know that if I push for what I want in the moment, it will only work against me and I will end up making the situation worse. I try to balance it out and get what I can from the discussion and at some point if my husband expresses the need to cool off, then I know to let him have his space, because nothing will be accomplished if I stay on him. In turn there are times when my husband is able to identify how deeply hurt I truly am, and he makes the effort in the immediate moment to place everything else aside and console me by hugging it out. It's important to try and give each other what is needed in the moment, and look at short term ways to cope with your immediate emotions.

That being said, you also want to ensure that you do not allow things to drag out and fester into bigger problems. If things go unresolved for too long, or if you rely on ineffective methods such as silent treatment, then resentment will surely follow. This only creates much bigger problems. It no longer involves the issue at hand, as it becomes a larger toxin in the union. It's a balance of not adding fuel to the fire, but also not sitting back and watching the entire house burn down. Sometimes a cooling off period is very much needed in order for the high emotions to defuse and for each partner to restore their mental clarity. A couple can agree to a time out, and also agree on a reasonable time to reconvene and address the problem in a much calmer environment. Most often you will find that many of your emotions and opinions will change after you have had a chance to cool off. When the environment is inviting, take head and get to talking.

7. Know How to Listen.

It's important to be as good a listener as you are a talker, and you shouldn't be using your mouth more than your ears. Unless it involves sex, because then this rule would definitely not apply. Being a good listener is one of the most difficult traits to embrace, and it takes a lot of work from both partners. Take the time to truly try and understand what it is he is saying. And you need to really LISTEN, don't just sit there with a pretend-listening look on your face, as you plot your next rebuttal and point in your head, one that you can't wait to blurt out as soon as the squirmy bugger FINALLY SHUTS UP ALREADY! Seriously, though, listening means no mental queue card preparations in the interim. You also have to be willing to hear him out, and give him the opportunity to communicate his needs and feelings. Don't interrupt or interject, and allow him to fully express how he is feeling. Not letting him express himself can be one of your man's biggest frustrations.

Sometimes, we are so set in our views that our brain tries to interpret what we hear in different ways. Don't try to redefine what he is saying, or try to guess what his true meaning is. People don't like to have their words twisted and they don't like to feel psychoanalyzed by their spouse. I of all people know this to be true, and it's often a challenge for me to stay in spouse mode, and not go into a psycho-analytical 'Relationship Coach' mode. I have to refrain from saying things like 'I'll tell you why you feel this way, and it's because deep down…' My husband will snap back 'Stop trying to tell me how I'm feeling or where it's coming from, it's coming from you!' I know how to recognize a relationship win, so I have retired this habit indefinitely. It's important to take what he says at face value and trust that what he says is what he's feeling. Remember, there are no wrongs or rights, and only personal views and needs that feel very real to a partner in the moment. Each side deserves to be fully heard and understood without interruptions. If you find the listening part a challenge, using a timer is a great tool. Each partner can be given the same amount of uninterrupted time to speak and be heard. This actually works, and it helps guide the discussion.

8. Be Honest and Keep it Positive.

When you do find the right opportunity to sit down and talk, take advantage of the moment and air it all out. Remember, stay realistic and communicate your needs in a positive way. You must also be completely honest, and speak your true feelings. If you are not 100% honest, then you will likely not find full resolution. Take a positive approach, and communicate what you "do want and need" and not "what I don't want, and what I don't need." It should be in the format of "This is how I feel, and why I feel this way." Let him know what you hope to gain with 'This is what I am looking for right now, and what will help me." It should never be in a negative format, or a barrage of things he did wrong.

Saying, "Well, you did this…and you always do that…I hate when you say…" will cause your partner to feel attacked and shut down. Focus on using positive words instead of negative ones, and on the overall positives of what you each hope to gain.

Remember, people are more receptive to hearing positive feedback, and negative words often fall on deaf ears and only cause more static friction. Remember, men are 'fixers' and as such you want to provide him with things he CAN fix and work on (he needs to find good use for his penis-pliers) Focus on the positives you would like to see, and don't harp on all the negative behaviors that you don't like. You can definitely express the things you don't like, but it needs to have validity and not just an airing out of your frustrations. You can say, "Sometimes when you say that, it makes me feel as though I am not doing enough." Or "It hurts my feelings because it makes me think that you don't appreciate….." Communicate clearly to your mate what it is you need from him and what will help you move passed this. Invite him to do the same and allow him to express what he needs from you as well. It's about giving positive solutions instead of negative criticisms.

9. Build Solutions Together.

A couple must always work as a team, even during an argument. Work with one another to find solutions that will meet both of your needs. This should be a collaboration of what you are seeking and what your partner seeks as well. I tell this to my husband often, and during an argument if I feel as though he's seeing me as the enemy, I'll remind him "Babe, we're on the same team here remember? You might not be happy with me right now, but we both want the same thing. We're just saying it in two different ways, and at the end of the day we want to be happy. So let's help each other out here." Compromise is key, and understand that you may not gain 100% of what you seek in the moment. However, if each partner gains progress in what matters to them the most, then this will help a couple work towards a beneficial unified solution for the relationship. It's all about negotiating our needs and identifying solutions that benefit both sides. Focus on the common grounds, and the things that you two can agree on. Each partner should walk away with a "To Do" list of things to work on, and each must commit to the promises that they make to one another. If not, then this exact situation will only come full circle and continue to resurface in the future. Remember, actions speak louder than words, and if we say "we're sorry" and we vow to change things yet don't follow through, it sends an indirect message for invalidating your partner's feelings and disrespecting the value of their needs. Make a pact to work on the requests that you have made of one another, and commit to it. Remember, IN IT TO WIN IT!

10. Find Peace and Let Go.

Once you two have resolved the situation, and you have moved forward, stay on a positive track and don't look back. When I say never look back, I don't mean that it may never become an issue in the future. However, once you have resolved a situation and found closure, look to move on only after you two have made the compromise to work on it. Never rely on rehashing, or digging back into this specific situation, when you are met with something else in the future. When we bring up old things that a partner has said, and try to use this as leverage for something else, it shows that you were not honest and still hold resentment. This is why it's important for both partners to fully find resolution and comfort, and not allow unresolved issues to linger. If you say you are good, you must truly be good and move on.

Keep Your Eye on the Relationship Prize:

I know that many things are easier said than done and in the heat of the moment it's difficult to remain level headed and keep all these factors in mind. However, one thing that has always worked for me in my relationship is that I always "keep my eye on the prize," and even in the midst of an argument I am mindful of the bigger picture. I think to myself "How important are my immediate needs right now? And how will my interactions in this very moment affect the overall relationship into the future?" By keeping my eye on the prize, being the long term success of my union, I am able to communicate more effectively because winning in the overall relationship is more important to me than winning in the moment. Let this be your motivation to remain level headed and open minded, and always be mindful that your goals are for long term happiness and not just immediate gratifications. Small wins in the moment are short lived, but small concessions in the moment pay out much bigger dividends for many years to come. This is the best investment you can ever make.

Good Reception: Effective Couples Communication

Our social culture teaches men that being emotionally expressive is not a masculine characteristic. This is part of the reason why men are not always well-versed as women are when it comes to communicating their emotions. Women often like when a man has a sensitive side and there does exist a happy medium between a penis that writes poems and one that crushes cans on his penis head, but most men still see this as an undesirable 'female' quality. It actually takes time to build good communication in a relationship, and for a man to be comfortable enough to expose his vulnerabilities and his emotions. This is why women should lead by example and create an environment that is supportive of the open communication we seek.

Always Say What You Mean and Mean What You Say

When we say that we are ready for a committed relationship, we must also be ready to retire our ineffective female practices. There's a reason why women carry a stigma for being "hard to figure out." Saying the opposite of what we mean (like "I'M FINE!" or "NOTHING IS WRONG" when in reality all is not fine, everything is very wrong) gets us in trouble every time.

I totally get why we do this, and when we feel as though *he* is the one who has affected our emotions in a negative way, it is *he* who has to make it right and if *we* have to tell him then he's not getting why we're mad. Makes sense right? TO A VAGINA, sure, but not to a penis. The reality is that men are incapable of two things: reading minds and making their penis grow. So you'd better hope you picked a decent size to hunker down with, and you're gonna have to speak up if you want to truly be understood. Don't let your emotions to get the better of you and prevent you from making smart choices that will help your cause and better your relationship. It's important to always speak up, say what you mean and to be completely honest and candid. If you expect your partner to be honest and forthcoming, then you too must do the same.

You also should lead by example when it comes to communicating in a positive way and not resorting to the use of hurtful words in the heat of the moment. When it comes to respect, it must always be honored even at the worst of times. My husband and I have always vowed to adhere to this practice and in all our years and even during times of quarrel, we have never resorted to name-calling or saying things that we don't mean. Couples should never resort to threatening the future of the relationship in an effort to raise the stakes in a heated moment. Arguments may not last long, but words can have lasting effects. It only leads to resentment and it really takes away from the quality of the relationship. The message is simple: indirect communication, non-communication and negative communication are all ineffective forms of communicating and provides no positive benefits to a relationship.

Creating the Right Environment

It's important to understand that if we have certain expectations of the relationship and our spouse, then we must know how to create the right environment that supports what we seek. We want a man to express his true thoughts and emotions. We have an expectation for him to be honest, forthcoming and fully candid. Understand that in order for all of this to take place we must maintain a relationship environment that will promote these behaviors. A man will freely and organically express himself as long as he doesn't feel pressured to do so, and he doesn't feel as though his words are being twisted and manipulated into something different. Supporting his style of communicating invites him to express himself in a way that feels natural to him.

When a man finds an inviting environment that allows him to be himself and express himself freely, it provides him with the comfort to be honest and fully candid in the relationship. If a man feels as though he will be judged or criticized, it causes him to have reservations about being fully forthcoming in the relationship. It's human nature for people to avoid negative reception, and when people are met with a negative reaction it causes them to become guarded in the future. Understand that our behaviors, interactions and reactions in the relationship are what set the tone for how honest and forthcoming a partner will be. I know that dishonesty is never acceptable and lying is never cool. However, choosing not to say anything or avoiding certain admissions is something that many people don't view as dishonesty. If a man feels like something is going to be met with non-acceptance and criticism, he will avoid it altogether.

Understand that there is a big difference between agreeing with what your partner says and being accepting of it, and that of simply being supportive of a partner and him having the freedom to express himself. You will not always share the same comforts with your partner on everything, nor will you always agree or accept everything they present into the relationship. The idea is that at the very least each partner has the comfort to come together and openly discuss how they feel, their ideas, like and dislikes without reservation or fear of judgment. How these factors get resolved and sorted out remains to be seen and it's up to a couple to work together to find mutual comfort and resolution. However, at the very least if we expect honesty and full disclosure then we must also be willing to bring forth a supportive environment that will help make this happen.

This is an area of opportunity that women sometimes don't recognize, and they don't realize how negative and unsupportive reactions often hinder a man's ability to speak freely. In a relationship it's a standard expectation that a partner will always be open and honest, but many women don't realize that half the responsibility is on them to be supportive of a partner when he is being candid and honest. Over the years I have worked with many male individuals who expressed their concerns of this being an issue in their relationships, and how they lacked the comfort to be completely candid because of their partner's disapproving nature in the relationship. Some of the common reasons behind this is "She would never be cool with that..." or "I tried bringing it up one time, and let's just say that it didn't go well." These types of negative experiences leave lasting impressions in a man's mind, and it teaches him to avoid these areas in the future just to evade the negativity that comes along with it. I've seen many relationships where a woman assumes that her partner is being completely forthcoming with anything and everything, yet such is not the case and her partner is actually reserved with certain things because he lacks the comfort to fully disclose candidly. There's never any certainty that a partner is truly being 100% candid in the relationship, but there is comfort in this notion when we provide a "risk-free" environment that invites this to take place. I'm sure we can both agree that this is something we don't want for our relationship.

Keep in mind, the idea that we discussed about a man gravitating to a relationship that is supportive of his needs applies here too. When a man finds a relationship environment that is supportive of his identity, allows him to express himself in a way that feels natural to him and provides him with the comfort and freedom to fully expose his thoughts, desires, likes, dislikes and most intimate emotions....This is a man that will latch on to this environment and relationship because such a deal does not come by as often as one would think. This stems back to the idea of knowing how to love freely and not allowing ourselves to be driven by our inhibitions or fears.

The reality is that it takes a pretty epic vagina to execute this one and maintain it. An epic vagina knows a good opportunity when she sees it, and she takes it upon herself to make it happen. This requires us to remain mindful of our common "not so desirable" female behaviors that we sometimes cycle and that negatively impact our relationships. Instead, we take a mature approach to the relationship and develop more effective and constructive tools that will work in our favor and produce us better results. Good communication is not as common in relationships as one would think, so it's important to keep these epic vagina factors in mind:

- **Emotional Maturity is Job One:** Avoid being emotionally reactive and resorting to common 'female' communication styles such as 'silent treatment mode'.

- **Be an Equal Opportunist:** What's good for the vagina is good for the penis, and what you expect to get is what you should be willing to give. This means no name-calling or hurtful words. It also means that you should never use certain offerings in the relationship as bait or a motivator for a man to produce the results you seek.

- **Keep it in The Relationship:** If you have a bone to pick with your mate, don't look outward to solicit support just so you can validate your position. This is counter-productive.

Instead, always go straight to the source. Hash it out, hug it out and move forward.

- **Build it and He Will Come:** If you want for your partner to always be honest and open about anything and everything in the relationship, then make sure you don't criticize him or scold him when he is forthcoming with his thoughts and needs. It's okay to have differing comforts and views on things, and no one side is more right or more valid than the other.

- **Think: "Unisex" and "Male Friendly":** If all of your interactions, reactions and forms of communicating are catering solely to your female needs and comfort, you will create a one-sided "vagina only zone" that's not supportive of his male needs. Remain mindful of the fact that men too need to have the ability to express themselves in their own male way and have the relationship acknowledge their unique needs. Always look to take the emotionally mature route and create a unisex-friendly zone that will be inviting to his male senses yet still supportive of your female needs.

Like I said, it takes a pretty epic vagina to make this happen, and a truly successful communication dynamic is not that easy to come by in relationships. When a man does find a relationship like this, he's holding on for dear life. And thankfully, you and I are fully equipped for the job, and we are focused on the overall picture and relationship prize and not blinded by the moment…right? Alright, enough blowing hot air into those epic vagina egos…let's get back to business.

Chapter Six

Sexually Speaking

Okay, so now that you understand how a man thinks and how he likes to argue, let's talk about his (and, let's face it, our) favorite pastime: sex. Sex is an important part of any relationship, and as we've established, one of a man's highest priorities in terms of his fulfillment and happiness. This section is not about perfecting your blow job skills and rotating new sex tricks, because, quite honestly, that's the easy part. Instead, we are going to focus on the real challenges in sex. We have sex, but we don't really talk about sex. And we often think we know our partner inside-out, but do we really? I like to focus on the aspects that helps keep a couple truly connected and that helps keep the chemistry flowing in the bedroom. The reason why I say that the sex tricks are the easy part is because when a couple is truly connected in the sexual relationship, the sexual exploration and variety of "new ideas" comes easy. You can grab Cosmo Magazine and execute every single vagina gymnastic trick they preach, but if the sexual relationship is not a truly connected dynamic then these tricks are worthless.

Talking about sex is even more important than the physical act itself, and the communication that a couple has on sex is uber important for many reasons. First, sex happens to be at the top of a man's happy list. Communication on sex and sexual compatibility is one area where couples experience the most challenges and this is often due to the lack of knowledge each sex has for one another. The biggest reason why sex is not always a priority on a woman's happy list, is because women don't always know how to communicate their sexual needs candidly, and they end up missing out on achieving true fulfillment in the bedroom.

People know damn well how to start fiery sexual relationships, and when the sex is new it's always on fire. However, what many couples don't know is how to keep it on fire and on track. In speaking to couples about their relationships, there's one observation that I've made time and again. When it comes to various aspects of the relationship such as the love & friendship, couples commonly share similar outlooks in these areas. However, when it comes to the sex, many couples have fundamental differences in how they enjoy and define it. This observation is also echoed in many of the emails I receive online from people seeking advice on their relationships. These folks confide that they don't feel comfortable opening up and speaking freely about sex with their spouse, or to ask for what they want during sex. The funny thing is that most of these people often follow that statement up with 'I love my partner very much…', but they feel as though this one element is missing in their life. This shouldn't be happening! Two people should both see the relationship in the same way and for what it really is. The reality is that many people in relationships are not lacking love or happiness, what they are lacking is the necessary comfort that the relationship should be providing them with so they can openly discuss their needs with their mate and feel 100% embraced by their spouse. Such a scenario creates a disconnection and eventually it is what leads to people no longer being happy.

The single most important factor in a sexual relationship is for someone to find both fulfillment for their needs and to find the comfort that they seek. The struggle that many couples experience is when one spouse asks the other to compromise a part of themselves in order to make this happen for their mate to be happy in bed. The biggest challenge for couples is compromise in the bedroom, and mastering the goal for both people to feel satisfied with the sex they're having, and to also have their comforts met. The first step towards a partnership in the bedroom is open communication and creating a positive environment, where both people feel comfortable to speak their mind and be honest. So how does this all come together and where the heck do we sign up?

Male Sexuality: From a Penis' Point Of View

Alright, after you open the lines of communication, what do you think you'll hear? Now I know that many of us already have our views on men and their penile ways. You can't exactly ignore their very obvious and often puzzling male rituals and sexual behaviors. Like seriously?! We get it guys... you love your penis! What we will never quite 'get" is the idea that a mere few inches has the ability to hijack an entire human being and take control of him. The male ego begs to differ of course...Not about the controlled behavior part, but about the "mere few inches." As women, we know damn well that you can crack a joke about a guy's height, job, car, even his mother and he'll easily laugh along...but poking fun at his pecker size, that's no laughing matter for the overly inflated twelve-inch male ego. We also know that when it comes to a man's "true" penis size, the quick little calculator conversion is to take what he says, divide it by two and round down to the nearest testicle...but, hey, these are the little things you ignore when you truly love someone. As long as a man never tells us that our ass looks fat, we'll keep telling him that his dick looks big. That's the unwritten rule.

Okay, so all jokes aside... A HUGE part of keeping a man happy, involves keeping the heat in the sexual relationship. It's important for a couple to stay connected and to keep the sexual relationship evolving. A man's sexual needs, desires, and fantasies are constantly changing and evolving, so it's important to keep the sexual relationship from becoming stagnant. The sexual relationship doesn't stay good on its own and good effort is required to keep the happiness flowing between the sheets. In order for a man to remain happy, the things he relies on the most need to continue to serve his happiness. And we all know that there is no auto pilot when it comes to a happy and successful relationship. When a woman remains invested in the areas that are most important to a man, a man in turn, remains invested in all the areas that mean the most to her. My husband has a great way of describing the sexual relationship between a couple in a long-term, committed relationship. He says, "When you're married to someone, you're married to their fantasies, their dreams and their desires. You want to see them happy, and you want to help them achieve their dreams, experience their desires and make their fantasies become realities."

There are certain elements that are embedded in a man's sexuality and that his sex brain strongly associates with. The brain itself plays the biggest role when it comes to sex, and this is why it's more important to appeal to a man's sex brain than his actual penis. By understanding the factors that contribute to a man's sexuality, it allows us to identify how and where to invest our efforts.

Male Sex Cycle: Understanding His Frequent & Prominent Need for Sex

The reason why men seem to always be ready for sex around the clock actually has to do with the internal physiological clock in their testicles. True story…and even though men don't really have a ticker in their balls, they do have a very prominent hormone cycle that builds to the point that it sets off a little sex alarm. Testosterone production takes place in a man's testicles, and for most men it takes about 3-4 days for build up to start peaking. At which point all of a man's senses are also peaking and he's in a heightened state of arousal. As a side note, it's at the 10-12 day mark when a man reaches his maximum peak, but let's go with the starting peak point and not kill the poor guy. Realistically speaking, a man can start feeling "in the mood" (aka horny) after just twenty-four hours of ejaculating. After three-to-four days of build-up, those balls are looking for the nearest vagina, or in an emergency even a simple hand would suffice. This cycle creates such an intense need to achieve gratification, that once a man experiences an orgasm and unloads the build-up, the cycle will start all over again. This is pretty much the cause behind a man's sex drive and his need for sexual frequency. It also accounts for the intensity of a man's sexual urges and his responsiveness to sexual prompters in his environment. That's right ladies, it's all courtesy of those intricate little testicles.

Sexual Fantasy: Understanding His Vivid Sexual Imagination

The reality is that all men fantasize about sex, and the reason they have such a strong association with sexual fantasy is even more important. We often identify a man's penis as being his most prominent sex organ, but it's actually the brain. Acting as the most powerful sex organ in the entire body, the brain responds to mental and physical stimuli, creates arousal and runs the whole damn sex show for a man. Exploring sexual thoughts and fantasizing about sex delivers the most intense dose of sexual stimuli both mentally and physically. Also, sexual fantasy is not just about a man "day-dreaming" about sex. Sexual fantasy allows a man to tantalize his sex brain and to mentally explore all the things that he associates with sexually and that he finds most erotic. Sexual fantasy can be about a person, an act or encounter or anything that a person finds sexually arousing.

If a man happens to have a thing for shoes and feet, then his fantasies may involve anything and everything to do with toes, stockings, heels, etc... He may be a guy that has a nurse fantasy and he finds the idea of nurse role play in the bedroom erotic. The next guy may not understand it, but if the nurse gig is this guy's thing and fantasizing about "Paging Nurse Becky..." prompts an erection then he'll revisit that one in his head as often as he wishes. Sometimes sexual fantasy can simply be about an act, and the idea of engaging in certain sexual acts as they play out in his mind. Sexual fantasy is the very reason why the online sex industry is a multi-billion dollar business, and it has a way of turning a penis dream into a virtual reality. Fantasy can also be based on reality, and on past sexual experiences that leave a lasting mental impression. Being able to relive the stellar experience mentally is a way to keep enjoying it over and over again.

Obviously, the ultimate scenario for a man is to have his sexual fantasies become a reality and that naughty nurse landing in his bedroom and becoming a part of sex life is a dream-come- true for the penis. However, not all sexual fantasies become realities, especially if the fantasy itself is pretty out there and far-fetched. Perhaps the hopeful male ego has some guys believing that their fantasy for an orgy at the Playboy Mansion has potential for becoming a reality. However, the true reality is that these "wishful thinkers" are probably a few inches short of making the cut on Hugh Hefner's VIPenis List. And so be it, because a man will continue to fantasize about the things he sexually identifies with regardless of whether or not his penis dreams ever transpire to anything more than just a dream and an erection....and maybe some solo sex with himself and his fantasies...but that's it...nothing more.

Sexploration: Understanding His Need for Sexual Variety & Exploration

We already discussed the fact that men enjoy sexual exploration. It's the variety and changing dynamic that helps keep the mental stimuli on high, and this is what men find most appealing about exploring sexually. The male sex brain is very aroused by the idea of taking a sexual desire and fantasy and exploring it in reality, in every different way and taking the stimuli to its maximum potential. Have you ever seen a dog's reaction when they are given the remnants in an empty ice cream container? To you and me, it may appear empty, but to the dog he has just been granted all exclusive access to the ice cream factory. That thing will burrow its nose in the container and lick that thing in trails and circles around the whole house until he has aspirated every last spec and his tongue has cleaned the entire inner surface of the ice cream container.

This is pretty much how men view the thought of sexually exploring their desires. A blow job is not just a blow job, their brain wants to feel and see every angle, every sensation, and experience every potential variable leaving no part of his penis unblown and no thought unexplored. And trust me, the male sex brain never runs out of ideas. A man may easily run out of date night ideas... "Well, what do you feel like doing? I'm game for anything." But, ask a man for ideas to explore in the bedroom and he can successfully continue to shoot off ideas long after the cows come home, and well after his penis ceases to stand on its own. Sexual exploration can involve anything from the simplest venture, like having sex in a new setting or trying a new sexual position, all the way to embarking on new sexual territory and exploring toys, props and visiting all the local sex shops. Sexploration appeases a man's curiosities and it keeps the sexual relationship exciting for him because the penis possibilities are endless!

Unpacking His Sex Suitcase: Understanding What he wants in his sex life.

Everyone that enters into a relationship comes with a full "sex suitcase." The "sex suitcase" represents a person's sexuality and sexual identity and encompasses all of their sexual interests and desires, as well as their sexual fantasies. When a man enters into a committed relationship, it's with the hopes that he will be able to unpack his sex suitcase in its entirety. If the relationship environment provides him with the support and acceptance that he seeks, he will find the comfort to be 100% candid and forthcoming with all of his sexual interests and desires and fully expose his sexual identity. And this is really what we all want. We like to think that the one person we choose to be with and the intimate personal relationship that we share is where we can find acceptance to be ourselves and be embraced for anything and everything that we represent.

Unfortunately, not everyone finds this in every relationship, and sometimes people face the challenge of being true to themselves and yet pleasing the one they love. The funny thing is that people often have a way of sniffing out danger, and if a man is met with any type of negative reception in the course of him attempting to unpack his suitcase (making mention of a sexual desire), he will mark the danger zones and avoid these areas in the future. If he is met with any form of disapproval, judgment, criticism, or even ridicule, he will guard himself in the future and only unpack the things that he deems as 'safe' or that he won't catch heat for. Anything else stays locked away in the sex suitcase.

When a man feels that the relationship is not accepting of his entire sexual identity, it causes him to suppress parts of himself that the relationship does not support and he essentially morphs into two identities. The one he exposes to his spouse, and the other part that remains in his sex brain. People often have this misconception about human sexuality: the idea that someone can simply choose to disassociate themselves from something that is embedded in their brain. This is where many men experience a struggle, and they are often torn between honoring the relationship and the personal comforts for the one they love, and remaining true to who they are and what they represent. Quite honestly, no one's to blame in such a scenario. When a man finds love, he opts to honor the love and please his partner by also honoring her comforts. Eventually when he has found his comforts, he looks to continue unpacking his entire identity. It is very possible for a couple to navigate through this successfully, but it does require us to shift our focus into an area that many couples often overlook.

Sexual Compatibility: Negotiating the Sexual Relationship

We often assume that if the overall relationship dynamic is supportive of open and honest communication this connection will naturally spill over into the sexual relationship as well. The reality is that openly discussing sexual compatibility is something that a lot of people don't really think about when they're going into a new relationship. When the sex is new it's always great, people assume that great sex equals great compatibility. It's not until relationships settle in and people start looking to explore and unpack their sex suitcases, do couples start to really talk about their sexual comforts and find out how well they mesh between the sheets. When you think about sexual compatibility it really is a unique negotiation that takes place between two people. The goal is for both partners to achieve fulfillment of their sexual needs and also have their sexual comforts and boundaries honored at the same time. Well, this truly does require creative negotiation, and depending on how effectively and successfully this environment is built will determine how in sync a couple will be moving forward.

When it comes to talking about sex, every little variable counts, our actions and reactions, even our body language. All of these signals contribute to the type of environment we create. This is why it's super-duper important to know how to build it right and to make the right contributions that will help you achieve the results of truly having an open and honest communication on sex. Taking the time to build good communication on sex and create an inviting environment will become your greatest asset in the relationship. You're basically tapping into the one area that a man identifies with the most, and a side of him that he pretty much hides from the entire world. When a man knows that he doesn't have to hide any part of himself or his sexuality from his relationship, he has found his truest security for life. I can't stress the benefits enough, and creating a good dialogue on sex is what helps keep a couple connected, the sexual exploration flowing and the happiness on high.

Sexual Compatibility: Meeting Your Partner's Needs and Honoring Your Comforts and Boundaries

Sexual compatibility is where it all starts. It's a proven fact that sexual variety and sexual exploration contributes to a much healthier and happier sex life. Keeping things spicy and rotating new ideas in the bedroom helps keep the spark ignited and the chemistry flowing. Successfully executing all of this and defining the identity and parameters of the sexual relationship is one of the most important negotiations that a couple makes in their union. It requires creative negotiation and a unified effort to build a solid line of communication that will provide both partners with the necessary comforts to be themselves and speak their mind. This right here is where many people mess up and they don't even realize it. I'll give you an example, and we'll use good ol' Larry and Becky… Mr. Larry has a thing for role play in the bedroom, and his biggest sexual fantasy involves Becky dressing up as a school teacher. It would be a dream come true for his penis, if Becky schooled him in the bedroom…and taught him a thing or two about some 'made-up' course, which really doesn't matter because it's less about the lesson and more about the glasses and stern look that Becky is going to be sporting. Unfortunately, Larry is hesitant to even bring this up to Becky, because the last time he tried bringing up a new idea it didn't go so well.

He had come home with a surprise for Becky, and while they were getting it on one night, out pulls Larry a sparkly ten-inch rubber penis. As he sat there with a big grin on his face, eager to see her excitement, Becky's face turned to a look of disgust as she snapped, and "I hope that's for you because it's definitely not for me"....aaaand that was the end of that night, and the end of Larry and his surprise gifts. The true reality of it all is that Larry and Becky simply didn't have the type of communication that's required for such a sexual venture. Had their relationship been more open and candid, Larry would know that Becky wasn't opposed to the idea of sex toys or vibrators altogether. She was however not okay with the obnoxious ten-inch size that Larry picked out and found the size factor disturbing (Hey, vaginas are like shoe sizes and it's gotta be the right fit). Had they discussed this, and identified one another's comforts and interests, they may have happily embarked on a sex toy journey that involved a more reasonable six-inch compromise and one that made them both happy. This miscommunication has now left Larry with the impression that Becky is not comfortable with any big changes in the bedroom and any future interests and thoughts will be rejected so they stay locked away in his sex suitcase.

Becky will never know that Larry has a school teacher fantasy, and it may be something that she is totally into and okay with. When she asks Larry if he's happy and content with their sex life, he will say "yes" because he loves Becky and he wants her to feel comfortable. Maybe Larry is happy, maybe he will stay happy or maybe one day he will wake up and feel that he has sacrificed a big part of his sexuality for the relationship. All of this because Larry and Becky didn't take the time to build the right environment in the sexual relationship, one where they would both have great comfort and stay connected. And quite frankly, sometimes, the roles are reversed and it's the guy who loses his shit when his female spouse tries to bring home a ten- inch rubber penis. I mean truth be told, it's a tough one to swallow for a guy (as in tough *idea* to swallow and not a tough *dick* to swallow…mind you at 10 inches, I don't think it's physically possible for anyone to fully swallow that!) Regardless, the fact that there's penis competition in the room and it's twice the size of his penis may be a little overwhelming for some dudes.

The Becky/Larry scenario is exactly what we don't want, but unfortunately it's reflective of many relationships out there. There's no denying that negotiating comforts in the sexual relationship is more of a challenge for women. Think about it" it's a cycle where our comforts in the sexual relationship relies on our security, yet our security is dependent on our finding the courage to fully embrace the sexual relationship. WHAT THE HELL BECKY?! Wasn't this supposed to be easy? Like, pull out a vagina, wave it in the air…penis nose dives into it like fly paper and Bob's your Uncle! … Okay, let's take a vagina breather here and regroup. It's very possible to build something that honors both partners. A good negotiation is one where you give a little to get a little, but not to the point where either partner is ever required to sacrifice themselves or their comfort zone.

Synchronized Sex: Building the Right Environment and Staying Connected

Perfecting sex is not found in *Cosmo,* with their "Blow his dick and his mind all in ten easy steps." Not every guy likes the same stuff, and every man has his own unique curiosities and fantasies. Working on the communication and building an environment that allows a man to speak his mind freely and ask for what he wants to explore, is what will give you the most valuable sex tips ever. The best sex tips don't come from *Cosmo,* they actually come from him! There are two things I totally endorse for all women to embrace in their relationships. One is to create the right environment in the sexual relationship, one that supports open and honest communication. The second is to get to really talking, and thoroughly explore every discussion, thought, desire and any sexual variable that exists in his brain and yours.

Taking the time to build it right is the best thing you can ever do for your relationship, and it will ensure that you truly are aware of your partner's sexual needs inside and out. Identifying the sexual compatibility in the relationship is job one, because it not only helps identify where there are commonalities but also areas of opportunity to grow and explore together. A common mistake that people often make in relationships is that they focus on the areas where they do share compatibility, and they simply dismiss the areas where they do not share the same comforts or views. Ignoring these discussions is such a missed opportunity for couples to truly get to know one another. Even if the differences are there, by exploring ideas and having discussions, it can take couples in new directions and they can discover new territory together and perhaps meet each other halfway in areas that are often ignored. Trust me when I say that these opportunities should not be missed. It only strengthens the bond a couple shares.

I can tell you that this is the very approach that my husband and I took when we first met. We committed ourselves to working on the sexual communication and by helping each other achieve our necessary comforts we were able to create an environment that promoted candid and honest discussions about our sexual needs. This meant complete honesty, as in no faked orgasms, and no offense taken when one of us was being honest. Instead we took this shared knowledge as valuable information that would help us grow and explore the potential for greatness together. My husband has always said that he appreciates the dynamic of our sexual relationship, and the freedom he has to be himself and speak his mind. This is something that he says he never truly had in any other past relationship, and he never felt 100% comfortable in candidly disclosing all of his sexual thoughts and desires. Openly communicating about every aspect of the relationship promotes sexual exploration and it creates a truly unified bond. No partner feels as though they have sacrificed a big part of their sexuality. No aspect of the sexual relationship should ever be ignored, because this is how couples become disconnected. Also taking the time to create an inviting setting sets the pace for what the relationship will be like moving forward in all aspects of your lives.

Regardless whether you are celebrating your one year anniversary or your twentieth, there's always benefit to frequently evaluating the sexual relationship and ensuring that you and your mate stay connected and happy. The following is a guide to help initiate the process, and help create an environment for candid discussions on sex and sexploration:

1. Setting the Sex Stage: Initiating Candid Discussions & Identifying One Another's Sexual Interests, Comforts & Boundaries.

The best place to start is to put it all out on the table and to figure out exactly where each one of you stand. Quite often couples think they know one another, when in reality there are many things they know very little about. That old school "Newlywed Game" show comes to mind, where husbands and wives would come to find out that their spouse didn't see things as they did (she'd hit him over the head with a couch cushion on national television and try to maintain her composure for the remainder of the show) The reality is that knowing your partner inside-out means being able to correctly answer such questions as "What is your partner's single most biggest sexual fantasy?" or "To date, what is the single most memorable sexual experience that your partner has ever experienced?" or "What does your partner love most about sex?" or "If he had to pick one sexual act as his most favorite of all, what would it be?" Knowledge is power, and these are all things that couples need to know about one another.

I have included a Sexual Compatibility Questionnaire (Chapter 9: Toolbox) that you and your spouse can each complete individually and then review together. This exercise will help guide the discussion by identifying the areas where there are shared interests and comforts, and that can be explored together further. It will also help identify areas where you discover new things about your spouse, as well as opportunities to work together and explore new ideas. At the very least, this exercise will help you gain a full understanding about one another and maybe learn new things that you didn't know about the relationship. Now, I will say this…before a couple can initiate a truly beneficial candid discussion on their compatibility findings, there are certain factors to consider…So keep those Epic vaginas put and keep reading to the very end before you do this exercise…

2. Keep an Open Mind and Don't Pass Judgment.

The reality is that you may not share the same enthusiasm or the same comfort level for sexual fantasies or positions your partner likes. And sometimes when something challenges our sensibilities, our immediate reaction is to reject the idea. No one says that you have to accept or like something simply because your partner expresses an interest in it. That being said, even when something doesn't coincide with your views, it doesn't put your partner in the wrong simply for his preferences. Both sides hold equal importance, and you deserve to have your views and comforts honored in the relationship, as much as your partner deserves to find equal treatment and reception in the union. For many of us our views are heavily influenced by societal views towards sex. And society's take on someone who identifies with anything "unconventional" is to label it as "taboo" or "unhealthy." Two consenting adults have a wide variety of things they can do together, and no one should judge them for it.

This is why it's important to know the facts and understand the behavioral psychology surrounding human sexuality and to truly define what is unhealthy and wrong. **Sex is wrong:**

- **If the act or behavior is illegal**. If a person identifies with, expresses an interest for, or has desires to engage in any sexual act or behavior that involves illegal practices or activity, then this is unhealthy and this person should not be encouraged or supported.

- **If a person has "obsessive" sexual tendencies or behaviors.** If a person has obsessive sexual habits that prevents them from being able to function normally in society, or they become socially isolated, and it infringes on a person's ability to live a normal and productive life (like go to work and perform everyday duties and responsibilities)... Then this is a problem. For example, if someone has an addiction to pornography and they have an excessive need to watch it all the time. This is considered unhealthy and can damage a relationship. If the behaviors are excessive and a person devotes all their free time to feeding this habit, then this is unhealthy and a problem.

- **If it causes distress on a spouse or the relationship**. If a person has sexual interests, tendencies or practices that cause their partner mental or emotional distress, or it makes a spouse feel alienated or rejected in a negative way…then this is a problem and unhealthy for the relationship.

Obviously, if a spouse fell under any of these classifications, it's understandable that their partner would be unaccepting and rightfully so. However, "out there" and "whacky" sounding sexual thoughts and interests don't necessarily make it wrong. Somewhere out there is a guy who fantasizes about having a massive orgy involving him and six blow-up dolls… and a bucket of Nutella. Now you and I may think that this is whacky, and maybe his wife does, too…but it doesn't make it wrong. I mean sure, if I were him I probably wouldn't run around with Nutella in my ass crack and bragging to all my friends that I just nailed six blow-up vaginas, because maybe his friends don't share the same fantasies or even like Nutella. However, if his spouse is totally into it, and she's willing to hold the video camera and catch all the blow-up Nutella antics on tape, then more power to them. What it really comes down to is that you need to make sure that regardless of how you feel towards something, it does not invalidate how your partner sees things, nor does it classify him as "abnormal" simply because it's not something you're into doing.

3. Staying Supportive Helps Build a Positive Environment and Promote Honesty.

Regardless of what a spouse brings to the conversation, it's important to always keep a positive and supportive mindset. Remember, it's not what you say, but how you say it. If your partner expresses an interest for something that you're simply not feeling, you can keep it positive and explain how and why it does nothing for you. Even when our sensibilities are being challenged it's important to avoid immediate knee-jerk reactions like "Ew! That's disgusting! I would never try that!' Keep in mind that this is still a man you love, someone who feels comfortable enough to confide in the person that he loves and trusts. Negative reactions will only make a partner feel shameful and rejected for what he wants. It will also send a message to him that it's not safe for him to be open and honest, and he will avoid doing so in the future. I can tell you this...that if my husband popped into the bedroom holding a jar of peanut butter, a pair of skis, a sack of marbles, a bottle of lube and a big grin on his face....My immediate reaction may be to smack all that shit out of his arms and the grin straight off of his face all with one swift open hand. However, I know that he's only displaying his excitement to try new things, so I will try to find positive ways to negotiate the situation and say, "Babe, didn't I tell you about my severe vagina peanut allergy?" At the very least I'd probably agree to use the skis as a ski bunny theme, but unless he was planning on using the marbles on himself then those would probably be out. Just know that being supportive provides him with comfort and it further endorses the honesty in the relationship.

4. Listening Costs You Nothing: at the Very Least Hear Him Out.

It costs you nothing to listen to what he has to say, but it does cost the relationship if your partner feels as though he cannot speak freely or simply be himself. At the very least, he should be able to express anything and everything that's on his mind. If he wants to share in a discussion about his past sexual relationships, even if it involves something or someone you don't want to hear about, let him. Don't let your own insecurities get in the way. This is a guy who is committed to you, and is comfortable enough to confide in you. Plus, these people and things are in his past...you have the ability to explore anything with him now, perfect it, and put your own twist and signature on it! I'll be the first to admit that when my husband and I first implemented this open communication concept in our relationship, there were times where I did feel uncomfortable. Who wants to hear about him having sex with his ex? However, I realized that an ex is an ex for a reason, and his willingness to share provided me with valuable information. By learning about the things he liked and didn't like about past relationships, it gave me insight into cultivating a sexual relationship that truly fed his happiness.

The same goes for his willingness to freely speak about his fantasies. Understand that listening to what he has to share does not imply acceptance or that you need to meet every single suggestion he puts on the table. Just hear him out. Remember, knowledge is power, and understanding the key to all his penis dreams is the most powerful kind of information of all. Again, all the same applies to a man, it's a two way street and he too should be supportive.

5. There's No Need to be Super Cool or Superhuman to Still Be a Superwoman in the Bedroom.

If you understand the simple science between a guy, his penis and his brain, you'll understand that there's no need to be an over-achieving vagina. When it comes to sex, men want nothing more than to explore their fantasies and their sexual curiosities. Yes, in an ideal penis world, if a guy had ten fantasies then all ten of those fantasies would become a reality in his sex life. However, in this perfect world every guy would have a full head of hair, a nine-inch penis and would be driving a fancy sports car. And we all know that in the real world, you have a much better chance of encountering a unicorn than you do a well-endowed successful man who has it all, including hair. The reality is that not every fantasy that transpires in a man's brain will be experienced by his penis, and there are many male sexual fantasies that remain just that...or at best become material for a solo sex session between him, his thoughts and his left hand. There are no guarantees that two people will always see penis-to-vagina on every single sexual interest and fantasy, and that's perfectly acceptable. Just because it exists in his head, doesn't mean that it's your duty as a spouse to tackle it and turn that shit into reality.

Are you kidding? You shouldn't feel as though you need to be some sort of super human Dick Fairy, forcing your comforts out of bounds just to deliver on every single fantasy and request your partner will ever have. Men are very realistic when it comes to this, and any guy with a good grasp on reality understands this. All a man could ever ask for is a spouse who is committed to giving where they can and when they can. The only thing you owe your spouse (and that they can happily expect) is the freedom to speak without being judged, and at the very least to simply consider and entertain what is being shared and requested. Anything more than that, like committing to exploring and incorporating ideas in the sexual relationship, is solely up to your comforts. If out of ten fantasies a woman had the comfort and ability to make even two or three of those a reality, any guy would shit himself from excitement. True story. So if you two see eye-to-eye on the handcuffs and blindfold, wearing a wig and pretending to have a French accent one night, but don't agree on his idea of you popping grapes out of your vagina…trust me, he's elated by everything else that there's no need to even try torpedo- launching grapes from your vagina. What's more important is for a man to feel accepted by you so he can be himself without reservation.

There is one amazing thing that works to your advantage in the relationship, and that's the love that a man has for a woman. When the human brain shares an emotional connection with someone, chemicals are released that make everything amplified and much more intense. In vagina terms, when a man loves a woman, the little chemicals in his head have him seeing her as a sex vixen. Every sexual thought he has, he wants to explore with her. And when he does have the ability to explore any of his desires and fantasies with this woman, it makes her a freaking super hero in the bedroom… She is Superwoman, Wonder Woman and Super Epic Vagina all in one. So just know that you don't need to bring it all, and the simple fact that you're willing to listen, and bring any part of it is a dream come true in his world.

6. Don't Harp on the Differences. Focus on Your Strengths. It's important to keep your focus on the areas where you two share commonalities and not in the areas where you simply don't share the same interests. It's about focusing on the positives and not the negatives. Staying focused on where you two match up helps keep the energy positive in the sexual relationship. The reality is that we are women and we are only human, and it's not uncommon to feel a sense of uneasiness when we are pushed out of our comfort zones. Many of us have been there, becoming fixated on the bad things, or differences, to the point that it starts to eat away at our sense of security. We feel inadequate because we cannot find it within ourselves fulfill our partner's requests.

Comforts vary for us all, be it embracing his request for incorporating sex toys into the mix, watching pornography together, videotaping your own personal sex sessions, or even tying him to the bed and smacking his testicles around during an interrogation role play. Everyone has their limits and two people won't always share the exact same comfort for the same things. If something is discussed and it's not "all systems go" on both sides, don't over analyze it or obsess over why you're different. It is what it is, and your energy is better invested in the areas that you two do share similar interests.

Women often get caught up in what's wrong, rather than what's right. Taking something insignificant, like him expressing, "That would be a hot scenario...." and turning it into "Is that ALL of what you secretly want? You're attracted to that type of woman aren't you? I'm not her, so you must not want me!" And while she continues on and allows these thoughts to eat away at her sense of security, he's already thinking about the next idea that has his penis twitching in his trousers. It's important to understand that the male sex brain has the ability to simply identify with the thought alone and with the idea of something being arousing and erotic. It's that simple, and most times they don't place much in depth thought into all the specifics. If anything, a man is excited by the idea of exploring new and erotic ideas with the woman he loves and who he is most attracted to. If one hot idea doesn't pan out, he's got plenty more. A woman shouldn't feel inadequate simply because she cannot find it within herself to embrace one particular fantasy. No man finds enjoyment in something that causes his partner distress, and if it's not a truly enjoyable experience for his spouse then it does little for him as well. This is HUGE for men, and a guy needs to know that a woman is truly into something in order for it to truly do something for him.

Focusing on the differences is only wasted energy that could be better spent and invested into the areas where there are shared interests and likes. Let's say that your partner expresses an interest in ten ideas that his penis wants to explore in the bedroom, and your vagina is all for three of those penis dreams. There would be no benefit to focusing unnecessarily on the seven ideas that you simply cannot embrace. Instead you invest your energy in the things that you are willing to explore and that you can fulfill. You take those ideas and rock them out in the bedroom, and turn those penis dreams into reality. Focus on what you can deliver, not what you can't. When a man is able to explore his sexual desires in any capacity, he's not thinking about the things he doesn't have. He's thinking about what he does have and how lucky he is to have a woman in his life that makes it all possible.

7. You Need to be 100% Honest and Have Total Transparency. Honesty in any relationship is an expectation that we all have, and the funny thing is that women will only make an exception to this rule when it comes to sparing a man's feelings or ego. In certain instances this would make sense, because no good ever comes out of telling a man his penis is so small that it needs a GPS locating device just so it doesn't get lost. Women often see no harm in overly embellishing the "truth" when it comes to the added theatrics during an orgasm, or completely faking it all together just to stroke his ego a little. Instead of being truthful, women often feel the need to tell a guy what they think he wants to hear. However, when it comes to a committed sexual relationship even little white vagina lies can actually affect the quality of sex in the union. If we're not honest with our partner they'll never know what it truly takes to fulfill our needs, and we'll never achieve ultimate sexual gratification in the sexual relationship. Being candid and honest in the sexual relationship is important for many reasons, and it not only affects the quality of sex but also the connection that a couple shares. This means that even the "harmless" Oscar-worthy fake orgasm performances can in fact harm the quality of the sexual relationship.

We already discussed the idea that if we say we want complete honesty in the sexual relationship, then we should never criticize a man when he is being honest and speaking candidly about his sexual needs. And if it's honesty that we expect from a spouse, then we too need to always be forthcoming and honest about our needs and our comforts. Honesty supports real growth and it helps preserve all the greatness in the sexual relationship. So this means that if you ever feel as though something isn't working for you, you need to be honest and communicate this. Never suppress or downplay your feelings. Doing so will only end up causing you distress and it will negatively impact the relationship in the long run. Being true to the relationship and your spouse, also means being true to yourself. The same applies in reverse and you should always be honest about your sexual needs and what you want from the relationship. It's very possible to speak candidly without hurting your partner's feelings or bruising his ego, and there's a HUGE difference between being honest and being brutally honest. Sometimes there's no benefit to being brutally honest, such as mentioning the fact that your ex's nickname was "Cockzilla," and that the orgasms he gave you were even bigger than his penis. So you can spare a partner's feelings by foregoing mention of this, or perhaps shaving a few inches off of your story when you retell it. With that being said, I know that many of us think "what's the harm in a little faked orgasm?" We're looking to boost a man's ego right? Wrong! Fake orgasms have no place in a committed sexual relationship, and it only gives him misguided feedback in the bedroom.

The infamous 'fake orgasm' has created a male-culture of falsified perceptions and inflated egos. When I canvas men on this topic, I'm always astounded by the number of men who believe that no sexual partner, past or present, has ever faked an orgasm. Pretty much 99.9% of the male population believes this to be true, despite the fact that statistics show that 80% of women have at some point faked an orgasm. It's comical actually, but it's also misguiding and these men will never be motivated to step it up in any other way because they believe that they have tapped into their best sex game. Women often complain that men don't invest enough efforts into a female partner's sex needs, yet how can we expect a man to raise the bar when we've created a fake lowered standard. In his eyes, he's Donald Trump in the bedroom and he's making shit happen (minus the penis comb over)! There are so many other ways to inflate a man's ego without shooting ourselves in the vagina. It may provide his ego with immediate fulfillment, but the overall relationship will be affected in the long run. Over the years, fake orgasms lead to less than great sex for a woman, and this leads to a lesser desire to have sex, which leads to less sex being had. Ultimately we know where this goes, and when we sense that a man is not happy in the relationship it starts to affect our security. Faked orgasms lead to failed relationships. If we want ultimate sexual satisfaction, and want to have a successful relationship that will last a lifetime, we need to stop lying to men.

A man relies heavily on feedback in the sexual relationship to know whether or not he's doing a good job. He also gages his efforts on the feedback he receives, and he looks to repeat those same efforts to get the same results. Think about it, a committed and long-term relationship means having sex with one person for a REALLY LONG TIME…Like years upon years! Why would any woman want to give her vagina a lifelong death sentence with the possibility of never seeing a real orgasm for eternity? You owe it to your vagina and her happiness to communicate honestly in the relationship. This allows a couple to work together and develop techniques that truly work and that make sex amazing. Keep in mind that if a woman doesn't find sex truly gratifying, she's less inclined to want to have more of it. So in the long run, you'd be doing your vagina and relationship a disservice by not being truly honest. In order for a man to truly find sex fulfilling he needs to know that a woman finds it equally gratifying and that she too is enjoying every experience.

Again, it's all in how you say it and you can totally be honest and tell him of something is not doing anything for you without hurting his feelings. Hurting his feelings would be saying something like "um, I think your dick is broken,", or mentioning that his 5.14 inches are not exactly hitting all the same spots that your nine- inch ex-Cockzilla used to reach. By working together to explore new ways to have sex, you can turn his 5.14 (on a good day) into a stellar nine- inch experience. Okay fine, maybe that's a bit of a penis stretch, but it's a hell of a lot better than having to fake orgasms for the rest of your life. Heaven forbid that you're not paying full attention one day and you may really bruise his ego when you're belting out an orgasm opera not realizing that he stepped away to grab a glass of water. I mean, hell, even Cockzilla's reach wasn't talented enough to cover the spread from the kitchen to the bed. Remember what they say, when you tell one lie, you have to keep telling lies to cover the first one. And before you know it you're estranged from your vagina and that bitch isn't talking to you anymore because you robbed her of all the fun she could have had. Trust me, it's all fun and games until your vagina stops talking to you…so, the moral of the story is that you always want to give honest feedback, and you want to give solutions and ideas too. Suggesting something different that you think may work for you, and trying it out to see how it goes. Trust me, when it comes to sex, no penis is complaining about having to put in extra hours on the job.

8. Give Where You Can and Don't Be Afraid To Try New Things.

I am always the first to tell women that they should never compromise themselves or their comforts simply to accommodate a partner's sexual needs. However, it's human nature for us to sometimes be reluctant in embracing change or venturing into unknown territory. We are often creatures of habit, and we find comfort in what we know. Sometimes we simply hide behind our what we know because of this 'unknown' factor, with no real justification. When it comes to your non-negotiables you have, you should never force yourself to cross any lines if it causes you distress. That being said, don't deprive yourself or your vagina from the wonderful benefits of exploring new things. It can be a great growing experience for you and your mate, one that can deepen your bond and enhance the sexual relationship. Sometimes when you allow yourself to step out of that comfort zone, you can discover a new world of sexual gratification and fulfillment. You never know unless you try, and it's no different than trying new foods. Sometimes we may be unsure about something, and before you know it it's your new favorite food…or sex position.

Who knows, you may learn new things about yourself and your sexuality that you never knew and it could stand to improve the quality of your sex life. Don't be closed off to something simply because you don't know much about it. If something piques your curiosity but you don't know enough about it, you owe it to yourself to investigate further before you decide for certain that it is or is not for you and your vagina. When my husband and I first embarked on our sexploration journey, I'll admit that there were times when he'd surprise me a new toy or gadget and my initial response would be 'is that a car part?' Keeping an open mind gave way to many delightful discoveries, and nowadays I'm unwilling to part with my magical car parts (car parts implies sex toys and I'm not firing up that vagina with spark plugs, so please don't try this at home.) A great way to explore curiosities is to jump on the internet and to read up on all the ins and outs. It can be a great bonding experience for a couple if they embark on the entire process together. Grab a glass of wine (or whatever your drink of choice is) and make it a date night on the couch. Online, you can discover new ideas, shop for sex toys and gadgets and even learn how to them. The wonderful thing is that when it comes to sexploration the possibilities are endless. If you're someone who's never tried sex toys before and you have some curiosities, then start exploring the possibilities. No exploration or experimentation (or vibrator) is too big or too small, and you can start out with a few things that fit your comforts (and fit your vagina). Whether it be a blind fold, handcuffs or even a mini-vibrator. There's no need to come busting out in fierce vagina mode and jump right into sex swings and rubber orgies involving a bunch of ten-inch dildos. The simple fact that you and your partner are open to trying new things is enough to keep the chemistry flowing and the sex hot and spicy.

I can tell you from first-hand experience that the biggest strides my vagina has ever made, all started by stepping out of my comfort zone. When I look back to where I was just over ten years ago, my comforts were nowhere near where they are today. Are you kidding me? If I happened upon a rubber ding-dong dildo back then, my vagina would have gone running for the hills straight to the nearest Nunnery or into a Vagina Witness Protection Program. However, over the years it's been a steady progression of growing and exploring. Through the years my husband and I have always been open to sexploration and to trying out new ideas in the bedroom. I'd have to say that this alone is the biggest reason why our sexual relationship has remained so intense and it's because it constantly evolves. The great thing is that it doesn't always have to be "something new." It's all about having a handful of favorites that you rotate and reinvent every time. In our sexual relationship, no two experiences are ever the same, even when we are repeating and rotating some of our favorite sexy pastimes. The sexual relationship should really be a balance and an exploration of both partner's interests and curiosities. Sometimes one partner's interests can open up their spouse to new experiences and they discover a world they never knew before. It's all about a couple growing together, helping one another explore each of their fantasies and creating a truly stellar sex life that provides both partner's with the ultimate sexual fulfillment in their lives.

9. Behind Closed Doors You Make the Rules and This World Doesn't have to Resemble Life Outside of the Bedroom.

One of the most wonderful aspects of a committed sexual relationship is that you can explore anything and everything your little vagina heart desires. In the privacy of your intimate relationship you can do whatever you want to do and be whoever you want to be. It's a world where fantasy meets reality, and there's no need to emulate who or what you represent to the outside world. There's a reason why the book *50 Shades of Gray* stirred up such a crazed vagina movement, and it's because the world of sexual fantasy and sexploration was finally acknowledged in a public way. Vaginas across the country found a mainstream outlet to finally embrace the world of sexual fantasy. A world where a woman could explore her sexuality and her desires, and create a sexual persona that was unlike the person she exposed to the outer world. The crazy thing is that this book really started a social mainstream Vaginalution, where vaginas across the globe all exhaled and started an evolution and revolution to explore our female sexual desires. As I mentioned earlier, the mental aspects of sex is the most prominent part of the sexual relationship, so our sexual persona and the characteristics that we explore is far more powerful than toys and sex itself.

In the comforts of the intimate relationship, a couple has the ability to define their own identities and boundaries. As long as it suits the comforts of both partners (and it's not breaking any laws or bones) anything goes! A woman who is normally a power house executive and someone who is always calling the shots and running the ship can transform into an innocent submissive sex kitten and explore her desires of being dominated and sexually ravaged from head, to vagina, to toe. On the flip side, a woman who normally likes to hold a traditional "wifey" role in her relationship and loves to have her husband steer the ship, can transform into a fierce sex diva and dominatrix…making that penis submit to her commands. As a side note, this is a great time to milk foot massages, pampering, being doted on… A submissive penis is a blessing to come by so full take advantage of it.

When it comes to a world of fantasy, it's a great opportunity to also explore sexual role play. Whoever said that playing dress-up is not for grown- ups never had a half-naked cop pull their vagina over for speeding in bed. There's something about a badge, handcuffs and an erect police-penis that seriously makes a vagina want to break the law and be put in penis prison. From playing cops and robbers one week to "Paging Nurse Betty…" the next, sex role-play can sizzle. Going to the doctor's office may not be a momentous occasion in real life, but there's something about a naughty nurse that has a man wishing he had a different ailment every day of the week. Trust me when I say that there is no need to have any prior medical experience or know any doctor lingo… When an erect penis is in the presence of the naughty nurse, saying something like, "We're going to have to do a penis physical because you may be suffering from Penile Erectoritis." totally jives. Just keep in mind that it is "fantasy play," and even though made-up medical terms may sound real and be totally cool, made-up medical procedures that involve real life instruments can turn shit into a real-life emergency that neither you nor his penis needs. It's all fun and games until someone REALLY ends up in the ER with a severed left testicle....and with you standing next to him dressed like a hooker nurse, holding "said left testicle" in a plastic baggie.

These are things that are best discussed prior to, and where you can both define your comfort zones and boundaries. Not to mention also come up with a "safe word" that he can blurt out, in the event that shit gets too real and his penis needs a time out and a way out. And like I said before, it doesn't even have to be all that elaborate. Something as simple as wearing a wig or creating a sexy new character that he's never met before. I can tell you that I have had many nights where things started out with no real plan in mind, and before you know it...out pops a character that no one expected. Sometimes just playing it by ear and pulling a persona out of your vagina works out the best. My husband always jokes about the fact that he never quite knows who or what will emerge from my closet on any given night. The next day my husband will say, "Man, what was that last night? I had some hot chick come visit me who only spoke French...I have no idea what the hell she was saying, but man that sounded hot!" The funny thing is that in real life I don't even speak fluent French, but high heels make a great translator in the bedroom. Mix a couple of real words that I do know, in with gibberish and a French accent...and VOILA! His penis translator hears "you're a bad boy mister and I will spank you my little French muffin"... when what I really said was, "I parked my yellow elephant outside...blah, blah, blah...Bonjour...if you can please pass me a toaster, blah...blah...French Fries...blah...I'd like to order a spatula and comb my toilet...Merci." Hey, whatever, it sounds hot in the moment and he loses his French toast over the fake French Bitch... so we go with it.

The penile point I'm trying to make is that you shouldn't allow yourself be limited by the outer world and think that there's a need to stay in your "normal character." Behind closed doors, there's only one rule, and the rule is this… that THERE ARE NO RULES!

10. Use Your Vagina Voice and Listen to what the Penis has to Say.

The funny thing about women is that we are never short for words when it comes to expressing ourselves outside of the bedroom. However, for many women the second that the bedroom door closes, their vagina all of a sudden becomes a mute mime. Okay, maybe not totally mute, because moaning and yelling does count as sexual communication. However, many women do struggle with communicating their needs in the bedroom, or coming out and asking for what they want. Having a vocal vagina is the only way a vagina gets what she really wants, and it's also the only way a man will get to know exactly what it is the vagina truly needs. Contrary to what many men may think, men are not vagina experts and only you know your sexual needs the best. He may be all up inside that vagina, but he doesn't really know what you're feeling, whether he's hit the right spot, or whether he's taking stabs in the dark and in the wrong direction.

The best way to perfect your sex life is to communicate your needs and to teach a guy exactly what it is you need in order to have an optimal sexual experience. Our vagina needs are very different than the needs a penis has, and we require our own unique stimulation and build up. This especially holds true when it comes to foreplay, and a woman relies on a much longer period of sexual build up before she reaches climax. A man can easily get his penis engine revving in three to four minutes, and he's ready to race. Where as many women require up to thirty or even forty minutes of foreplay just to get that vagina warmed up. So while he's already spinning his penis-wheels and burning rubber, that vagina bitch hasn't even made it out of the driveway. This is probably the real reason why they invented rubber penises and it's because when the vagina is finally ready for action, he's already out of commission, had himself a sandwich and snoring away. Okay, perhaps that's being a little harsh on the penis, and I apologize.... I take it back, because not all penises snore.

Okay, penis jokes aside, it's your job to teach your partner what you need, and what works best on your specific vagina model. A mind-boggling fact that many people are not aware of: a study conducted in recent years shows that only 25% of women consistently climax from sexual intercourse alone, and that the majority of women require clitoral stimulation in order to achieve an orgasm. Many women are actually aware of this need, but are not comfortable to come out and suggest using a sex toy, or even their own helping hand during sex. They think it may offend a guy and make him feel that his penis alone is not enough to do the job. The reality is that a guy can't take offense to factual science, and it's simply a reality. My husband has always said that he appreciates the fact that I have always been honest in our sexual relationship. I have always been forthcoming from the very beginning, and I explained that I was not one for faking orgasms, and that he needed to place his male ego aside if we expected to create greatness. My husband always says that he realizes now that most of his past relationships lacked a good sexual connection. Sexual discussions were never candid and most of his partners weren't very vocal with their sexual needs. He also thanks me sarcastically for bursting his male ego bubble, because all these years he was of the impression that no woman had ever faked an orgasm with him. I try to console him by telling him that perhaps he was lucky and dated only within the 25% pool of orgasmic women.

The reality is that for most women, we have intricate vagina needs and it's important to have comfort in coming out and asking for what your vagina requires for ultimate satisfaction. Even in the midst of sexual play, it's important to be vocal and provide feedback. You can guide him with your words… "Faster, slower…to the left, to the right…right there… OH SWEET NELLY DON'T STOP!" Okay, before this turns into a smutty sex novel and a shirtless Fabio comes galloping in on a horse, I'm sure you get the idea. Communicating your needs is the only way your vagina will ever truly experience the most mind altering orgasms of all time. There's a reason why one-third of women have never experienced an orgasm. Many women think they are incapable of doing so, when the reality is that they have never really taken the time to learn about their vagina needs and experiment with what works. Every vagina is different, and some need that extra clitoral stimulation, while others rely on unique rhythmic motions be it fast or slow. A woman should know her vagina inside and out. There's always a benefit in learning about the female anatomy and taking to the internet will help you become a vagina expert. Women have many erogenous zones and you need to know about all of them, so you can teach him about all the ways he can make your vagina sing her own rendition of the "Star Spangled Banner.", and do cartwheels off the ceiling. That being said, no amount of sex education literature can replace hands on experience. So take full advantage of the penis apprentice that you have, because he will happily partake in any lesson that involves sex.

Men want to know that their partner is truly enjoying the experience and that it's truly gratifying and fulfilling. When a man knows that his partner is truly getting the most out of the experience, it's a huge dose of mental stimulation for him as well. Not to mention, men love a woman who is vocal in the bedroom and who has the confidence to ask for what she wants. It's also a huge ego stroke as well, and like a pat on the back for the penis. Keep in mind that the penis is a perfectionist and if he knows that he can do something even better, perfect it and deliver an even more stellar orgasm for his partner, this is the biggest achievement for the penis perfectionist. So take full advantage of this and keep the dialogue flowing throughout the sexual relationship, as this will ensure that the sexploration is always serving to your vagina needs.

That being said, the greatest asset to perfecting any and all of your sex skills lies right at your fingertips. Well sort of, it's more so located in his pants…but easily accessible and at your fingertips anytime you're handling the penis. The point is that your partner and fellow penis owner is the only source that will ever grant you the knowledge needed to perfect your sex skills in the relationship. Cosmo doesn't know what his dick needs, and Cosmo can't tell you what truly tickles his fancy, or whether he likes to have his "fancy" tickled, stroked or even smacked. Your greatest resource for what he wants and what he likes is found by going straight to the source. This is why it's important to listen to what the penis has to say. It's your job to ask for feedback, both in and out of the bedroom. As long as you're open to listening, the penis has no problems being vocal and asking for what he wants.

Ideally, you want to become an expert on his penis and his sexual needs. And it doesn't end at just his penis, because men have many erogenous zones that totally turn their crank. Some men thoroughly enjoy having their testicles stimulated, while others don't like it at all. Obviously, it's a lot easier to identify if a guy is not one for any type of ball play, because he will likely let it be known should you venture anywhere near those bad boys. However, if it is something he likes, it's something you want to know. When it comes to physical stimulation, there are so many variations and sensations that you really need to openly discuss it and experiment with all the potential pleasures. Now I know that I just got done saying that other resources won't give you insider knowledge, but there are benefits to learning about the male anatomy and finding out about all the male erogenous zones.

Taking to the internet and researching some of the more reputable medical sites can help teach you and your partner what all the potential offerings are and how to embark on exploring these areas. Once you have the basics, you can tweak it and customize it to just the way he likes it. The amazing thing about it all is that with good communication, and experimentation you can take a "super blow job" experience and perfect it into a stupendous fantabulous experience one that will have him smacking his own ass in disbelief.

11. You Need To Talk about Sex Often and Then Talk about It Some More.

Talking about sex both in and outside of the bedroom is crucial to the sexual relationship and having a good line of open communication is the best way to keep the sex on track. There's no such thing as "too much" when it comes to how often a couple communicates and the depth to which they discuss sex. Everything from sexual fantasies, to desires, likes and dislikes…From the tip of his penis, the inner most regions of your vagina, to the back of his scrotum. No testicle remains unturned, no nipple goes un-stimulated and no fantasy goes un-talked about. Talking about sex is a great way to initiate new ideas and sexploration. And it's just as important to talk about sex both before and after any experience. Evaluating and re-evaluating the sexual relationship keeps a couple connected. Sharing thoughts on what you liked most about an experience and what you found most erotic bonds you together. This provides valuable feedback for future experiences and helps a couple navigate into new directions and sexplorations. It's almost like having one of those suggestion boxes that companies rely on for feedback. They use this valuable information to improve their business and to ensure optimal customer satisfaction.

My husband and I take any opportunity we can find to talk about sex and have "post sex wrap-up" discussions. It's a great learning experience, because you gain insight into everything that runs through your partner's head during an experience. Obviously, in the moment with all the sex being had, there are many aspects that don't get acknowledged. By having post-sex talks, you find out all the little added things that stimulate his sex brain. Like the fact that he gets so aroused by watching you undress, how you flip your hair, or even a certain look that you give him. Having this knowledge, you can play up all of these little extras in the future, and give an extra hair flip, or give him that piercing sex stare that will deliver that added blow and mental stimulation from his brain straight through to his penis. This may sound corny, but these are things that the penis pays close attention to. My husband has told me that I have a certain look that I give him, one that I had no clue that I did. Knowing this now, I make sure to totally play it up during sex. It's so effective that even in the moment he will blurt out "OH, GOD! THAT LOOK!" It may be his brain and mouth sharing this information, but its coming straight from his penis who's sending up a message loud and clear… "TELL HER TO STOP STARING AT ME LIKE THAT BECAUSE I'M BOUND TO EXPLODE!" I kind of feel bad for doing so, I mean who likes to purposefully torture a guy?…Said no woman ever. This kind of torture is the good kind, and it's pleasurable suffering so we keep that trick tucked in our vagina sock for safe keeping.

Frequently re-evaluating the sex in the relationship ensures that it continues to serve each partner's needs. I often ask my husband all sorts of questions. Things like: What do you like most? What don't you like? What could I have done differently? More of? Less of? As the relationship grows and the dynamic changes over the years, so do people's sexual interests and desires. Something that may not have been prevalent in his sex brain last year, may now be a new found desire and something that your partner is curious in exploring. Frequently discussing the sexual relationship allows a couple to stay connected with the evolution of one another's sexuality and sexual needs. It also helps ensure that each partner continuous to find the sexual relationship gratifying and serving to their happiness. If the sexual relationship is one sided where one partner is finding fulfillment yet the other finds themselves lacking true fulfillment, then the communication hasn't been built right. And it can cause a disconnection in the sexual relationship.

The thing is that when a person feels as though the sexual relationship is no longer serving to their needs, they lose momentum and lose motivation to stay fully-invested, or maintain a high level of effort towards sex. People stay fully engaged only when they find a true sense of fulfillment. This is why an ongoing dialogue in the sexual relationship is crucial, not just because you want your partner to stay invested, but also because it will affect your own interest in the sexual relationship. All too often women find themselves becoming disconnected from sex because it's not really all that enjoyable. And it's because they have never taken the time to truly explore their own needs and to teach their partner what these unique female needs are and what the vagina requires in order to be truly happy. Mind you, every guy already thinks he knows what a woman wants in bed, and sadly this is what years of being exposed to fake orgasms does to a guy. Ask any man about his skills in bed and the common reply is always 'I've never had any complaints and every woman I've been with has had multiple orgasms.' It's both funny and sad, funny because they all say the same thing, and sad because bitches like us now have to set the penis straight and then retrain him to our liking. Fake orgasm jokes aside, when a woman takes the time to learn about what her body really needs, she's very capable of having a multitude of orgasms and as often as she'd like.

Whether your vagina has already found happiness and belting out orgasm operas, or you're still teaching the penis how to handle her, it's important to keep providing your partner with feedback and openly asking for what you want and need. It's important to make the vagina happy and keep her happy, because when she's not happy she has no interest in keeping his stupid penis happy… before you know it you'll be the owner of a grumpy vagina and he'll be her miserable penis side-kick. And a frown- face is not a good look for the vagina…lord knows that she needs all the help she can get just to keep a pretty smile on those vagina lips.

Okay, enough about the vagina for now we can fiddle around with her later. Let's get back on the penis and do a quick recap of all the important penile points. As I mentioned throughout this entire chapter, communication in the sexual relationship is crucial and there's no such thing as too much when it comes to talking about sex. Our goal is to create a supportive and inviting environment that promotes open and honest communication. Remember, a man looks to find a safe haven in his relationship, a place where he feels accepted for his sexual identity and all of his sexual desires. Keep in mind that a man might not always be forthcoming and candid until he has full comfort, so it's up to us to initiate sex talks and get the ball rolling. It's important to keep the energy positive and supportive, and even when our own comforts are challenged we must never receive him in a negative way.

Take the time with your partner to complete the Compatibility exercise I've included, as this will promote many great conversations and give way too many new ideas. And remember, sexploration is a key factor in successful relationships. Couples need to stay committed to keeping the sexual relationship evolving, to keep exploring and finding new ways to keep sex fiery. Communication is just as important in the bedroom, and providing feedback is the best way to achieve sexual gratification. It's your job to guide your partner and let him know what you want, what feels good and what doesn't feel all that great. Honestly, this is your vagina's happiness we're talking about here, someone's gonna have to take a hit somewhere. So if his oral skills suck and it feels like there's a mackerel fish flapping in your crotch, then pull his fish tale out of there and get him to try something else that you do like. Whether it's feedback in the bedroom or talking about sexual fantasies you want to discuss it all. And it doesn't matter if you've been together for sixty days or sixty years, you keep communicating about sex until the end of time and until the day he can't get his dick to stand up anymore and you can't find your vagina because of your dementia. At that point there's no need to talk about sex and you two can focus on fighting over Bingo dabbers and prune juice brands. When a couple stays connected on all the things that gets them hot between the sheets, they keep the chemistry and fire burning in the sexual relationship. And where there is fire, there is always happiness.

Chapter Seven

Sex Shop Maintenance

We've been talking a lot about what the penis wants, but what about the vagina? One of the biggest reasons couples experience a "lull" in their sex life is because the female partner starts to lack fulfillment. It's in our nature to be nurturing to those around us, and we often sacrifice our own needs for the ones we love the most. Women see this as a selfless quality, but it can actually harm the sexual relationship when a woman is not ensuring that her sexual needs are being met. What sets us apart from men, is that a woman can still find the overall relationship fulfilling even when the sexual relationship is somewhat lacking. There's no denying that our vaginas are true warriors and even in a sexual- hiatus that vagina can go dormant and yet we can still remain happy. A woman may be able to stay emotionally connected during such times, but for a man it affects his emotional connection much differently. So even when we feel as though our vagina is faring well during a sex drought, the poor disconnected emotional penis feels much differently.

This is why it's super important for a woman to ensure that the sexual relationship continues to serve her needs and that she always finds it enjoyable. There are specific elements that directly tie into all the areas where women are commonly affected, and these are the factors that every woman should be aware of in order for her to ensure that they are being maintained. There's a huge difference between "maintaining" the sexual relationship and that of "maintenance sex." Maintaining the sexual relationship is about nurturing the elements that help keep things on track and enjoyable, as opposed to simply engaging in unenjoyable sex just to keep the sexual relationship going. Think about it, if our vaginas are signing on for life, shouldn't it be a wonderful life that's truly serving to the vagina's happiness? Of course it should! And this is why every vagina needs to be mindful of the factors that will help provide her with sexual gratification and happiness. When it comes to the sexual relationship, people often focus on the act itself and overlook many of the important variables that tie into keeping the sex gratifying. We could easily run down a list of sex tips and vagina tricks, but our focus here is to address the areas that often cause a couple to become disconnected in the sexual relationship. Our focus is to solidify these elements, and the rest will come when you and the penis embark on a unified sexploration journey. Only when a woman is truly content and connected with her sexuality is she able to fully provide sexual happiness for her partner. Making this happen, requires us to keep the sex maintenance up by focusing on the following key elements:

1. *Navigating the Sex Drive: Keeping Your Vagina Tuned Up*

<u>THE CASE OF THE MISSING SEX DRIVE</u>

Husband: Hello, I'd like to report a horrible theft.

Officer: Okay, when did this theft take place?

Husband: I'm not exactly sure, but I think it happened sometime after my wife started her new job. Well, it kind of went missing around then, but it definitely went totally missing after our son was born. Actually hold on, I may have seen it once or twice since then, but it most definitely has been MIA in the past seven months.

Officer: And what exactly was taken?

Husband: (short pause followed by a trembling sound in his voice as he breaks down in hysterics) HER SEX DRIVE!!!!...er, um...IT'S GONE! They just came and took it. It's horrible. Who would do such a thing?

Officer: I see... That's horrible, and I'm sorry to hear that. You're not the first to call about this, and there has been a string of such occurrences for some time now. Listen, buddy, I feel your pain. The same thing happened to me about two years ago (Cops voice now too starts to tremble, as he tries to keep his professional composure). The worst part is that in my case, it was never recovered (pulling away from the receiver, so he can mask his sobbing).

Husband: That's awful, I'm sorry to hear that. Well, I'm actually willing to do anything and everything in order to find it. I'll put up a reward, maybe if I contact the local news station? There's gotta be something we can do? I even tried calling our Homeowners Insurance to file a claim, and I'm just waiting to hear back from them.

Officer: Don't bother, I already tried that, and they told me it's not covered. The only thing you can do, buddy, is pray. And if you're lucky it will come back periodically and visit you maybe once a month, or on your birthday if you're lucky. In the meantime, we can file a report, but I'm not sure when we will get to it, as we have another 550 similar unsolved cases before yours.

Okay, so maybe this is a little far-fetched and filing a Missing Vagina's report, or sending out a blow job search party are not an option. I know that it's sort of comical when we can make light of the common problems surrounding our female hormones and the challenges that women often face with vagina ownership. Albeit funny, it does pose a struggle for many women in relationships and it's something that we don't always recognize as having any real effects on the overall relationship. There's no denying that the hormonal fluctuations we experience from our female monthly cycle alone affects our libido and female sex drive and often governs our mood and desire (or lack thereof) to have sex. Throw in all the other added stressors from our everyday lives and life events, and it truly becomes a struggle to navigate that vagina and maintain a consistent sex drive. The reality is that many of the responsibilities we deal with in our daily lives, comes with little choice as to whether or not we're "in the mood." Things like doing laundry, cooking dinner, showing up at the office, and driving the kids to and from all of their kiddy events. Somehow our super hero vaginas are not only expected to juggle all of this, but at the end of a long-ass day we're now supposed to bring the sexy, by driving this vagina bitch straight on into the bedroom. Great, just what we need: one more pit stop to add onto our already hectic carpool schedule.

The funny thing is that it's our hormones are doing the driving, and the vagina is just along for the ride. Not all vaginas are built the same, some women experience no issues with their sex drive, and some even have an overdrive vagina engine, while others struggle with no drive at all. There's no denying that even with a healthy libido and sex drive, everyday responsibilities and stress is enough to have any vagina tank running on fumes by the end of it all. I always say that if I had nothing else to worry about and if the only item on my daily "To Do" list was "Penis," it would get done with little to no effort each and every day and with great drive and enjoyment.

We're really not focusing here on temporary vagina ailments, and the short-lived fluctuations that the vagina can easily recover from. The great thing about a loving committed relationship is that even during the course of monthly cycles or even major life events such as pregnancy and motherhood, a woman finds great support through these "periods" and periods. It only becomes problematic if a woman experiences a lack of sex drive for a prolonged period of time or even indefinitely. It can affect the quality of the sexual relationship, and how can it not when one partner has little to no desire for sex? Our female sex drive not only fuels our desire to have sex, it also creates the chemistry that connects us to a mate and an overall desire for their affections. This is why it's important for a woman to never ignore such a circumstance and if you find your libido lacking or sex drive non-existent, you need to do something about it. It goes beyond just sex, and when there's a lack of desire for intimacy it can affect the emotional connection in the overall relationship.

It can also affect a woman's self-esteem and confidence, as well as her partner's because of the lack of affections being shared that makes them each feel desirable in the relationship. Ignoring a compromised sex drive creates a new disconnected norm, where a woman lacks the desire to have sex and to connect with her partner on an intimate level. It's only human nature for a man to begin to take this personally, as he starts to feel unwanted and even rejected both sexually and emotionally. The difference between men and women is that a woman can still maintain a great sense of fulfillment in the relationship even with the absence of her libido. However, for a man it can affect his fulfillment and the sense of connection he has towards his spouse.

As women, we tend to be selfless and our need to nurture those around us, often has many women ignoring the signs of a diminished sex drive. It's your job to ensure that this never takes place, because in the long run it can affect your happiness and the overall relationship. Your vagina's health should always be a top priority, and it's important to ensure that she's always tuned up both mentally and physically. We can't always control hormonal factors, but we can control many factors that help keep our libido and sex drive in check. Having a healthy lifestyle is the easiest way to maintain a healthy vagina and drive, and maintaining a good diet and exercise regimen is important. Eating foods that fuel good energy are beneficial to the body and the brain. Physical activity alone puts us in a better state of mind and it helps the brain release chemicals that make us happier. Not only does it make us feel better about ourselves, we feel sexy, look sexy, but it also makes us want to engage in more sexy time. Taking care of yourself both inside and out has a way of changing your outlook and it supports the brain to produce a steady stream of chemistry and feeds your sex drive.

When it comes to maintaining greatness in the relationship, you should stop short of nothing. This means that if you are experiencing challenges with your libido and drive, and you've tried everything to kick start that bitch with no success...then there may be underlying reasons why your libido is dormant. This doesn't mean that your vagina is broken, but it does mean that you should walk that bitch right on over to the doctor's office and find out what the issue may be. It's no different than taking your car in for an oil change and tune up, and sometimes there may be a medical explanation to why you're experiencing a lack of sex drive. Most often it's a quick fix and you can have that vagina engine back to revving on high in no time. Even though men appear to never suffer from lacking any sort of drive when it comes to sex, they are not immune to such a circumstance. A man can also suffer from a lack of sex drive that's attributed to medical reasons, and this too should not be ignored. I know that men are often reluctant to acknowledge that they have an issue because of their whole male ego thing. However, if it's affecting your sex life, then it shouldn't be ignored. Think about it: if a guy had little desire to engage in sex, or had issues in keeping an erection, most women would take this personally. We shouldn't take it personally, but it's hard not to when that penis is not doing cartwheels in the presence of that magical vagina. Having a healthy libido helps keep that chemistry flowing in the relationship. This is something that should always be openly discussed, and if you ever feel as though your drive is not where it should be then you should communicate this to your partner. It may be situational, and it could be due to your strenuous schedule. This could be easily remedied just by working together to establish new shared roles, or changing schedules around. Maybe reserving certain days where there's less going on, having date nights, or anything that helps put your mind and body in the right place.

A healthy sex drive and libido prompts us to be more affectionate during intimacy and provides us with the desire to express our emotions more liberally. There are certain happy chemicals produced by the body and brain during sex. And the great thing about having sex is that the more sex you have, the more sex you want. When we engage in sexual activity, it releases endorphins in the brain, and this creates that happy feel good sensation that we experience. It actually has lasting effects long after the sexual experience is over. It leaves us in a good mood, we feel re-energized and refreshed. It also is a good stress reliever, and rids the body of negative toxins. By repeating this elated state of euphoria, it creates an ongoing cycle and sense of elation and mental happiness. Keep in mind that the vagina is very intricate in how she operates. When there is a prolonged period of no sexual activity, those chemicals are not being released and it causes the vagina to go dormant. Sometimes the simplest remedy to kick starting that drive and breaking a dry spell, is easily brought on by simply doing the good deed. It's like a jump start to the libido, and it gets the mental stimulation flowing again. This breeds our mental chemistry, and it creates a sexual presence in our minds. The more sex we have, the more sex we want. And before you know it, your super charged turbo ride is pulling into that bedroom all week long. There's something about a great orgasm that has a vagina coming back for more. So the best way to keep that libido in tune is to keep it well exercised. And if you feel as though you can't get her jump started, then you owe it to your vagina's happiness to find out why and get that bitch back in check.

2. Committing to Sex 100%

You've probably heard the saying, "You're either all in or all out." This totally applies to sex, and there's no vagina points awarded just for showing up for the main event if she's not going to be fully tuned in to the experience. The biggest culprit for tardy attendance is most often the brain and not so much the vagina. When it comes to engaging in a sexual experience, if you're not present "mind, body and soul,"' then you're not getting the most out of it. And if this is a common occurrence where the vagina doesn't get the most out of an experience, it decreases her desire for future experiences. This goes back to the idea of "maintenance sex," where sex is being maintained more as a relationship chore than anything else. Now, I know that many of us can agree on the fact that when it comes to real life with real responsibilities and all the added stressors, it's often a challenge to fully clear our minds from all the noise and simply focus on the experience. Sometimes, we carry this guilt of wanting to please our spouse, and we figure that something is better than nothing. Sex should never be about one partner seeing it as "Operation: Let's Get It On" while the other sees it as "Operation: Let's Get It Over With." Women sometimes feel the need to maintain certain offerings, even when it's not serving to our immediate needs in the moment. We feel as though the least we can do is spread some cheer and happiness for the penis and absolve ourselves of the guilt. It's not so much that we are having sex against our will, because obviously we want to have sex with our spouse, it's just that the required mind set and energy is not in place.

There have been studies conducted where women admitted to having sexual encounters where they couldn't wait for it to end. The feeling that their partner was taking too long to reach climax, and they were ready to call it quits. It would be ideal if orgasms were synced, and a couple would find gratification at the same time and wrap up the show. Sex takes place in many ways, be it a multitude of orgasms, foreplay, extended play, you name it and you can play it up between the sheets. The reason why I say that it's important to stay true and fully commit to the experience is because it needs to be enjoyable to both partners. One of the most common reasons that women admit to faking orgasms, is because they want to speed up the process and get it over with.

That being said, it's important for the vagina to know that when she does commit to sex, she owes it to herself and her mate to be truly present and fully invested in the experience. Women often don't realize how a lack of commitment and investment can actually harm not only our own enjoyment in sex, but also the enjoyment that a partner gets out of the experience. We often think that if we "throw him a bone" or a vagina, that we are doing a good deed. What we don't realize is how this lack of full investment is often evident, and how it affects our interactions in the sexual relationship. Not every sexual encounter will always be endless hours of penis and vagina Olympics, and sometimes even a quickie can be just as erotic and gratifying. Whether it's a ten- minute affair or one that lasts for hours, it should always be an enjoyable experience for both partners.

If a woman is reluctant to have sex and feels like she can't wait for it to be over, then she does not have a fully-satisfying sex life. Sex should never be viewed as a chore or tedious and unenjoyable. Yes, I totally know what it's like to be a woman, and all the crap that we deal with. There have been times where I myself wasn't feeling the whole sex thing in the moment, yet somehow just by laying around in bed and being all touchy feely, I suddenly get hit with an urge to do a little sexy tango between the sheets. Sometimes, the mere energy in the room is what ignites the chemistry, and sets off the vagina fireworks. That being said, a woman who feels as though she is doing her spouse a favor by giving him sex, as she sits in mental agony waiting for it to be over, is really doing herself or the relationship no favors.

Women don't always have an understanding of how delicate the male ego is, and how a man's libido works. Some of the women I have spoken to, joke about the fact that they often get to the point where they verbally express their feelings in the moment, and tell their spouse "Alright, but hurry up, you've got 10 minutes," A man's erection is controlled by his brain, and when a man feels pressured in the moment to perform, it causes him mental anxiety. The pressure of being on the clock distracts the surge that is sent from his brain to his penis, and the anxiety is transferred down to the penis. Unfortunately, the penis doesn't work well under pressure. At which point he will lose his erection, or he will experience an inability to have an orgasm just based on the mental sense that he is being pressured to do so. If a man feels as though his partner is not fully invested or that she views the experience as a chore, he too will start to view the experience as unenjoyable.

There are many reasons why women find themselves not fully committed to the experience, and regardless of the hows and whys, it's important to always be honest and communicate how you're feeling. If you find yourself pooped at the end of a long day, and you simply don't have it in you, then be honest and ask for a raincheck. My husband always tells me that he'd rather have a handful of quality sexual experiences, rather than a slew of sexual encounters that are somewhat lackluster and unfulfilling. We are very honest with one another and if either one of us opts for a raincheck, it's always a great make up session the next time around. Another common reason that women are often not fully invested is because they find that their experiences are not serving to their sexual needs and that they're not getting much out of it. If you feel as though your vagina needs are being neglected, then it's important to communicate this and work together to resolve the issue. It may require a longer foreplay experience that focuses on getting that vagina warmed up and fully aroused. Keep in mind that his balls are not made of crystal and he's not a mind reader.

When you do commit to a sexual encounter, it's important to shut out all other mental distractions and fully immerse yourself in the experience. This is where foreplay comes in handy, and it's a great way to set the mood and help clear the mind before the big event. In the midst of a sexual experience you should never find yourself running down a mental grocery list while he's feverishly plugging away at that vagina....Or while he's down south trying to deliver a great oral experience, you're staring at the ceiling and picking out paint colors that would complement the new bed spread. Sex should always be an enjoyable experience for both partners, and it requires a full investment on both sides. Remember, if a woman starts to see sex as a chore, she's less inclined to want to have more of it. So when you commit to the physical experience, you need to fully commit mentally as this ensures that your vagina always has fun during every experience, and that she will always look forward to the next experience.

3. Unleashing Your Sexual Persona and Letting it All Hang Out

One of the greatest gifts that a committed relationship bestows on us is comfort and security. This provides us with the ability to expose ourselves entirely and to be embraced by the comforting arms of the relationship. The outer world places so many unrealistic demands and expectations on women, that we often find ourselves juggling so many different social masks in an effort to conform and please all of these worlds. Think about how good it feels to come home after a long day, and to shed those tight ponytails, strangulating pants and constricting Spanx and girdles, and to simply slip into comfy clothes. This is the exact same sense and feeling that relationship security provides for the vagina and a woman's sexuality. The ability to finally let go and let it all hang out, without any inhibitions whatsoever.

In the privacy of the intimate sexual relationship, no woman should ever have reservations with her sexuality or her sexual offerings. Your vagina has waited a lifetime for this opportunity and it's her time to shine and let it all hang out. Men aren't the only ones who get to share their fantasies. You do, too. This is your chance to tap into your own sex suitcase and start unpacking it all. The only way to discover true sexual gratification and fulfillment is when you allow yourself the freedom to fully explore your sexuality. We all have a unique identity that represents our sexual persona, and it's defined by what a woman identifies with sexually, and all the qualities that represent her sexuality. And here's the amazing thing about it all: we are not restricted to just one sexual persona. A woman can have various sexual personas, each representing qualities that she identifies with sexually and each uniquely serving to specific sexual desires and fantasies. When you allow yourself to unleash your sexuality and explore these sexual personas to the fullest, you are able to discover true sexual gratification. This is what makes a woman want to stay engaged in the sexual relationship and it's because of the happiness that it provides for the vagina and her needs.

I know that for some women, it's not always easy to find the courage to simply let it all hang out and unleash that sex vixen persona, because it's not something that they identify with in their everyday lives. Understand that your sexual persona doesn't have to be representative of who or what you are to the outside world. A woman who identifies with the role of being a great wife, a wonderful mother, and even a respectable business woman, can maintain these roles separate to what she represents behind closed doors. These outer roles may be ones that we hold proudly, but once you cross that threshold behind closed doors, they are not invited to the sex party and they have no place in the bedroom. Trust me when I say that men totally gravitate to this quality, and find it quite desirable when a woman is able to confidently transform into her sexual persona and unleash her sexuality with no inhibitions.

If you've ever had any reservations or perhaps felt timid to fully let go and explore these sexual personas, rest assured that a man sees things much differently in a sexual setting. Sexual arousal causes a man to become dummied down by his dick. Yup, that's right ladies, when the male sex brain is experiencing a surge of stimuli he sees everything through his penis spectacles. Everything before his penis eyes is covered in lust dust and sex fairy glitter. What you and I see as a naked body, or one dressed in lingerie, he sees is a sex goddess and porn star status. This in itself is the biggest ego and confidence booster for a woman, and it pays itself forward because this confidence allows you to unleash and explore even more. His responsiveness alone is what feeds a woman's confidence, and it spills over into the entire relationship as he walks around thinking back to all the antics that transpire behind closed doors. Women often have a need for solid relationship security before they feel totally comfortable to fully unleash their sexuality and explore sexually with no inhibitions. If you ever feel as though you need help in fulfilling certain needs that will give you that added comfort, then come out and communicate this to your spouse. If you'd like more affections and romance or need to feel a little more emotionally connected, then ask for what you want. The idea is "help me so I can in turn help you." And it's about a couple helping one another achieve ultimate fulfillment in the areas that mean the most to each of them, so in turn each spouse can have full comfort and motivation to fulfill the areas that mean the most to their mate.

Tapping into your sexual persona(s), starts simply by initiating conversations with your spouse and talking about both of your sexual fantasies and curiosities. It can be built in layers, as one small exploration leads to another, which eventually creates an entire sexual identity and persona. There's no need to simply bust into the room like a sex super hero proclaiming "I am sex goddess, hear me roar! Pass me a penis!" I can tell you from my own personal experiences, the journey of discovering my sexual persona(s) is something that has transpired over *years.* I'd have to say that it wasn't until I met my husband, that I truly had the comfort to fully unleash and explore my sexuality. This is something that my husband and I have nurtured through good communication over the years, and unified sexploration in our relationship. Through these discussions, I learned that my husband was very attracted to the image of a strong dominant female, one that had the confidence to take charge in the bedroom and control the sexual play. This was something that I too found appealing, and it's because it was an alter ego to my everyday persona that the rest of the world sees in me.

Having the ability to take charge during sexual play, ask for what I wanted and have him comply with my requests was very empowering for me. It was also a huge surge of stimuli for my husband as well, who normally has control in his everyday life and usually calls the shots. This allowed me to unleash a sexual persona who was confident, fierce and uninhibited. I'd have to say, that out of all of the sexual discoveries I have made throughout the years, this is one sex vixen persona that has truly allowed me to take control of my sexuality and discover true sexual gratification.

Having a sexual persona and alter ego allows you to explore any and every sexual curiosity and desire you may ever have. It allows you to create alter egos and sexual fantasy characters, and it's a great way to role play in the bedroom as well. It also plays into the visual and mental stimuli that the male sex brain is so responsive to, and the idea that you can transform into a persona that plays into his sexual fantasies. Think about it, any vagina can slap on a wig or nurses outfit and jump into bed. The excitement and allure is in her presence and in the persona that she assumes. The wonderful thing about it is that it can be as simple or as elaborate as you choose, anything from uninhibited naked bodies to elaborate costumes and make belief sexual play. Take for example, the idea of an erotic striptease, and how easily you can transform into this persona if it's something that you and your partner both find erotic. Dressing up in sexy lingerie and heels, you can put your own spin on it and do it up any way you choose.

I know for some women, it may seem intimidating, and a tough pair of stilettos to fill especially if you feel as though you don't really have all the dance moves that the pros have. The thought of having to "perform' is enough to give a vagina stage fright. It doesn't have to be a professional dance show, or involve super dance skills like the pros. Remember, his sex goggles have him seeing you as his own private dancer, and this real life experience allows his fantasies to materialize. There is no need to be running out and taking pole dancing classes, just to master working the brass pole you just ordered for your bedroom. Nor is there a need to spend endless hours secretly studying porn and taking notes, and practicing on bananas and stair bannisters. Don't put that type of pressure on your vagina, and you don't need fancy tricks just to put on a sexy dance. Remember, it's all fun and games until somebody pulls a vagina. And what good will your tricks be then when your vagina is in a sling and on six= weeks bed rest. By simply unleashing this sexually inviting persona, it not only creates sexual tension but it is such an empowering feeling for a woman. The thought of being the object of his desires, as he is fixated on your every move.

Sometimes an idea is born simply through a characteristic that both partners identify with. This is a great opportunity for you to tap into the sexual characteristics that you truly identify with. Whether you have a desire to explore your sexually dominant side, or a kinky and submissive sex vixen. Exploring your sexual persona also feeds into a world of sexual role play. Sexual dominance comes in handy if you decide to play nurse, and having a sexually submissive side comes in handy if you decide to be a naughty school girl one night. The great thing is that you can begin to create fantasy experiences, and escape into a magical world filled with sexual make belief characters. This in itself has allowed me to fully explore what I truly identify with sexually. I have discovered a sexual persona that enjoys taking the lead and being dominant, and also one that enjoys being submissive and dominated in the bedroom.

Exploring your inner sex vixen truly creates an element of excitement in the sexual relationship with all the endless possibilities. It also gives you the opportunity to engage in sexual encounters that solely focus on your sexual needs, and have the experience cater exclusively to all the things that are truly gratifying to your vagina's pleasures. When a woman allows herself to let go and fully unleash her sexual persona, she not only discovers sexual greatness for herself, but she also creates sexual greatness for her spouse. The sexual empowerment and confidence becomes a woman's greatest asset in the sexual relationship. It allows her to create a sexual persona that is serving to her needs, one that he becomes fixated on. I can tell you from first-hand experience that this in itself has a way of feeding the entire relationship. My husband is quite appreciative of the fact that I have truly found the comfort to let myself go and to take control of my sexuality. This prompts him to often show his affections and appreciation in all aspects of the relationship. It really has a way of making a woman feel like the sexiest woman alive. And the more a woman exudes this aura, the more a man feels as though he is the luckiest man alive, and that his partner is the epitome of sexiness. It's the best of both worlds! The vagina discovers the best sex life imaginable and also becomes the object of her partner's desires and affections. And remember, the sex vixen persona that you represent in the bedroom, is one that no one ever has to see. It's not as though you have to exit the house dressed like a super sex hooker hero while you grocery shop.... Or walk into your parents' house during the holidays and say, "Sorry we're late, I had Ted tied to the bed and we were playing CIA agents...I thought it would be a quickie and well one penis interrogation led to another... six orgasms later, and here we are.... Merry Christmas, Mom and Dad!" This unleashed sex vixen is one that will allow you to discover sexual greatness, and ensure that you will stay invested in the sexual relationship because it's truly enjoyable and gratifying to your vagina needs.

4. Make the Time

I'm sure we can all agree that one of the greatest challenges of all time is actually finding the time to juggle everything in our lives. Wouldn't life rock if we had our own personal vagina assistant? Kind of like a helping hand that could assist in the daily juggle, just so we could get it all done and still have some juice left in us to throw down those vagina tricks at night. The funny thing is that any woman reading this is probably thinking of the benefits to her daily schedule...while a guy would likely read this and get an instant erection at the thought of a threesome with this "helping hand' assistant. Gotta love the penis and his overzealous imagination.

Time management is something I myself always struggle with. What often starts out as a day with good intentions and high hopes ends up becoming derailed with many unexpected tasks and added responsibilities. We've already touched on the very real responsibilities and stressors that life throws our way and not just on a day to day basis, but also the overall very real responsibilities that come with being grown up. When a relationship is new and fueled with all that chemistry, finding the time for the penis and vagina to frolic together is of little to no effort at all. You gotta love the logic behind that, and no matter how hectic life is, anytime is the right time to schedule in a penis and vagina meeting. The reality is that every relationship finds its pace…even when multiple daily sex sessions evolve into a multiple weekly schedule…there's no love lost and good times are still had by a unified and happy penis/vagina duo.

Like I said before, it's not always about quantity as much as it is about quality, and the perfect quotient is when there's a balance of both variables. The reality for most couples is that the growing dynamic in the relationship eventually expands to many new responsibilities such as becoming parents and taking on many new roles in their lives. We touched on this earlier, about the importance of a couple making the time for one another…especially in the sexual relationship. Sometimes "making the time" for sex can be challenging, and it can't come down to penciling in 'have sex with husband at 9pm" on the calendar, as this too can kind of kill the vibe. It's not so much about having to schedule sex sessions in order to ensure that sex is being had, as much as it is making time for intimacy a priority. One of the reasons people often struggle with "making time" for sex is because they see it as having lesser priority to many of the other things they manage in their lives. People often view sex as an "extracurricular" activity and as something fun that is reserved for when we have free time. Obviously, when there are more important things on the agenda such as picking up the kids from school, you're not going to scratch that in lieu of sex…and make the kids walk home four miles just so you can squeeze in a few midday orgasms. It's totally understandable that going to work and picking up the kids takes precedence over your vagina and her needs.

With that being said, the sexual relationship shouldn't be viewed as a just a fun pastime that falls at the bottom of our list and only after everything else has been managed. Sometimes we become so caught up with everything in life that we don't realize how delicate the relationship really is. People assume this sense of invincibility, and see the relationship as iron clad and unbreakable. The notion that 'ah well, there's always tomorrow," where today is always pushed back and becomes just another hopeful tomorrow is not the right approach. Remember, that the sexual relationship is not only about the physical aspects of sex, it's a way for a couple to intimately connect on an emotional level as well. This is why the sexual relationship should be just as much of a priority as any other aspect of the relationship. I once coached a couple that had separated and were no longer living together. They attributed the cause as them having grown apart because they stopped spending time together in their busy lives. The kicker in this story is that they were now living apart yet still having sex and even more sex than ever before. Now they find the time? They couldn't find the time before, but now that they're no longer together somehow they managed to make time for one another? This is a prime example of how important this element is, and quite often when relationships fail couples still have love for one another, but they've allowed life to take precedence over the love.

I know that it's often easier said than done, and expressing our affections throughout the day with a simple phone call to say "I love you" requires a lot less time and effort than marching that vagina on up to the bedroom just to physically sign all these gestures with naked body parts. Trust me, I totally get it! There are days when it's simply not possible to squeeze in a game of naked twister in the bedroom. And this is understandable, as these days will always exist. The old adage of "where there is a will, there's a way" comes into play, and willfully making sex a priority ensures that time can and will be made for one another in the sexual relationship. It's important to understand that even when we balance roles as a parent and a spouse, each can hold equal importance in their own unique way. Think of it as a monarchy, where the King and Queen sit at the top of the pyramid, and in order for everything to remain intact the King and Queen must remain united. Many women often struggle to balance both roles as spouse and parent, and because it's natural to put our children's wellbeing at the top of our priority list, we often sacrifice anything and everything else before we ever compromise our motherhood role. Trust me, I get this and my son is job one in my life. However, there is no need to choose. Both roles can be equally nurtured without either being compromised or neglected.

Again, this goes back to many people often seeing the needs of children as being much more delicate than that of a spouse and a grown man who can fend for himself. This is a common struggle for many couples, and it's because of the mindset I mentioned earlier. I've worked with couples that struggled to find a balance in their relationship, and where many partners didn't see the effects it had on their spouse or the relationship. In one family unit that included a husband and wife who also were mom and dad to three kids, a dog, a cat, and three goldfish, the parents would work a long day, only to come home and juggle dinner, homework, sporting activities…along with nightly routines of bathing, brushing teeth and bedtime stories. Understandably, this couple had a lot going on and their biggest struggle was knowing how and when to shut it off. They managed their routine quite well, but what they lacked was managing the transition from "Mom and Dad" to that of "husband and wife." There was no consistency when it came to bedtimes for the kids, and many nights involved these parents pooped out on the couch while the kids still bounced around at 10 or 11pm. Family time is a great way for a family to connect, and there's always great benefits to family fun nights. However, having structure in the family unit is not only beneficial to the children, it's also beneficial to a couple who can manage their alone time with more ease.

A couple needs to have alone time, uninterrupted time to share intimately with one another, and to simply connect with each other. It doesn't always have to be about naked Olympics and kinky sex and something as simple as lying together, kissing and being affectionate with one another is just as beneficial. I mean, sure this may lead to sex... I'll be the first to admit that what sometimes starts out as me offering to massage my husband's feet, often ends up turning into a penis massage... The penile point I'm making is that the importance is in making the time, no matter how that time is spent. People often fail to realize the importance of making the sexual relationship a priority, and it's often the cause of why many couples become disconnected with one another. A relationship where two people no longer identify with one another on an intimate level and as a couple, and their only connection becomes that as co-parents, and then they pretty much are no more than roommates. This is not healthy for any relationship, and quite often it's very difficult to recover from such a circumstance. I always say, it's a lot easier to keep a flame going and burning by putting logs into the fire, then trying to reignite it after the flame has dwindled and gone out.

The reality is that it's never our intention to neglect any aspect of our relationship. And I'm placing emphasis on this because of the fact that many of us often view sex as that "fun" activity we do when we have finished tending to "real life." Sex is real life! And there are real life implications when a couple doesn't make the time (and often) to nurture the sexual relationship and connect with one another on an intimate level. The best way for a couple to avoid becoming disconnected, is by making the time to stay connected! Lock the door, draw the curtains, and shut off the ringer....because no one's home! It's uninterrupted sexy sexy time. Even if it means just laying naked and cuddling in bed while you listen to music. The penis LOVES playing naked dick jockey with his coveted vagina. The great thing is that you can steal intimate time in many different ways! Whether it's saving on water and taking a shower together, or making "movie night" a naked movie night in bed and ditching the popcorn for some penis instead. The funny thing is that having added stressors in our lives is often a cause of making time for sex. Well guess what? Sex is a great way to relieve stress! More sex means less stress! And who are we to deprive those stressed out vaginas right?

Like I said, there's no need for it to always be an elaborate affair, and you do what you can. Even if it means synching schedules and squeezing in a "nooner" where you can. A 'nooner', also known as a lunch time activity of swapping soup and a sandwich for cock and cookies instead. Half the calories and double the benefits! Okay, maybe not half the calories, and skipping meals isn't healthy...but it's a lot easier to take a sandwich on the go and in the car than it is to manage a penis while you drive...and if you get pulled over it's also a lot easier to explain a sandwich, rather than getting caught with a penis in hand and trying to talk your way out of that one. It's about being creative and making time when and where we can. For example, a quickie midday matinee sex romp doesn't always require a lot of time and it's a great way to create excitement in the relationship. It's that sense of being naughty, and doing something that we really shouldn't be doing...especially when there are so many other things we should be doing in the midst of a busy day.

This is something that one of my girlfriends takes full advantage of in her relationship. She and her husband have crazy schedules, but they always try to squeeze in a lunchtime romp whenever they can find the time. Her husband has come to LOVE these coveted lunch sessions, and he often jokes about his wife being his favorite meal of the day. When the clock strikes twelve, his cock-mobile is pulling into the driveway and headed straight into her garage. The great part is that the kids are in school, and they have free reign over the whole house. This sure has a way of breaking up a long day, and putting a smile on his penis face. This may not be a realistic possibility for us all, especially if we don't work close to home and location is a factor. The last thing you want to do is try to make this happen in the parking lot at your husband's office. It's all fun and games until security comes tapping on the steamed up window of your minivan (that's sporting a "Proud Soccer Mom" bumper sticker) and you get cited for public indecency. Anyway, the goal is to simply make the time for sexy time. There's no need to be a Wonder Woman…and as long as he's not "wondering where his woman went" and time is being made for intimacy and connecting one on one…then this is all that matters. And remember, a couple that makes the time and plays together… stays together!

5. Sexual Pursuit: Initiating Sex

When we think about our sexual relationship, many of us don't place much thought on the initiation process leading up to the actual sex deed. It usually plays out with either partner feeling frisky or in the mood, and making it known by propositioning their partner for some sexy time. Initiating sex comes in many forms, both verbal and non-verbal. Sometimes all it takes is a suggestive gaze and devious grin, or a little sensual petting to imply a desire for intimacy, or simply just coming out and saying, "Hey, wanna have sex?" When it comes to initiating sex, men have no issues in articulating their desires and making them well known. Most often, we are pretty in tune with a partner's sex signs, and you know how and when he's eluding to sexy time. Like when he's taken out the trash all on his own, replaced all the bulbs in the house and offering up a foot massage, it's often a tell-tale sign that this penis has ulterior motives.

The general consensus is that men are in the mood a lot more often than women, and generally speaking this is often the case due to the fact that men have a higher level of sex hormones and a more prominent sex drive. For a man it doesn't take all that much to get him in the mood, and when it strikes he's bringing sex up the second his penis pops up. The penis often doesn't require much persuasion and before a woman even has a chance to fully send out a sex smoke signal, he's already burning carpet upstairs, naked and erect, anxiously awaiting your arrival with bated penis breath. In an ideal world, the sex stars would align and a couple would share synced sex drives always be in the mood at the same time. However, in the real world such is not the case and there are times when one partner may be feeling frisky while the other is simply not feeling it. It's understandable, and it's always better to be honest and take a raincheck for another day when moods align and the experience will be equally enjoyable for both partners.

It's pretty evident in any species, that males are the ones to pursue females in their sexual conquests sex, and as females we become accustomed to this sexual pursuit. When you really think about it, does it really matter who's doing the pursuing and who's being pursued? Truth be told, it really makes no difference as long as both partners are equally finding fulfillment in the sexual relationship and having their needs met. However, there are certain aspects to the concept of sexual pursuit that many women often don't recognize. This goes back to our discussion on sex and how it ties into a man's emotional needs. Believe it or not, a man receives the same form of fulfillment from being pursued sexually as a woman does. You see, being propositioned for sex in the relationship is not just about having sex and a way to fulfill our sexual needs.

When we are pursued in a sexual manner, it sends a message of "Hey, I am attracted to you. I'm aroused by the thought of you and by your presence. I have a desire to be with you, and being with you sexually, satisfies this desire and it provides me with physical, emotional and mental gratification." That's a pretty loaded hidden message that's encompassed in a simple "Hey, wanna have sex?" It's true, and this is exactly what is being expressed when one partner pursues another for sex. Women often take for granted how much we actually rely on this pursuit from a male partner, as a way of making us feel desirable and wanted in the relationship. It's not so much that we take it for granted, as we have simply become accustomed to it. We don't give it much thought and it's simply what we've come to know in the male/female dynamic of sexual relations.

With that being said, men may be natural hunters when it comes to sex, but it's not to say that they too don't gain fulfillment in the same way. It's important to recognize this opportunity and provide a male spouse with the same type of fulfillment. The male ego has a need to feel both desired and desirable. To feel wanted, and needed by their mate…and most importantly a man needs to feel as though he brings something unique to the sexual relationship, something only his male presence and masculinity can provide for. I know that this may sound like he's swapping his penis for a vagina, and as touchy feely as it may seem, even the most masculine penis gains fulfillment from being pursued sexually.

Even though women are identified as having lesser sex hormones, it's not to say that we less frequently in the mood for sex or even less horny then our male counterpart. Trust me, you may or may not be one of them, but I have had enough exposure in my line of work to attest to the fact that women can often be the horniest sex crazed little creatures of them all! I'm sure we've all heard the reference of a female being "in heat." And it doesn't just apply to dogs, because when that vagina bitch is fully ripe and on cock patrol…look out! There's a new Sex Sheriff in town! The only reason why women don't do a lot of the initiating in the sexual relationship is because we often don't even have a chance to. When the mood does hit us, and before we even have a chance to open the sex door, there's the penis! Standing there all bright-eyed and bushy-tailed, saying 'Hey, wanna come out and play?' Well what do you know? The penis can read a woman's mind! Man, when you really think about it, the penis can be a bit of a stalker…a little vagina breathing room would be nice wouldn't ya say?

Okay, enough poking fun at the penis and the stigmas surrounding men and their sex drive… back to sex business… What I'm saying is that there needs to be a balance in the relationship when it comes to initiating sex. This way both partners can enjoy the fulfillment of feeling desirable and wanted in the relationship. It's as simple as a woman speaking up when she is feeling "in the mood" and sending out smoke signals to get his ass in the bedroom STAT! Well, not just his ass per say…bring it all! And don't forget the penis! As women we may have become accustomed to being propositioned for sex, but it's important to not neglect the opportunity to stroke his male ego and his penis at the same time! It also has a way of taking the pressure off a man as well, because quite often he doesn't always know how you're feeling. There may be times where he's in the mood, but reads your mood as not being in the mood so he hesitates to say anything. And maybe he misread you, and it becomes a lost opportunity to have sexy sexy time and connect with one another.

As I mentioned earlier, two people won't always be in the mood at the same time and sometimes we opt for a raincheck and politely decline the offer. When there is a balance in sex initiations, it also balances the roles of who is asking and who's declining. If he's the one always sending out the sex invites, this means that he's the one to always be turned down. When a man starts to feel as though he's the one who's always asking, being turned down and having to wait for her to come around, it starts to affect his emotional male ego. Eventually a man can perceive this as sexual rejection, and this is something that the male penis ego doesn't like. Are we sure here that he didn't swap that thing in for a vagina? If this becomes the norm, he may start to feel as though his advances are bothersome to his mate and he's become a nuisance. At which point, a man will back off and take a passive role, waiting for her to come around when she's ready. And this is where women often don't realize that when we start to feel as though our partner is no longer making us feel desirable or fussing over us, it's because he too is feeling the same way and in need of all the same attention and affections.

The moral of the story is, don't ignore the penis! Actually, it's about making the effort to hit him up, and knock on his sex door. Remember, you're the only friend he has and that comes calling on him to play. Trust me, in this case the penis doesn't mind when the vagina is being a stalker. This is where good communication comes in, and a couple can quickly identify if each partner is content with the dynamic of sexual pursuit. Ask your partner if they are content with the sexual pursuit, and use that feedback to ensure that there's a balance and provide your partner with what he needs. Keep in mind that sexual pursuit also involves hosting to the experience and playing host to your sexual encounters. Taking the initiative to not only proposition the penis for sex and also hosting the entire event and taking charge of a sexual encounter.

I make it a point to ensure that there is a good balance in our relationship, and I surprise my husband often by playing host on special sex nights. My husband always says that he appreciates the fact that I take initiative and it takes the pressure off of him. He likes to simply show up and enjoy the experience. Men find it a desirable quality when a woman takes initiative and asks for what she wants, and this translates into many big points for the vagina in the relationship. As I've mentioned before, it doesn't take much to get the penis excited. Sending him a text before he gets home that reads 'Dinner in bed tonight, we're having your favorite', is enough to have him fly through traffic with his penis at the wheel. When both partners equally feel sexually desired in the relationship it feeds the sexual chemistry they share and it intensifies how they interact with one another. Who knew that so much could come from simply asking a penis if he wants to have sex? And if he doesn't always accept all of your sexual advances and decides to take a raincheck from time to time, it's no big deal. Who needs him anyways, this vagina bitch has options, she can throw her own party even if her dance partner happens to be made of rubber…hey at least he vibrates and can dance until the batteries run out. Okay, seriously speaking, make sure you take advantage of initiating the sex-festivities and stroking his ego. The importance is in the balance of efforts and keeping the love-chase going by chasing each other's tails…because it's no fun chasing your own tail, just ask your dog.

6. The Love Den on Lockdown

This is another variable that feeds into the quality of the sexual relationship, and one that many people often overlook. I often make reference to the "bedroom" when talking about sex… and obviously it's not the only place where sex can be had. There's something about having sex in unconventional places that makes it exciting and naughty…be it in the shower or on the kitchen counter. And although the bedroom is not the only place where sex always takes place, it is the one location where a couple spends most of their intimate time together. Whether it's actually having sex, cuddling, hanging out or best of all sleeping! The environment that hosts your sex life is an important place. It's one place that you can escape to, locking out the outer world and being with together with one another in unified solitude. This is why it's important for a couple to preserve the sanctity of the bedroom.

We have many distractions in our lives, things that create mayhem in our home and in our heads, and these can also impact the relationship. One area that needs to be protected from all of life's external influences is our sex life and the environment that hosts to it. The bedroom is one place that needs to be reserved for this intimacy. It's very easy to lose sight of this, especially when it comes to convenience, or simply a lack of living space. Before we know it, our bedroom can become crammed with a treadmill in one corner (which we had good intentions on using daily, but now serves as a holding place for yet to be folded laundry)...The massive TV that hangs on the wall, laundry baskets lined up by the door and waiting to be laundered (which has been pushed back on our "To Do" list three times in the past week)... tons of knick-knack's and non-essential crap that litter our night stands and dresser... and that not-so-compact computer desk in the corner that's overflowing with papers and files (what was once a vision of turning the third bedroom into an office, unexpectedly became a baby's room instead...so much for the pulling-out method). It may not seem like it, but all of these things start to take away from sexual experiences. Obviously the bedroom is not a twenty-four hour sex room (despite how a penis often wishes it be). However, you should have the ability to transform the bedroom into a sexual environment with ease and not have any added distractions affect the flow of sexual energy during intimacy.

The reality for most of us is in our daily lives we often gravitate to convenience and practicality. Having our bedroom serve as a multi-purpose environment is convenient and functional for many of us, especially when the family dynamic includes kids. If you've experienced motherhood, you know all too well how easy it is for the entire house to quickly become cluttered with toys all over the place. Obviously, the bedroom is no exception and often those little plastic balls and doll heads find their way under your bed. Such is life right? And truth be told, one or two toy cars or plastic baubles under your bed is not going to make or break a man's erection. However, if you're trying to host to a sexy striptease dance in heels, and you're tripping over Lego pieces and stumbling over stuffies...

this may be a buzz kill. If you're having to stop the pumping action in bed, just so you can pull out a rubber ducky that's wedged in your ass cheeks…this can be distracting and also kill the mood. One or two toys may not break the mood, but throw in enough stuffies and it's enough to kill his stiffy.

The thing about sex is that it involves a shitload of mental stimulation, and the brain relies on all the surrounding visuals as a great source of stimuli. A man can love his kids to death and his kids may be the only thing he ever thinks about… but in the heat of the moment when he's focused on his erection and all things sex…he doesn't want these thoughts to enter his sex brain and divert his focus away from sex. It's not to say that the kids will never step foot in the bedroom, and many of us enjoy a family night in bed watching a movie. However, the family element should never overpower the bedroom, and turn into a "mommy and daddy' zone. Work related stuff, things like desks, files and computers, are a huge buzz kill when it comes to sex. These things symbolize 'work', which is often associated with stress and all things "unfun." Now, I know that everyone has their own parenting style, and many couples practice co-sleeping with their children. Obviously, there will always be accommodations required for the family dynamic, and it's important to try and develop solutions to such variables and carve out exclusive time and space for the sexual relationship. This is a common struggle for many couples, when they don't define boundaries and at some point they have over grown children sleeping in between them indefinitely. This is very symbolic, and without moderation the "kids in the middle of the bed" can eventually create a wedge and disconnection between a couple. The reality is that having our kids in bed is a wonderful bonding experience for us as parents, and is no harm done as long as it doesn't affect the bond that a couple shares with one another.

Extra furniture pieces, such as a workout machine, not only take up space, but they bring the outer world of all things unrelated to sex, and they affect how we mentally associate with this space in relation to sex. Unless that treadmill doubles as some form of sex apparatus, and he's turned on by running on it while you're smacking his ass, then it has no place in the bedroom. Along with all the other mental and physical distractions that bring the outside world into this intimate setting. These things change the energy in the room, and how a person mentally associates with the space. A couple's bedroom should essentially be about serenity and viewed as an escape. The two elements that the bedroom should essentially host to are "intimacy" and "sleep" with minimal distractions.

When it comes to sexual encounters and sex play, you shouldn't be limited to just the bed. De-cluttering and keeping the space simple, allows for many potential erotic forms of play. Taking the sex play to the floor, or having the space for an erotic sexy dance… Or perhaps you really want to turn up the heat and use the extra space for a removable exotic dance pole, or even a sex swing. There may be a "no kid toys" rule, but there are no rules when it comes to adult play and any toys that enhance the sexual experience. Something else to consider if you have other occupants in the house (aka curious kids) is a locking door. What good is the thought of escaping to the love den if there's a risk of a little someone barging into the room and shouting, "There's a monster under my bed!" There's nothing more distracting to a man's hard on, like the constant fear that someone may come busting through that door. Being buck-naked with your legs thrown behind your head is not the ideal image for a mother…and scarier than any monster lurking under little Johnny's bed. Having a lock on the door gives peace of mind and the security in knowing that you'll never be sitting across from little Johnny at breakfast when he asks, "Mommy, I didn't know you're a nurse. Is Daddy's peepee going to be okay?"

Speaking of locks and securing things, not only should you make every effort to keep kids toys from making their way into the bedroom, you also want to keep the kids from getting into your "toys" should they find their way into your bedroom. The idea is to keep the bedroom environment transitional and have things easily accessible. In the midst of a steamy sex session, it can kill the moment if you have to break and scrimmage through your sock drawer just to locate those nifty hand cuffs or trusty vibrator. Reserving a specific cabinet or drawer for all things sex makes them easily accessible and keeps them safe and hidden. You want to also have a lock on this little treasure chest as well, and ensure that no little curious five-year-old gets their little sticky-fingers into your personal sex toys. There's nothing worse than showing up to a parent/teacher meetings and hearing that "Little Johnny has quite the imagination. He tells us that mommy is a secret super hero because she has a cape and mask, handcuffs, whips and special spike shoes." And perhaps it doesn't even go that far, but just the thought and image of little Johnny whisking around the house with the cool "Zorro" mask and vibrating *Star Wars* lightsaber he happened upon, is enough to permeate in any guys sex brain.

The rule is simple, and there should never be any cross contamination between all things outside the bedroom and anything relating to the love den. This ensures that the sexual environment is serving to all things relating to sex and that the sexual energy is preserved. This applies to ALL distractions, especially relating to work and anything associated with stress. Think about it, no one goes to their place of work, and plops a massive dildo on their boss's desk. Hence, any work the boss gives you, does not belong in your sex space at home. If it doesn't serve a purpose for sex, it shouldn't clutter the sex space.

The funny thing is that many of us don't often view something like a television as being a distraction to our sexual environment. Granted, if the TV is hosting to a "Porn and Popcorn" night, then this could be a very welcome distraction for many couples. However, always having the TV on in the background during sexy time, takes away from the sexual energy and a couple's ability to take in the entire experience mentally. It's difficult to enjoy the mental stimuli of all the sights and sounds when the nightly news is reporting, "Sixteen dead, no known survivors and a massive search underway!" The goal is to try and preserve the sexual energy and eliminate any distractions. It's about busting out sex toys, and not busting your strip-tease ass when you trip over Barbie's Pink Ferrari and your stiletto decapitates Ken Doll in the passenger seat. Not only do you end up killing Barbie's husband, but also killing the mood and your husband's erection.

When you preserve the sanctity of the bedroom and sexual environment, you also preserve the quality of your sex life. The best way to preserve the quality of your sexual relationship is to invest good efforts in maintaining every single variable that the relationship depends on. It's important to ensure that the sexual relationship is always meeting your needs, and when you have ultimate sexual gratification it motivates you to stay connected and fully invested in your partner's needs. Remember, nothing gets overlooked and every single element is important to keeping the sexual relationship intact. If at any time you find yourself lacking a drive or motivation to have sex, communicate this to your partner and don't let it linger. People often think that things will pass, or that it's just a phase and before you know it the phase turns into the new norm and a new disconnected reality. Explore your sexual persona to its fullest and tap into a world of sexual fantasy. This is what helps keep the sex spicy and keeps couples connected, as every experience gives way to something new. Make sure that you keep the sexual initiation balanced by taking initiative and hosting to special nights with his penis as your guest of honor.

It's important to always make time for sex, find the time and make it happen. It's about committing 100% and always being fully engaged in every experience. The only time it's acceptable to not be mentally present during sex is when you've had such an earth shattering orgasm and you can't remember what day it is or even your own name. Now run along and go bury Ken's head in the backyard before little Suzie wakes up, but hurry back because our vagina work here is not done.

Chapter Eight

Love Lockdown

Alright ladies, this is where we put the finishing touches on those vaginas so they can last us a lifetime! Initiate "Operation: Dazzle His Dick Off!" Okay, well, we don't exactly want to dazzle him to the point that his dick actually falls off, because then we won't have any use for him. I mean, sure someone still has to take out the trash, but someone still needs to service those vaginas! Speaking of servicing, we've pretty much touched on all the important factors involving men, their penis, their penis's happiness and a man's overall happiness. And of course, the idea that by taking this approach, a woman and her vagina find happiness too.

Earlier on we touched on all the elements that go into building a solid relationship foundation, everything from love and friendship, to respect, honesty, loyalty, sex, and the list goes on and on with all the things that honor each partner's values and needs. All of these variables hold equal importance, and they all tie into one another. The idea that where there is great love, there is respect, loyalty and trust...Where there is intimacy, there is a great friendship and unified bond. A successful relationship is one where each and every aspect is equally maintained and nurtured. If even one element and aspect of the relationship is not maintained with a great amount of invested efforts, it can compromise many of these other elements and affect the overall relationship. This is what makes good communication so vital to a relationship, as it allows a couple to remain connected and it ensures that the relationship is always serving each partner's happiness. The reason why the overall union is affected when even one link is broken, is because each link holds importance to each partner's sense of fulfillment and it contributes to their overall happiness. Just one broken link can affect that sense of fulfillment, and eventually it can erode one's happiness into a state of unhappiness.

When you look at it as a whole, it can seem like a shitload of responsibility to take on, especially when maintaining a relationship is not our only job. The reality is that in real life we have real life responsibilities, many other jobs and roles that require just as much investments and efforts. Throw all of this into the mix and it's a juggling act that can give even the most skilled vagina panic attacks. How can one vagina be expected to maintain all of this, and at a level that's supposed to dazzle his dick off? There are not enough hours in the day to go to work, tend to the kids, run errands, feed his penis, go to the gym, and tuck your pooped out vagina into bed each and every night. We need a vagina assistant, or else this simply isn't going to work. Do they even give bathroom breaks around here? How's a vagina supposed to find time to get her nails done and roots touched up?

Actually, the good news is that it's a lot easier to maintain a good relationship, than it is to try and fix a crappy one, or even worse live in a broken one. When a relationship comes to rely on the greatness that it has been built on, there are little things that we can do each and every day that can help keep it that way. The reality is that every single day is not always going to include having sex, talking about the relationship, taking time to share in cuddles and affections, mow the lawn and feed the penis. It's all about tapping into effective and valuable mini efforts and ideas that can be sprinkled here and there and throughout the overall relationship from day to day. It's about finding ways for a couple to stay connected even when they are not face to face. Knowing how to maintain the sexual relationship even when a couple is not having sex... And by bringing that sexual energy out of the bedroom and into the overall daily relationship. How cool is that? A vagina has the ability to appeal to a man's penis needs, without getting her hands dirty or even doing the dirty deed! As women, we often don't understand the full magnitude of our vagina capabilities. Something as simple as being present can have a powerful impact. We can assert our female sexuality through the simplest ways and make an impact.

It's all about knowing how to keep that chemistry flowing in our daily lives, and finding new ways to keep reinventing all the little things that feed this chemistry and that help recreate it time and time again. Man, you'd better bust out that vagina cape, because this shit is golden! Okay, maybe not so fast...one thing at a time, because my vagina has a hard time staying focused and sticking to the important penile points. So, what are all these little magical vagina tricks we speak of, and are there any door prizes? Okay, maybe no door prizes for the vagina, but there is benefits in this for all vaginas and every relationship. Be it a relationship that's sparkly and new and only one year old, to a relationship that's a golden classic and celebrating twenty years in service. At any stage and at any age, and no matter how great a relationship already is...there's always benefits in continually investing new and creative efforts that help keep things exciting and inviting! There's no such thing as "too much" when it comes to all things good in the relationship. Like seriously, has any vagina ever complained about one too many lovings? Or of a penis having one too many inches? Exactly! So let's get rocking and dive into all the ways a couple can keep that fire burning and keep things hot and spicy! I've put together a "Top 10 List" of the most important and effective factors for keeping the chemistry flowing in a relationship.

1. The Power of Persuasion

It's a well-known fact that the male species is quite responsive to any form of female sexuality. It's been said that "The female persuasion is powerful enough to bring the entire civilization of man to its knees." Love 'em or hate 'em for their penile behaviors, by nature men are easily prompted by their sex brain. The male libido has the ability to overtake his brain's entire operation and control his behaviors. Thankfully, somewhere up in that little male brain is logic, and (believe it or not) impulse control. However, even when a man appears to be poised and unaffected by his penile urges, his sex brain always has its eyes and ears open and is always open to receiving stimuli. As women, we often don't appreciate the true value of our female presence in the relationship, and it's because our female libido is not as powerful and it doesn't hold us captive under its control. Unless we are experiencing a spike in hormones during our monthly cycle, we are consistently less responsive to sexual stimuli and much more responsive to emotional and mental stimuli. This is why they say that foreplay for a woman starts from the break of dawn. And it's the efforts that a man puts in outside the bedroom, things that make us feel appreciated and that help make our life easier that we find more of a turn on. Not so much is the case with a man, and all that's often required is to break out those heels and dawn a cute little lace number…BINGO! Mission accomplished.

By gaining better insight into this powerful influence, a woman can better appreciate how this unspoken interaction works and how it impacts the interactions that take place in the relationship. Most of us already have a pretty good idea of how easily men respond to sexual stimuli, but often not to the fullest extent. It's all about a woman familiarizing herself with how it works, knowing how to assert her female presence and influence a man's behaviors and interactions in the relationship. Trust me when I say that it doesn't require an obvious and overstated sexual effort, or the need to pull out a vagina and slap it on the table in order to illicit a response. It's about learning the unspoken language of the penis, and speaking in his native tongue even when the vagina lips aren't moving. Cool right? Well, you can add vagina ventriloquist to that resume! Okay, maybe not, because that doesn't sound sexy… Let's stay on the penile point…. One of the greatest benefits of appealing to a man's sex brain is that it satisfies not only a man's sexual taste buds, but it also intensifies his attraction and appreciation for his mate and it feeds his sense of being emotionally connected to her as well. Well, I'll be damned! So, there's no need to pull out any vaginas, no need to even talk, and yet he still gains all of that. We're some fierce powerful pussies, I tell ya!

The best part about it all, is that a woman has the ability to directly influence how her needs get met, and increase fulfillment of her needs. The art of unspoken mental sexual seduction is what men gravitate to, and they have no idea that any of this is taking place. Yup, that's right! How a woman conducts herself, and her artful sexually infused interactions is penis hypnosis. It can reprogram a man's sex brain and alter his behaviors. Okay, I know that this may sound like a cruel science experiment, but rest assured that this has nothing to do with taking advantage of a man's weaknesses, using our vagina as kryptonite or abusing our sexual powers in any way. Who would do such a thing? All we're simply doing is utilizing this knowledge and asserting ourselves in a way that maximizes our interactions in the union and betters the quality of the relationship. Now, I know that this section may not seem fitting in this chapter, when were supposed to be talking about keeping the relationship spicy. The reason why I have chosen to include this topic here is because it involves the daily interactions that a couple has in the relationship. The quality of our interactions either add to the relationship when it's a positive exchange or they deteriorate the relationship when common daily exchanges are negative experiences. Knowing how to create more positive energy by tapping into what the male brain is most responsive to, optimizes the quality in the overall relationship.

There's no denying that when it comes to penis and vagina negotiations and communications, navigating such tasks can often be challenging. He's got his penis earmuffs on, and her microphone is tuned into an emotional frequency that's causing foreign static feedback to his penis ears. The reality is that men will never fully comprehend the vagina mind and women will never fully understand how the penis brain sees things. It is what it is, and if we expect to overcome this then we must learn how to tune into a man's frequency and articulate our vagina needs in a manner that his brain can comprehend and appreciate. How many times have you found yourself trying to articulate your feelings, yet somehow you just feel misunderstood? Times when you want to discuss something that's important to you, and you want to dissect all the variables involved and explore all the feelings tied into it? Yet, it comes across as you just saying the same thing over and over and he's just not hearing you. How about when there's something you need assistance with, like repairing something around the house... you've had to remind him three times and it's yet to be done? This doesn't imply that he's a poor listener or lazy, and it could simply mean that he doesn't see the same importance on the things you place priority on. So how does a vagina change these things, and how can she get the penis to see things her way?

Before we start strutting our female stuff all over the relationship, it's important to understand exactly how the male brain works. This goes back to the male sex cycle that we discussed earlier, and the build-up of testosterone in a man's body. Men may not be exposed to the suffering of female monthly cycles and periods, but a man's cycle can affect his moods, and influence whether or not he's in an attentive and doting mood, a laid back mood or even an all-out crabby mood.

It's not an exact science that would apply to each and every male, but as I stated earlier the average sex cycle from an empty post orgasm state to the state of being fully topped up and seeking relief is approximately three-four days for most men. By the third or fourth day, he's once again starting to peak and this continues to peak until he finds gratification. Now, the valuable information in this is not exactly about knowing how often he's looking for sex, but knowing exactly what stage he's in as this has an effect on his overall mindset and mood. You see when the testosterone build-up has been released, his mind is clear, he's able to think much more logically and his perception is not clouded by his sexual urges. As the build-up continues to increase, he begins to have less and less clarity, his brain starts to become more and more clouded and controlled by his sexual urges…up until the point that he peaks and it can pretty much almost blind his perception and affect his ability to have sound judgment. He is literally dumbed down by his dick! It's like a build-up that causes a fogginess in his view finder.

Essentially, as it relates to his moods, he is in his least tolerant and responsive state when his balls are empty, and he is in his most tolerant and responsive state when he's pent up and in need of relief. In a filled-up state, having been dummied down by his desperate dick, he sees everything through rosy penis goggles. It's not that he's desperate per say, as he is in a heightened state of arousal and awareness and much more responsive to his surroundings. It's almost like his brain is on happy drugs. So basically the penile point here is that when a man is in that elated happy state, he is much more sensitive to his sexual surroundings. It changes his perception of his spouse, as he obviously sees her as the ultimate solution to his backed up balls problem. He becomes fixated on her presence. He's more affectionate during these times, and all in all, he's much more inclined to be in a position to please his partner and tend to her needs. This is all in an effort to make her happy, so he too can gain his reward and satisfy his urges for sexual gratification.

I'm sure we've all been prey to a guy that seems to have ulterior motives when he's being overly affectionate and extra kissy kissy. A woman will easily identify this and call him out with "Why are you being so nice? You never massage my feet and wash the car all in one day?" It may be obvious, but a man may not acknowledge any notable changes in his behaviors or see it as being motivated by sex. There is great value in it for a woman, and the benefits are in the process and days leading up to and inclusive of his cycle peaking.

By becoming more aware of a man's sex cycle clock, a woman can better predict a man's mood and state of mind. Think about the range of moods and responsiveness that the average male has. Post sex and after an orgasm, what is the most common male behavior? He is tapped out, and if he has enough energy to make himself a post sex sandwich he will, otherwise he's fast asleep and snoring away. Hey what can he say, it takes a lot out of a man…literally! However, sandwiches aside, by identifying the stages in these cycles a woman can utilize his varying levels of attentiveness to her advantage. Sometimes there's benefits to not having sex every day, as they say a huge part of sexual stimulation and satisfaction is in the art of seduction and giving a little but not giving it all and all the time. Sure having sex everyday can be just as fun and keep the relationship just as connected. However, when it comes to a woman's needs for affections, or her overall emotional needs, this is often fulfilled through communications and a couple engaging in discussions about their feelings and overall relationship.

They always say that timing is everything, and it's not always what you say, or how you say it…but when you say it that makes all the difference in the world. Obviously this whole idea is not a science, because truth-be-told a man could easily hijack the entire operation and abort the mission with a simple solo session of relieving himself in a pinch and in a state of emergency. Damn that masturbation trump card! That's okay, because there's no need to sit and create penis pie charts, or use a testicle scale to record daily weight findings, in an effort to track how many times sex took place and how backed up his balls may be. When you spend enough time with someone, you can judge their moods. The simple knowledge of knowing that he's looking for sex and at his maximum level of attentiveness, can help in times when you are looking for extra affections, or want to sit down and talk about the relationship. Maybe even break some bad news to him, as his backed up balls will probably take the news better.

This may sound loopy, and perhaps some of you may be thinking that I'm off my vagina rocker....but I assure you that this is very real and it has real benefits to the relationship. After being with my husband for so many years, I can easily read his moods. Based on this and knowing our sexual frequency, I can even tell if he hijacked the navigation of his build-up cycle, and veered the operation off course by flying solo without his trusty vagina co-pilot...and relieved himself. Especially with the very obvious sign of him taking an extra-long shower. I know that something is up because he's bald and has no hair to wash, no penis showers for 30 minutes unless he's romancing himself with shampoo! Rest assured that even though the cycle can take up to three-to-four days, it doesn't mean that most men are willing to let it go this far. Regardless, the reality is that this is not about the acts themselves and more about the varying moods and state of mind. Now, I'm not implying that when a guy is tapped out that he's a jerk. A man can easily have varying shades of pleasant moods, some just more intense and tolerable than others.

Knowing this all too well, I know that if I want to sit and have a productive discussion about the relationship, my needs or anything else that I want to dedicate a great deal of time towards... Or if the matter involves something stressful like money being spent or finances, I will not strike up this discussion right after sex. No, ma'am! I'm no foolish vagina! I have learned first-hand that a penis brain that is seeing with total clarity, and doesn't have the padded cushioning of that dummied down dick state of mind, such a time is not an opportune time for such discussions. Nor is the right time, a time when he's walking through the door after a long stressful day, and needs time to decompress and de-stress. If I choose to have these conversations at a time like this, I may not get the same favorable reception that I would get if he was in a more relaxed and attentive state of mind. Reserving such conversations for when the time is right, and his mood is right, will provide me with what I'm seeking. He will be more inclined to express his affections, explore my needs and feelings and give me what I need in the moment.

It's amazing how much more responsive a man is when there's a source of sexual influence or sexual stimuli involved. When a man is in a "Dummied-Down Dick" or what I like to call a state of "3D," it changes everything. Actually, this state is exactly like 3D, because everything in his presence is larger than life and a much more intensified experience for his mind. During a state of sexually amped 3D, a woman could do no wrong! While your man's in a distracted state and wearing his horny 3D glasses, this is now the time to slap on those heels and break the news to him that "Honey, I sort of backed the car into the garage door by accident today." A normal man's reaction when he's in a clear state of mind, would be to run out to the garage and assess the garage door and car damage. However, in a state of 3D, his reaction would be, "Awww, babe, that's okay…don't be upset. It was time for a new car anyway." Despite the fact that this may have been the third time in one month that you forgot to actually push the garage door opener before you tried reversing the car out of the garage, he won't care. His need for sexual release supersedes the need for your house to even have a garage door, and it has him rationalizing that perhaps that garage door was just an added nuisance, and he's glad that you got rid of it. In this very moment, he couldn't give two testicles about the garage door or the car, because he's preoccupied by all the sensory overload in his sex brain. Now's a good time to tell him about the $400 high heeled shoes you put on the credit card.

Realistically speaking everything is in moderation and these phases come and go. I mean, at some point you're actually gonna have to have sex with him! All is not lost! Obviously, the sexual relationship is just as important, and nothing replaces the bond that is created through sexual intimacy. Not to worry, the build-up stages will come again and in the meantime you can slap on those $400 heels and put them to good use. Trust me that sexual satisfaction and the endorphins that are created from such an experience also have lasting impressions. After a night of great sex, moods are happy and needs are satisfied. It's really about enjoying what both stages have to offer. Having great sex, and utilizing the art of sexual persuasion that acts as a buffer from one sexual experience until the next great sex romp.

Understanding the power of sexual persuasion allows a woman to assert this persuasiveness with a simple underlying tone in her everyday interactions. It's amazing to see how easy it is, and how it gets the job done. It's easy for me to identify how quickly it works with my husband. In the midst of a busy day, if I text him with some sort of a reminder or some mundane task, he often will respond when he has a free moment at work. Now if I send him a text that's sexual in nature (AKA, "sext"), no sooner do I push send, do I get back an auto-reply from his penis that says, "Oh Wow!" which is quickly followed up by him ringing my phone, wanting to further "discuss" the "Sext" I just sent. The penis is never too busy to take calls from the vagina. Funny enough, you ask a man to pick up milk after work (even with three follow up reminders), and there's still a 50/50 chance that he shows up at home without the milk. Now ask a fella to pick up some ice and candles which are for the mixed drinks you are making that night and a special sexy surprise you have planned. That penis is on it with impeccable precision! He's bringing home ten candles (one of every scent), five bags of ice, an icemaker as back up, and an Eskimo to churn the ice while you two are having sex. Sure, the Eskimo may be overkill, but his dick isn't taking any chances! Oh, and he also brought home the milk you asked for two days ago, because all of a sudden his memory is working again.

Like I said, it doesn't have to be overstated and obvious, and sometimes a woman can pretty much say anything to a man, just as long as she says it in heels. This doesn't mean that in order to get him to change a light bulb or do stuff around the house, that we constantly have to raise the temperature by dressing like hookers decked out in heels every day. Mind you, you could put on the heels and reach the light bulb yourself, in which case there's no need to put on the vagina charm. Then again, the mere sight of you in heels and changing a light bulb, will likely spark a bright bulb idea in his penis head....with him envisioning a real life porn scene starring 'Handy-Job Hooker." Like seriously, does the penis ever sleep? Yes, he does! So it's important to take advantage of times when he's clipping on your vagina heels and dotting on your every move. Instead of seeing this as an invitation for sex, look at it as an opportunity to engage in an exchange of sexual persuasion that will only intensify the sexual tension and when sex does take place it will be all that more appreciated as the build-up will be a huge dose of mental stimuli.

Now's the time to get some extra affections, ask for a foot rub as he sits and tells you what he loves most about you. A pent-up penis will run you a bubble bath, hold doors open for his lady, and even take your car in for an oil change. He'll happily sit for as long as your vagina heart desires, expressing his affections and doting on your presence. And of course, the vagina too will dote on the penis...and we'll get to that in a moment... (Typical penis always trying to make it about him and his needs...). Simply put, take heed of these opportunities and times where you can achieve much better results and gain fulfillment in the process. All it takes is knowing how and when to assert your female presence and your needs...and when to throw in a vagina here and there so everything remains balanced. Who knew that there was SO

MUCH greatness in two little pent-up testicles? Now just make sure that if you leave this book laying around the house, you glue the pages in this section together so he can't get his sticky little penis fingers on what we just discussed. It's of no use to us if those backed up balls catch on to us, because it'll only prompt him to secretly take long showers and drain his sorrows just to stay at the top of his game… at which point, it'll lose its effectiveness. Ah fuck it, let's just title this section "Vagina Hymns and Poetry for the Vagina Heart"…that's enough of a penis deterrent in itself.

2. Penis and Vagina Celebrations

The most gratifying feeling in a committed relationship is found in the love that a couple shares. When we find that special someone, we want to celebrate their love and celebrate all that they bring to our lives. And that's what it's really all about: a celebration of love and an ongoing celebration of one another. It's important to never let this momentum fade, and never stop showing our appreciation for having that person in our lives. When we celebrate the love we have for our partner, it's our way of saying, "Thank you for being you. Thank you for choosing to share your love with me…and thank you for continuing to be you, continuing to still choose me and love me." Now, perhaps someone who's yet to find such a love may look at this and think *Why should I be so grateful for someone picking me? Or loving me? He should be the one that's grateful, and why wouldn't he choose me? He's lucky to have me too!* And, yes, it's all of this too. This is exactly how both partners should always see things. A partner's love should never be seen as an entitlement. Sure, we should be able to rely on the security of knowing that they will always be there. However, when two people commit to one another, they are bound by their hearts and all that they share. It is an emotional tie, and not a physical binding that prevents someone from leaving if they so choose. That's the thing… With each passing day, a person chooses to be in that relationship. Every day, a person vows to renew their commitment to remain invested in the relationship, and to continue to stand by their partner's side. This is a conscious decision we make each day, and if someone really wanted to, nothing is stopping them from up and leaving if they really truly wanted to. And any two people can live together but not be committed to one another. Commitment is a choice, not a title...And it's expressed through our actions and our efforts. And a committed union should not be seen as an entitlement, but as a privilege, the privilege to be given another day to stand by one another's side and to celebrate the love that is shared.

All too often couples lose sight of this. Life gets hectic, years pass and people come to rely on the fact that what has always been, will always be. We come to expect what we have always known. At some point a couple loses momentum, and the celebrations start to dwindle. Sure, it's unrealistic to assume that throughout the entire course of a relationship it's going to be an overly elaborate fussing over one another with the penis blowing party favors and the vagina shooting confetti and streamers all over the place. The idea of celebrating one another is in the daily efforts of simply saying, "Hey, have I told you how much you mean to me? And the reason why I'm so happy that you're in my life is because..... You have a big penis."... Okay, scratch that last part....But trust me, his penile ego is eating that up! Which is exactly what I'm getting at, actually. When I talk about celebrating one another, it's not an 'Oh yeah! Look at us, we're in love!" A partner needs to be celebrated for the unique offerings they bring to the relationship. We as women, totally have a need for this. We like to feel as though we are recognized and valued for our unique female representation, and that our partner appreciates the unique offerings that we as women bring to the relationship. We want to feel as though a partner honors our unique female needs. And that he's willing to invest in the efforts to fulfill these needs in the unique female way that is required.

This means that if we're ever feeling vulnerable or that our sense of security needs topping up, a man would recognize the importance of providing this fundamental need that a woman brings into the relationship. He treats her heart with delicacy, and uses a gentler hand and approach when tending to her needs. He has a little more patience when she is in need to explore her emotions and regain her sense of comfort from time to time. Celebrating a partner can be in the form of expressing appreciation for their uniqueness, or simply providing affirmations when they require reassurance. When a woman asks, "Do I look frumpy in these pants? Gosh, I feel so bloated and blah today!"....A man's celebration of her is when he responds with "Are you kidding me? You always look beautiful...You're the sexiest woman around. That's why I married you."

It may often seem that men don't have as much need for such celebrations, but rest- assured, men are no different. A man needs to feel as though he too is recognized for the unique male offerings he brings to the union. He wants to know that he is appreciated for his unique male presence in the relationship, and he needs to be honored and respected...and that his female spouse has a need for his offerings that only he as a man can provide for her. I know, trust me...It's a lot. You thought women were complicated... The male ego has vagina-sized emotional needs! It's inherent to their nature, and no different than when a gorilla comes on the scene and attempts to assert their male presence by pounding on their chest and stuff. Whatever, listen, when you love a guy you do what's needed. A guy may not come packing with impressive six- pack abs or bulging muscles... He may not be the tallest in the pack, and he may not even be packing an impressive twelve- inch penis...But in his male (twelve- inch ego) mind, he wants to feel as though he's packing a punch full of masculinity and that his female partner sees him as a full twelve- inch package.

Keep in mind, this isn't all about fussing over his penis size. Well, actually, it is all about fussing over his penis size... Remember, sex is also an emotional need for men. A man relies on sex to express himself emotionally, to connect with his partner on an emotional and intimate level, and to assert his sexuality and satisfy his partner sexually. All of these things make a man feel as though he's serving his purpose in the relationship. And if he's unable to do so, he feels as though he hasn't fulfilled his role as a man. I know, I know... This is why affirmations and celebrations both in and out of the bedroom are important for a man. He too wants to feel desired and that his partner is attracted to him. He wants to know that he's satisfying her sexually, and when he gets feedback in the bedroom, it feeds his male ego. This one is easy! Something as simple as moaning and groaning, and sounds of pleasure are enough to inflate his ego to that full twelve inches. Being verbal and expressing what it is you enjoy during sex, how it makes you feel and all that fun stuff... inflate, inflate, inflate...

Outside of the bedroom he likes to feel as though he has what it takes to be a good leader, a protector and a good provider. Not just physically protective or financially providing, but even emotionally and any other effort he puts into the relationship. Essentially, no effort should ever go without praise. I know this may seem like a shitload of vagina confetti flying his way, but rest assured that it pays itself back two fold. When a man feels honored and celebrated in the relationship, it boosts his confidence and feeds his happiness. It prompts him to share in the celebrations and in turn honor the woman that fusses over him. Trust me, it's not just for gorillas and not found just at the zoo. This is your man, and in your home. Except unlike the zoo, where we're not supposed to feed the animals, it's "PLEASE FEED THE EGO" and often. No need to be over the top, and make it look unrealistic... like bringing a bag of peanuts into bed and throwing them at his penis just to make him think that you mistook it for an elephant's trunk....because he may have a twelve- inch ego mindset, but he's no idiot and trust you and me, he's probably already measured his penis one too many times and confirmed that it probably belongs more in the otter exhibit than in the elephant exhibit at the zoo.

It's important to understand that a man expresses his appreciation in his own unique way. As women, we have our own way of showing our appreciation, and we naturally become expecting of the same vagina sized efforts from a male partner. He may not be well versed in verbally articulating his emotions, and if he has his own way of expressing himself it's important to see his efforts in even the smallest things. My husband happens to be somewhere in the middle. He often verbally expresses his affections and emotions, but not to the elaborate extent that I do. I can recite an entire wedding speech from the top of my head and on the spot. However, he does little things for me each and every day as a way to show his affection. He is great at providing a woman with her much needed female affirmations. And when I'm having blah days, he's always quick to fuss over me and put those qualms to rest. Sometimes he'll stop at the store to pick up one of my favorite chocolates (a man after my vagina heart), and he'll come home and surprise me with little treats. Even after he's had a long day, he will still offer to give me a foot rub at night as we sit and chat. When he senses that I am having a down day, he'll make the effort to initiate a face to face pow-wow and invite me to share in how I'm feeling. If I have a ton of errands to run and I'm frazzled trying to juggle them all, he will offer to knock a couple of them out for me just so he can make my life easier. He encourages me to go out with the girls and have a fun night, or go to the nail salon and get my nails done. He recognizes the importance of what it means to be a woman, the things we like to do and that make us feel sexy, and the unique female needs I will sometimes have that require a little extra topping up.

Sometimes, it's even the small effort of him texting me a photo of ME! With a little note saying, "I love this picture of you, I'm so proud to have such a smart and beautiful wife." This makes me feel beautiful and sexy with one simple text. And there are times where he will come out and voice his adoration for the fact that he thinks I'm a wonderful mother, and an amazing wife. In the midst of a conversation he will stop and say, "Man, you're so smart!" And in return, I tell him each and every day that he has the biggest penis I have ever seen in my whole life…and everybody's happy! Okay… maybe not the biggest per se…

And it's not the only celebrations I throw his way… However, the fact that he fusses over me the way he does, literally gives him a twelve- inch penis and heart in my books. And that is the best part about it, because when someone feels appreciated, fussed over and celebrated…it enhances their sense of happiness and appreciation for the source that's blowing all the hot air their way. And the mental fulfillment that this happiness provides them with, actually enhances their perception of how they view their spouse. When I say that I have the best husband in the world, with the biggest penis in the world…it doesn't necessarily have to be true, it doesn't have to be believable to anyone else but me. And because my husband fusses over me and celebrates me in the relationship, I see him as the epitome of greatness and male partners in all the land. Just the same, I may not be the most beautiful in all the land, or the sexiest around… bit as long as my husband is appreciative of the woman who puts him on a pedestal and celebrates him each and every day, his perception is that he is married to the greatest and sexiest woman alive. No one else needs to see that but him…and his penis…and we're all good. I mean, quite honestly, he already had me with the chocolates…but who am I to turn down an opportunity to be fussed over?

When a couple celebrates one another, and they raise each other up in adoration and appreciation of each other…that celebratory sensation is contagious, it prompts each partner to continue in the celebrations and invest in the efforts each and every day to reciprocate the appreciation and the love. This is something that should be continually invested in daily. It helps keep the chemistry flowing and it recreates the mental stimuli that is often found in new relationships and that 'honeymoon stage'. The very reason why couples lose that honeymoon feeling is because they stop investing in the honeymoon efforts. All the things that were once in place when things were new and exciting. Continuing those efforts and finding new ways to express our appreciation is what recreates those new and exciting feelings and places them on repeat indefinitely. Okay, so epic vagina homework for tonight, is to tell him that he has the biggest penis you've ever seen! If he asks why you've never told him this before, just tell him that you reran your numbers and forgot to round up at the testicle point last time (feel free to throw the peanuts for added effect.) Okay fine… maybe we forgo the massive penis deal… I'm sure by now we all get the penile point and we can all find our own unique ways to inflate his ego. The only restriction is that a vagina never resorts to faking an orgasm as an ego booster… because you don't want to rob your vagina in the process. Alright! Pull out that vagina confetti and get to celebrating some love!

3. Affection is Sex for the Heart

This too ties into the little efforts a couple makes in the daily relationship. We often don't appreciate how some of the smallest efforts actually feed many other important areas of the relationship. When it comes to showing our affection in a relationship, we often tie this into expressing our love and see it as a way to connect emotionally. And yes, it is exactly just that. The sexual relationship is also a way of expressing emotions, affections, and connecting on an intimate level. Now, in an ideal world, there would be a high frequency of 'sexually connecting" going on... And having a lot more sex means a lot more intimacy, which also means a more solidified bond in the relationship. However, in the real world and in real life, every day will not be an opportune day to have sex.

Keep in mind that the emotional bond that two people share is the strongest link that ties them to one another. Every other aspect of the relationship relies on this emotional connection to remain in place, in order for all of these other areas to continue to thrive. When a couple experiences an emotional disconnection, it can affect the state of the sexual relationship and this too can quickly become disconnected. The friendship that is shared can become strained when two people no longer feel as though they share a common bond. There will be times where other areas of the relationship are forced to take a back seat due to life's circumstances (such as a bad flu and ailment that sidelines either partner and puts the vagina or penis out of commission for two weeks straight and with no desire to have sex). I mean, honestly, what vagina can even stomach the thought of ingesting a penis when she can't even keep a damn cracker down. Not to mention, the thought of his coveted vagina suffering from a case of diarrhea is a total buzz kill for the penis and causes erectile dysfunction. Such is life, and it's times like this where the sexual relationship may need to be put on hold. All is not lost, and the relationship does not simply fall to shit just because you have the flu and shits for two weeks. It's the wonderful comforts of commitment that see us through these trying times, and the emotional bond that helps keep the relationship thriving and unaffected through real life and real shit.

And this, my dear vaginas, is why it's important to nurture the intimate relationship even in the absence of vagina and penis playtime. The best formula is always found in a new relationship, the days of courting and all the little things that give us butterflies.

The little strolls in the park, writing love letters and spilling our hearts out on paper or in an email. Sitting in front of the fire-place, and cuddling with a cup of tea or hot chocolate. Taking bubble baths together (that's if you and his newly found massive penis both fit in the tub together). Something as simple as sitting on the couch and giving or receiving a foot rub as you talk about your day and express heart felt emotions. Lying in bed with some candles and a glass of wine, listening to love songs and making out....Or simply spooning before bed and laying nestled in each other's arms. Actually, those last two are somewhat sketchy, and could quickly veer off course. Anytime the penis gets too close or starts to feel any sort of friction he can become easily excited. Throw in another glass or two of wine, and that Lionel Ritchie cuddle session turns into a naked lambada sexfiesta!...and with his drunk penis taking jabs at that vagina-pinata. Man, no one expected this party...had we known we could have stayed with the whole Mexican theme and made margaritas instead. Maybe even have turned it into a role play with a penis sombrero... OLE! Oh well, can't get mad at the penis for being so sensitive to stimuli. This is always a risk anytime you're cuddling with the penis, and a simple spooning session can turn into a real pain in the ass...with his erection poking and trying to gain entry. Better limit the alcoholic beverages if you're hoping to keep it to just cuddling.

The great thing about these little affection sessions is that it doesn't require a lot of time, a lot of energy or effort. Even after a long tiring day, lying down and connecting one on one doesn't require much, but the benefits are much more than the efforts put in. My husband and I always try to make the time to connect one on one and just enjoy each other's company. Talk about our day, perhaps share our feelings and simply take each other into our hearts and enjoy the moment. Sometimes we'll return home from a date night, park the car in the driveway... turn up the radio with some love songs and have ourselves a good old-fashioned make out session in the car. You know, just like those days back when we were dating, and he was dropping you off at home. Except this time your mother isn't spying through the front window.... And there's no need to jump in the backseat to have sex, because now you have access to your own place and don't have to worry about getting caught! Mind you, sex in the backseat can also be hot and recreate those old memories, and the idea of getting caught may be exciting to some people...but not all penis' work well under that pressure...and after so many years perhaps your vagina is not all that flexible, and throwing your legs behind your head and using your hoop earrings as stir ups like you used to may not be a viable option... So we'd better stick to making out in the front seat...

Anyway, all I'm saying is that a couple should make the effort in the daily relationship to nurture the intimate bond that they share, and to stay connected on an emotional level. It's good for the relationship, it's good for the soul and it's sex for the heart!

4. Unplugging From the Outer World and Connecting One on One

Now this one pretty much ties into what we just discussed, and it has to do with a couple spending one-on-one time together. The idea and importance of connecting is one we already touched on. In today's day and age, with all of the technologies that are available to us, it makes it easy and convenient to stay connected with just about anyone any time. It can be a great way to stay connected with our partner, during the day when we are apart from one another. It's as easy as sending a text, an email, or picking up the phone to say a quick "hello" or "I love you."

With that being said, even though there are benefits to staying connected with your mate, these conveniences can quickly become a distraction in the relationship. Nothing replaces the very important need for a couple to come together, face to face and to connect one on one with no added distractions from the outside world. Staying connected sometimes means disengaging from the rest of the world, putting the cellular phones away and having an environment that promotes communication. Having your cell phone chiming off in the background with "oh, it's my boss I have to take it" doesn't count. At some point everything has to go away and the only people invited to the party is you and your mate... and the vagina and penis as back up....just in case, 'cause you never know. Hey, spur of the moment impromptu sex can be hot. Oh hell, keep that phone nearby in case you want to snap a hot pic or two to send him at a later date... okay fine.... Focus...

It's important for a couple to unplug from the rest of the world, and to simply plug into one another... Damn...see, sex again! Okay, not that type of plugging in... and let's try to keep his charged up cord out of that vagina socket for just one session shall we? These distractions deteriorate the quality in the time a couple spends together. It may seem as though they are "connected" but not if there are things that take away from the mood and that prevent them from being able to communicate face to face. Talking is important and communication is the glue that binds everything in a relationship!

Another common distraction in relationships, and especially in the bedroom, is the television! Yes, it's cool to lie in bed and watch TV together sometimes and it can be a simple date night when you throw in some ice cream. However, bad habits such as always having the TV on in the background, and even falling asleep with the TV on, is a distraction. When a couple is sitting side by side watching TV, this is not quality one on one time. When we are watching, we are not talking... at least not the good type of talking and the communication that a relationship relies on. There's nothing wrong with a couple watching their favorite shows together, because this is time together. However, there comes a time, when you need to turn the TV off and you share in quiet and alone time, even if it is in the dark. And even if turning off the TV means that it may lead to his penis getting turned on. And if things lead to sex then hey that's great. Again, when sex is being had, having the TV on in the background kills the vibe. Especially if there are Housewives fist fighting in the background, or an infomercial blaring "NOT ONLY DO YOU GET TWO BUT THREE FOR THE PRICE OF ONE."

The only exception to this rule, is if a couple is into watching a little porn to set the mood, or simply letting it play in the background as "ambiance"....because this could be a good distraction and even provide for some new ideas.

Actually, visual sexual aids like erotica and pornography are also great for foreplay and setting the sexual mood. It's almost like seeing a commercial for food when you're hungry, and all of a sudden craving that burger on TV. Keep in mind that 'burgers' on TV are always a lot bigger than in real life... so your guy shouldn't feel bad if he can't re-enact the exact same theme and position. I mean, not every guy is blessed with a cock that enters the room two minutes before he does.... That's okay, it may not be "As Seen on TV," but we love our burger and it's always a satisfying meal. So be sure to take those ideas and perhaps improvise...because like we always say, "It's all fun and games until someone pulls a vagina...or fractures a penis." So remember, when we unplug from the rest of the world and plug into to one another...we keep the lights on in the relationship and the sex remains electrifying!

5. 9-5 Sex: Working the Sexual Energy into the Overall Relationship

Don't worry, the above captioned title is not to imply that any one of our vaginas is expected to turn tricks for money in the relationship, and there's no need to turn those over-priced $400 heels into a work uniform. Actually, working the sexual energy into the rest of the relationship doesn't require a lot of strenuous work on the vaginas part, so there's no need to train for the big event with vagina push-ups and start running that bitch on the treadmill. This has to do with the daily overall relationship, and the times when we are actually not having sex...so drop the vagina weights and let's get to work. Obviously, when it comes to nurturing the sexual relationship, nothing replaces the act of physically having sex and connecting on an intimate level. And although I often joke about us stressing over the idea of having more sex and as though it's a tedious and painful thought. We all know that the vagina loves sex just as much as the next penis and we're just poking fun. As I mentioned earlier, even when sex is not at the forefront, there are benefits to bringing that sexual energy out of the bedroom and sprinkling it throughout the daily relationship. This helps keep the sexual chemistry as a constant in the relationship and it adds an element of excitement to regular routine and daily lives.

There are ways to simulate sexual stimulation with the simplest of efforts. We may not always have the ability to physically touch the penis and appeal to his pleasures at all times. However, there are ways to reach out and touch someone even when were not in their presence. Remember, there is one powerful element that plays the biggest role in the sexual relationship...and that's his sex brain. When it comes to the pleasures of sex, the brain plays the most prominent role in sexual arousal. And when you appeal to the sex brain with a good dose of mental stimuli, it can send a physical surge down to the penis and create an intense sense of arousal. Pretty cool, right? Almost like the cool discovery of riding your bike hands-free... "Look Ma! No Hands!" I'm telling you, this right here is a golden vagina discovery, and one that works wonders! His penis can be all the way across the globe and on a business trip in Tokyo. And it's still accessible, anytime, anywhere...His penis is always at the tip of your skilled vagina fingers.

'Enter, The Mind Fuck Experience!'

Okay, so I know that the term "mind fuck" may sound a bit crass, and if such 'expressive articulation" (AKA Cursing) is not in your vagina-cabulary, just bear with me for a moment... It may sound like a bad term, but the idea behind it is all good and great for the overall relationship! So what exactly is a 'mind fuck'? This is often in reference to messing with someone's mind. Although it can sometimes imply in a negative manner, in this case it's all good! A 'mind fuck' is when a sexual idea or thought is put into a man's head, and it creates a process of triggering his sex brain that ultimately produces both mental and physical responsiveness in his mind and his body. By simply introducing a sexual element in a man's immediate environment, it acts as a surge of sexual stimuli in the moment and it creates an intense state of arousal. Normally, the sexual energy and sexual tension that a couple shares is often only found in the bedroom during sexual intimacy. The purpose behind the "Mind Fuck" is to recreate the chemistry found in these intimate experiences, and to bring that sexual energy into the overall relationship.

The reality for most couples is that they spend a good amount of time apart from one another, tending to their daily routines and responsibilities. Such time spent apart and focusing on other things, means opportunities for a couple to connect and to nurture the chemistry in the sexual relationship. It's almost like multi-tasking, and even though you may be away from one another, it doesn't mean that the chemistry cannot still be enjoyed and the relationship nurtured. It's important for couples to take advantage of such efforts, and invest in ways to continuously provide for each other's needs even when they are not face to face.

As women, we find it quite easy to put aside our immediate sexual needs when we are off tending to our busy daily lives. We naturally assume that men work in the same way. However, because of their unique male libido, men are often in a constant state of awareness when it comes to their sexual needs. Many of us have heard of the male stigma surrounding this, and of the popular belief that the average male thinks about sex 100 times a day. Actually, there are more recent studies out there that say on average men think about sex eighteen times a day. The male sex brain enjoys engaging in sexual thought and fantasy just as much as it enjoys engaging in the sexual act itself. Keep in mind that the mental aspects of sex play a much more prominent role over the physical aspects when it comes to sexual arousal. The idea of sexual foreplay is to appeal to just this, and the mental stimuli that is produced is what creates that heightened sexual state of arousal.

The male sex brain enjoys recreating this heightened state, even when the physical aspects of sex are not involved. Think about it, if a man is already prone to stop and think about sex eighteen times a day, and he actually enjoys the pleasures of a simple sexual thought, then how could an Epic Vagina not take advantage of this and deliver a tantalizing Mind Fuck experience that will get his sexual taste buds salivating. How amazing is it that a woman has the ability to penetrate a man's mind, even when she's not in his presence, and insert herself in the midst of his busy day. Leaving him, his sex brain and his penis, to enjoy in these pleasurable thoughts, one's that will help intensify the chemistry that they share and also intensify the attraction he has for her.

This type of effort may appear to serve solely to the sexual relationship, but it actually has a way of making the relationship even better...In every aspect. Keep in mind that the brain acts as a mission control center to everything, and it processes any and every type of mental stimuli that is received. Be it emotional, physical or sexual, the brain relies on all these collective mental stimulations as a way of forming perceptions towards our sense of fulfillment and our sense of happiness in a relationship. Each and every interaction and experience in the relationship provides us with some form of mental stimulation, and contributes to our overall sense of happiness. This is the very reason why in a new relationship, the chemistry is always intense and what we often refer to as the Honeymoon Stage. Anytime we have something new in our lives, the newness is what prompts us to invest great efforts into this exciting new find. All the Honeymoon stage really is, is a more frequent cycle of efforts and investments that naturally produce intense surges of stimuli to our brain. It has a way of creating an overall heightened sense of perception that makes the love feel even more magical, the sex stupendous, the attraction intense and the happiness euphoric.

Even when we are appealing to a man's sex brain, it is contributing to even the emotional aspects, and influences how a man perceives his overall state of happiness in the union. A highly stimulated brain is a happy brain. This is the exact formulation that goes into the Honeymoon Stage and a relationship can easily maintain such this sense of excitement and newness by cultivating an ongoing cycle that appeals to the brain and that helps keep this magical sensation alive. It can be the difference between a guy thinking 'Man, I love my wife and she's a great woman', and 'Holy crap! I have the sexiest, bestest woman in the whole freaking world!'

The great thing about executing a "Mind Fuck" is that even a simple delivery has the ability to create such an intense response. He may be stuck in his office and his penis may not be reachable, but his brain is always within reach and easily triggered. Sending him a sexually suggestive thought that's neatly packaged in the form of a simple message is quickly received by his brain and instantly relays the message down to his other "package" which processes it and turns it into an erection. VOILA! Mission accomplished! You've successfully inserting yourself into his day, and in a way that is so impactful that it's almost like your vagina landed smack dab right on his desk!. This is a very welcomed distraction to the penis's day, and the virtual sexual experience is enough to wake the penis from his flaccid slug like state. Men are enamored by a woman's ability to appeal to his sex mind even when she is not around. When a woman is unattainable in the moment, and immediate gratification of exploring these sexual thoughts is not a viable solution, it causes him to continue to desire her presence even more. They say that absence makes the heart grow fonder, and if you thought that this theory was effective, you should see how fond the penis grows in the absence of his coveted vagina when he can't reach her. This creates sexual tension, and a continuous build-up of anticipation for the potential gratification that's yet to come. This fuels his desires and intensifies the attraction that he has for a woman. He becomes fixated on her as the object of his desires, and as the source that can deliver him with ultimate gratification for what he's obsessing over.

When the male sex brain is exposed to such ongoing experiences throughout the relationship, it creates a heightened state of mental awareness for a man and it prompts him to crave her offerings and her presence in his sexual world. This is a great way to initiate the anticipation for sex, and it creates a foreplay experience even when we are not in our partner's physical presence. How amazing is it to be able to initiate sexual foreplay, before we even get home? It's like a sex crockpot, but even better, kind of like a cockpot! You know, like when you throw in a roast and some potatoes in the morning, and it's ready by the time you get home! These thoughts stew in his mind all day, and come night...Dinner is served! We're having your favorite, vagina with all the fixings! I assure you that this is one recipe that is always a hit, and that no mother in law can claim that she makes better than you. Hell, a woman can suck at cooking, serve burnt roast and lumpy mash potatoes…and as long as she's serving the much anticipated reward that he's been dreaming about all day, she's the woman of the year. Anticipation creates chemistry intense stimuli for the sex brain.

Keep in mind that the journey is just as important as the destination. Taking advantage of these opportunities to send little mind fucks in the middle of the day keeps things exciting. Remember, that sex is heavily influenced by all the mental aspects involved. Anticipation creates sexual tension, and sexual tension heightens a man's senses during physical intimacy, and it also intensifies the ultimate reward and sensations he experiences from sexual gratification. Basically, it can take an orgasm to stupendous magnitudes. Okay, so I'm sure by now we all see the benefits to appealing to a man's sex brain in the overall daily relationship. So, let's move on and get to the good stuff, and talk about all the ways in which a vagina can deliver a great "Mind Fuck" experience and get into his pants even when he's miles and miles away. Distance is no obstacle for an Epic Vagina, and that bitch knows how to make it work in her favor!

'Daytime Diva Sex Deliveries'

Unlike the Post Office, sex deliveries have a magical way of never getting lost, and always deliver an impact upon arrival. Delivering a sex dose to the penis during his busy day can be done in so many different ways, and it's really up to you on how you choose to clobber him over both his heads. No one knows a man's penis better than the vagina that services it. When it comes to what sort of things you could possibly send his way, it really comes down to what he finds most sexually appealing and arousing. Whether he's a boob guy, loves a great ass, has a foot fetish and gets an instant hard on at the sight of high heels, you can appeal to his deepest fantasies. As long as it tickles his fancy and tickles his balls at the same time and the thought of what you've placed in his mind causes him to get chills up and down his penis spine... then it's great resource material for daytime sex deliveries!

Daytime sex deliveries, or what I like to call "sexchanges," are a great way for a couple to stay connected, and keep that supercharge flowing in the relationship. It really comes down to how you choose to communicate and how you and your mate stay connected during the day. I, myself, happen to have a pretty tech savvy vagina, and I totally depend on my smartphone for anything and everything. In this day and age, we all pretty much have access to such technologies and this is the best way to get your little vagina fingers on his unsuspecting penis during the day. When it comes to the sexchanges and communications that my husband and I rely on, we take advantage of them all! Texting (AKA 'Sexting), emails, voice mails and even connecting with a phone call and chatting on the phone.

We always make it a point to partake in some sexchanges, and enjoy in the sexual energy that it creates in our daily routine. Sending sexts and sex-emails to that sexy male in your life is a great way to say, "Hey, my vagina is thinking about you, and I can't wait for your penis...I mean you to get home tonight!" When it comes to human relations, I know that we often view texting and emailing as an informal, and sometimes impersonal way of communicating. However, in this case it actually works to our advantage. Texting can create an element of mystery. It's like hiding behind a vagina smoke screen, and giving him just enough to enjoy in the moment, but not so much that it will disrupt his brain's ability to carry itself away to a nice little fantasy. The open-interpretation of a text allows a man to use his own imagination take it as far as he wants to go with it.

This is something that I often make a point of doing, and when I send my husband a sexy text, email or voice mail, I purposely make them short and to the point. There are times when I have sent my husband a naughty message that's infused with just enough penis potion...No sooner do I push, "send," than I get an auto-reply from his penis. It's amazing how quickly an erect penis can type. Sometimes, I will engage in a few playful sex-changes, fueling him even more and then leaving it at that. I will leave the thought with him to enjoy as I go about my day. Now, in his excitement, there's a very good chance that his erection will accidentally hit speed dial, as he desperately tries to get a hold of the vagina so he can attain the highest form of gratification available to him in such a limited moment. If he can't physically have the real deal, he at least wants to talk to her and discuss the all the wonderful terms of how this "deal" will potentially go down and when. In such a case, I often ignore his penis's call on purpose, and let it go to vagina voice mail. Sure, he will leave a message, a loooong one at that, and perhaps even make it a point to express the sense of urgency for me to return his call. Now, why would I want to do that? That would disrupt a wonderful moment for his imagination. Even if the penis makes it sound like the house is burning down, and he's making an emergency 911 call for the vagina to come extinguish his penis fire, letting the fire burn is a good thing and it helps keep the fire burning in the relationship too.

Sure, picking up the phone can lead to a sexy chat, and sometimes I opt to take the call, but I find that picking up the phone at a time like this can risk the discussion running its course when he has milked himself for all he's worth. And talks can quickly turn into "So, anyways, my boss is pissing me off today.... Don't forget to pick up the dry cleaning...and the dog needs to go to the Vet." By the time the call ends, so does the sexual energy and we're back to dealing with the daily mundane duties in our lives. Letting it ride also allows for the sexual energy to continue to build. Limiting the discussions sometimes has a way of being a good thing, and it's only when he gets home that he can finally express his pent up sexual tension with a "Man, you were naughty today. I really missed you! Let me wash up and I want to give you a foot rub." His heightened state of mind has him expressing his affections in any way he can. When it comes to timing and frequency of these deliveries, being spontaneous and inconsistent is a good thing. It creates an unpredictable and unexpected cycle, and this is what also creates excitement.

This is what we're aiming for, an unexpected sneak attack that catches him off guard. It's like pulling the pin out of a grenade, tossing it his way and then running for cover.... The male sex brain is aroused by the idea that the sexual relationship has such an unpredictable nature, and these deliveries create an even bigger spark in the relationship.

Now, this may be something that many of you are already well versed in, and you're vagina is putting out unlimited sexts on that unlimited penis plan smartphone. And if it's not something that you're already taking full advantage of, it's never too late to start. It's also easy to do, and it's up to you how and when you do it. Rest assured, that it doesn't take much to appeal to the male sex brain, and a penis is hyper-sensitive to even the slightest delivery that eludes to sex. There's no need to be sending him a five- minute movie clip of you and your vibrator having a solo sexfest just to catch his penis attention. Albeit, a personalized amateur porno clip featuring your bad ass, is probably the hugest surge of stimulation and arousal you could ever illicit out of a penis without physically touching it. Mind you, such over-stimulation is probably enough to send his penis into cardiac arrest...And with his erection taking up all the resources, the blood loss to his head could also cause him to pass out at the office. The last thing you need is for his boss to discover him passed out cold (or possibly dead) and still with an erection....Losing his job will most definitely cause him to lose his erection. Remember, stimulating the penis when you physically stroke it is a good thing. Over-stimulating the penis and causing him to physically have a stoke… not so good.

Okay, seriously speaking, no penis will ever complain about a personalized sex video, but the reality is that most vaginas don't have time for all that in our busy day, so let's stick with the basics because it's just as effective. From the time that pretty vagina awakes to the time she heads to bed, there are endless opportunities and moments that can provide us with good resource material. I never miss out on any opportunity to collect good resource material. During my daily morning routine, when I'm in the bathroom getting ready, I'll take a minute before I get dressed and snap a quick picture. Be it a naked selfie, or even dawning my bra and undies. Nothing says 'Good morning!' like a nipple shot to go with his espresso. A little goes a long way, and it's up to you to decide what you're comfortable with and how naughty you want to be. If your vagina happens to be a risk taker, and you feel like snapping a vagina collage with her in all her morning glory, then go right ahead and snap that vagina selfie. This is one time that kissy pouty lips, or that infamous duck face and fishy lips are a great thing. Such a pic may not be one for social media sites, but rest assured that posting this to his "Penisbook" is a welcome sight to his day.

You can opt to send just a simple picture, or even attach a naughty message along with it. Whether it's a simple caption, or a few words that tells a sexy story and helps create the fantasy in his mind. Like I said, as long as it appeals to his particular preferences, then it'll do the trick and turn his penis crank. My husband happens to be just like many other men who have a foot fetish and he's easily aroused by the sight of sexy toes. I take advantage of this and send him pics of my freshly painted toes. Anything goes, and it really comes down to what you feel comfortable with. Now, I know that along with the potential benefits of such technologies and resources, also come the potential exposures and risks that could cause concern for many of us. The idea of putting such private material out there means that once it leaves your little vagina hands, it's out there for good. There's never any knowing for certain that it will remain private, and it really comes down to discretion in the relationship.

Assuming that we are speaking on committed life-long relationships, where a couple's mutual mindset is to protect their interests and privacy, you have nothing to worry about. But there's no shame in less is more in terms of pictures you send. For those of us with kids, it's often hard to keep a phone private, especially when sometimes the best babysitter in a doctor's office is our own personal cell phone. We all have different variables to consider, be it shared computers at work, children, or any other exposures that may be cause for concern when it comes to being discrete. No one ever wants to explain to their child, why Mommy has pictures of her boobies on her phone, and why there are happy faces drawn in red lipstick all over her butt.

That said, when it comes to technology, there are many security features that can be used, such as lock codes. There are also applications that offer a private and safe way to communicate and send such intimate media. If the concern involves work computers or shared devices, you can create a personal email account that is used solely for personal penis/vagina use and never accessed from work computers. A guy may be able to talk his way out of the fainting erection incident, but having to explain nudies on his work computer may be a tough penis for his boss to swallow. It's all about being smart and staying safe. No one wants the risk of his penis 'selfie' pic popping up during a power point presentation at work. Mind you, if his boss happens to be gay, it might score him a promotion.

If it is possible to make it happen and find safe storage for that vagina media, it's a great way to stock up on photo shoot material that can be used in future sex deliveries. Nights where you get all dolled up for some sexy-sexy time, and you're dawning some lacy lingerie, snap a photo. As a side note, this is also a great foreplay opportunity. As he and his penis play photographer, you can pose for sexy picks and get him worked up at the same time. This material can be saved for another day, when he's least expecting it. What better way to relive an experience, than by sending him a larger than life reminder along with a little written reminder of all that took place that night. Not only will he relive this experience in his mind, but the penis is never left out as he too relives the same memories and erection he had then, as if he were right there back in that very moment.

It's little things like this that we can use to recreate passion. The ongoing renewal of excitement is what fuels his ongoing expressions of affection and his desire to express his happiness in many different ways. The ongoing heightened state of mind has a way of making a man fuss over his sexy mate, and it sure as hell has a way of making a woman feel even sexier. She becomes the object of his desires, and the showering of affections and vagina celebrations is what feeds a woman's confidence. Remember, that foreplay can be initiated any time of day, and such exchanges can be an exciting prelude for what's to come. Something like sending a photo of your clothes piled on the floor, attached with a message that reads, "Clothes are so over rated. I'm not going to wear them for dinner tonight. Did I mention that dinner is being served in bed?" And some added details of what is on the dessert menu and you'll have him thinking about "dinner" before he's even had breakfast! The excitement will build all day, and this is one time that traffic isn't slowing him down, not with his erect penis at the wheel.

Keep in mind that such daytime antics don't' only benefit the penis, and it's a great way to mutually enjoy in such naughty exchanges. Initiating it is the easy part, but getting his penis to shut up will be the challenge. Anytime you have a few vagina minutes to spare, you can send him a message that reads "Feeling frisky, and I'm open to suggestions…If I said I was up for ANYTHING tonight…what would your wish list entail?" Trust me, no penis will be at a shortage of ideas. Oddly enough, a man may be of little help when you say "What gift should we get my parents for their anniversary?" Now ask him what gift he'd like to give that vagina, and his penis will start shooting off ideas like a machine gun. These sexchanges are a great foreplay experience for both sides, and you too can look forward to all the gifts that are coming your way.

Like I said before, there's really no rules and you can be as creative as you like. Even a sexy voice message is enough to act as a foreplay tail gate party to the main event. When I get a good role play idea that I want to serve up, and unbeknownst to him I plan on playing nurse later that night…I will leave him a playful message saying, "Hi, this is the Naughty Nurse. I'm calling to remind you of your appointment tonight. Please don't be late." There's no need to leave cancellation instructions, because his ass is definitely making it a point to make this appointment. This instantly creates excitement and he now has something to dream about all day. Even when my husband is under the same roof, I will still rely on the mystery element and resort to texts. I will instruct him to pour himself a drink and when I am ready to call him up, I send him follow up instructions to come upstairs. Taking full advantage of creating sexual energy can also be done face to face. Sitting on the couch and sharing in a glass of wine and sexy talk is a great way to spark the chemistry.

My husband and I have these nights often, as we sip wine and enjoy in some sexy chat time. It's easy to get things going, and it's a great way for a couple to take a mental journey and explore sexual fantasy together. What starts out as "What is one thing you've always wanted to try, something that you thought about but never actually done?" The conversation takes off from there, takes many twists and turns and often has a way of landing us in the bedroom. Damn that penis, when he's at the wheel he always finds a way to veer off the turnpike and end up lost inside that vagina asking for directions.

Remember, that what often makes it so good is anticipation. A text can't actually deliver physical gratification, but it does delivery foreplay. You can use anticipation even if you're sitting across from one another at a restaurant. Tell him "I'm not wearing any panties." If he needs confirmation, you can even discreetly give him a little verification by handing him the panties you just removed in the little naughty ladies room… and let him cook on that for a bit. While the chef prepares your meals, his brain is already fried and he's prepared for action. He'll have to wait of course, and make it through his dinner courses before he gets a stab at his dessert. It's all about finding new ways to serve up the daytime sex deliveries and enjoy the same old reliable sexual energy that remains a constant in the relationship.

This is such a great vagina tool, that you could literally be in any place doing any other thing that's unrelated to sex, yet still feed the fire. Even if your vagina is at home doing laundry, you can have him thinking that you're warming that bitch up with some solo inspiration. Just make sure you don't shoot yourself in the vagina by painting such a believable penis picture that it prompts him and his penis to slip out of work early, just so he can race home for a 'nooner'. It's all sexy fun and mind games, until his penis busts through the door… and instead of the naughty nurse that he's been losing his penis marbles over, he finds you laid up on the couch eating potato chips and giving yourself a facial peel.

The penis doesn't like to be tricked, and it causes future sex deliveries to lose their appeal because he'll think that you're just bluffing and really waxing your ass. At the end of the day, taking advantage of daytime deliveries and sprinkling sexual energy in the midst of a busy day, is a great way to keep the fire burning and a man's mind yearning for that vagina all day long!

6. Dump the Frump: Dressing for Success Is a State Of Mind

When we hear something like "dump the frump," we think about a vagina make-over where she's ditching the old comfy sweats for more fashionable vagina wear that appeals to the penis's tastes. Even though we're not entirely talking about vagina make overs, there is some merit to a woman remaining mindful of the fact that men happen to be very visual creatures. The reality is that real life brings a lot of real shit our way. Sometimes there's no greater feeling than coming home, rubbing off all that make up and war paint, slapping that hair into ponytail and slipping into some comfy sweats. After a long-ass day, this can be wonderful soul food for the vagina and a much needed escape from our stressful world. And why shouldn't we be able to enjoy these days? We've damn well earned it. Not to mention, when we can finally enjoy the comforts of a committed relationship, one where there is great love… It's this very love that has a man appreciating a woman's natural beauty. A vagina waits her whole dating life to find this comfort. Long gone are the dreadful days of having to yield to such dating dilemmas like that "first over-nighter," where a vagina is sleeping over at the penis's house for the first time, and she has no idea how she will tackle the "morning-after" situation. At this point, the penis has never having seen the vagina with no make-up on and dressed down, so we set that vagina alarm clock at the break of dawn just so we can put on our face and make ourselves look sexy for when the penis wakes up. Little do many of us know, that a simple morning blow job easily erases the need for such dolled up efforts… forging the make-up and making it up with some morning sex can have that penis seeing all things Playboy, even when we really look like a hot mess.

Truth be told, sometimes the simple essence of a woman in her own skin and natural beauty is the sexiest thing of all. Not to mention, that the penis can find sexiness in many things, and guys find a dressed-down gal in sweats just as sexy as when she's suited up in lace and heels. Guys like a woman who is versatile, someone who can dress it up, dress it down, and even find comfort and beauty in her most natural state. It's really all about balance, about enjoying the comforts and having those days, and also making the effort to maintain all the wonderful elements that the relationship was built on. It's important to preserve these elements, not just because we want our spouse to continue to find us sexy, but because of what it does for a woman. It's about how a woman feels about herself, not only her physical appearance but also the sexiness and beauty that is found in her mind.

The funny thing is that they often say that women dress for other women. We often see our female peers as having more fashion sense than a man. Regardless of why we dress the way we do, the one important variable is that a woman should always find sexiness in herself. Of course the easiest way to feel sexy about yourself, is when your partner finds you sexy. That means that appealing to your partner will help you both. I happen to value my husband's opinion, and for me, it's important to not only make myself feel good, but to also appeal to my husband's likes. I've always appreciated the fact that my husband has always made it a point to express his attraction for me and take notice anytime he sees me looking sexy. Anytime we have plans to go out, and I am looking to pick an outfit for the night…I ask my husband for his opinion. I'll show him a few options, and when he sees something he likes he tells me, "Oh yeah, that one is hot! Wear that!" Obviously, I don't do this each and every time I get ready, but when it involves a date night, and the two of us are headed to dinner… I see this as an opportunity to set the mood for the entire night and to look sexy for my hot date (my husband being the hot date, of course).

I'm the type of woman who makes all my own decisions, and I never feel the need please others, except when it comes to my husband. I make it a point on special nights to make it about him, dress sexy for him and to appeal to all the things that help renew the appreciation he has for me in the relationship. This really isn't all about him, because this makes me feel sexy, too. We'll often be out to dinner, and he'll say, "Man, you look so sexy and hot tonight!" It works in my favor, because he spends the rest of the night clipping at my sexy heels and fussing over me. The thing is that "sexy" cannot be defined in just one way, and everyone has their own unique idea of what sexy is. We often assume that revealing clothing is what defines sexy… less clothes and more skin. And sure, cleavage always has a way of being sexy. For me, I happen to be that cleavage gal, and I feel sexy when I wear clothes that accentuate my curves and show off my figure. I like it, and my husband's not complaining, either.

The truth is that sexy is defined by how it makes you feel, and how it makes your partner feel. As long as it suits your comforts and appeals to your spouse, then that's all that matters. There's no need for a woman to dress like a hooker, if it makes her feel uncomfortable. And if a woman has great comfort dressing like a hooker and her partner loves the hooker in his life…then so be it! Hooker-Wife it is, and let her hooker it up to her heart's (and his penis's) content. There's no denying that a sexy pair of heels has a way of changing everything, included a woman's mood. And how she accessorizes that sexiness is up to her. When a woman feels sexy, and her mate sees sexy, all that sexy energy is what makes the mental aspects of the sexual relationship even better. If a guy defines sexy as a woman dressed in a ball cap, T-shirt and shorts, and sporting this cute get up makes her feel the same about herself…then take that vagina out to the ball game, and then take that sexy game and his balls back to the bedroom and hit a home run.

The reality is that physical attraction plays a big role not just in dating, but in the ongoing relationship, be it the visuals a man encounters on a daily basis, or the ones that are presented in the bedroom during sexual play. When a woman makes the effort to keep herself feeling sexy and keep appealing to her partner, it adds to her sense of confidence and happiness and it also influences the chemistry in the overall relationship. A man is quite appreciative of a spouse who stays sexy and that maintains all the greatness that has always fueled his attractions.

Like I said, you can't wear hooker heels and spandex every day, and even your guy wouldn't want you to do that. There are really no rules to how a woman should dress, how often she nurtures her sense of feeling sexy or confident and how often she fuels his penis fire. Keep in mind that sexiness is a state of mind. It's simply about making the effort to maintain our own sexy and happy state of mind, and also appealing to a partner's state of mind as well. Even on a day when I am heading to the gym, running errands or simply running non-stop until I get home and I opt to wear sweats or gym clothes, I still take the time to do my hair, put on a light dab of make up or lipstick and accessorize with a happy sexy smile. My husband enjoys all my looks, whether I'm sporting sneakers, and even when I'm in the bedroom wearing leather and lace.

The only rule that would apply is the notion that no woman should ever stop investing in herself. How we dress and how we see ourselves, directly influences the energy that we put out. So, when a woman stops investing in herself and putting in those efforts, she begins to stop putting out all the energy that comes with it. Men are quite receptive to how their partner carries herself, and they gage their perceptions and mindset on the energy that's being transmitted. If a guy comes home and finds his partner cuddled up in PJs and reading a book, he gages her mood as one where she feels like simply being cuddly or relaxing. Now if good ol' Larry comes home every day to find good ol' Becky in the same PJs he will be less inclined to pursue her as he thinks that he's bothering her. And he waits for the signs, or a day where she appears to be in better spirits… signs like her getting dressed up, being more chipper and sending out a different vibe and energy. When a woman finds herself in such a cycle, it will start to create a sense in her mind that he's no longer making the effort himself. He's not fussing over her like he used to, and why the hell is he not making me feel sexy anymore? Thus begins an endless loop for both parties to feel unsexy.

It's not to say that his feelings towards her have changed. He still loves her, he still wants to be with her…but it's starting to look like perhaps she doesn't even want to be with herself? He's not sure anymore, because most often our interactions are unspoken ones. Until a woman finally asks, why don't you fuss over me anymore? What is he supposed to say? "Because you don't look sexy?" That's not even what it's about. It's simply about the fact that he may feel that she has stopped fussing over herself mentally, and her perceptions of herself may also be affecting how she interacts in the relationship. It not only affects the sexual relationship, it can affect the overall relationship and a woman's overall perception of herself. I always say, the formula that creates greatness in a new relationship, is the very formula that will continue to create greatness as long as it's maintained and remains the same. Sure, real life brings real things, and it's unrealistic that any formula will remain unchanged through the course of time. As long as the changing and ongoing dynamic continuous to nurture the mutual happiness and fulfillment of both people in the relationship, then a healthy dynamic will continue to grow.

If a couple has always enjoyed the wonders of dress-up and play in the bedroom, then continuing to do so year after year will help fuel their chemistry. If this dynamic drastically changes, and once-upon-a-time sex becomes plain-Jane, missionary sex wearing a sports bra and hair scrunchie, well, such changes will naturally change every aspect in the overall relationship. Any time we stop appealing to the things that attracted our partners to us and us to our partners in the first place, then we'll naturally lose chemistry. Eventually it affects not only our state of mind and our desire to even invest in any elaborate ongoing efforts, but it starts to bring the entire energy and chemistry for our whole relationship.

Remember, that energy is contagious, and what we believe is exactly what we produce. And it can work the other way around, too. Sometimes, when we aren't quite feeling sexy or sort of blah, putting in the effort to change that around and dress for success has a way of creating the belief in our minds. Sometimes a blah feeling can easily be shaken with a little dressing up, a little lipstick and a little smile. It makes your brain smile, your heart smile…and it also makes his heart, brain and penis smile, too! It's not just about clothes and make-up, it's about any and all efforts we invest in ourselves. Even keeping up a good exercise routine, or any other health and wellness investment like a good diet and keeping active pays dividends in our relationship. All of these things keep good chemistry flowing in our brains and it fuels the desire to invest even further. The idea is that it's important to keep up the efforts and keep ourselves not only looking sexy, but believing that we're sexy…because when a woman believes she is sexy, her partner believes this, too…The penis will pretty much buy anything that the vagina is selling.

They do say that a sexy pair of heels has a way of changing a woman's entire sense of sex appeal, and a woman can say just about anything to a man, as long as she says it in heels. Sometimes all it takes is a sexy pair of heels and nothing on but a sexy smile… to get the sexy going and keep the sexy flowing.

7. Never Stop Dating Your Mate

I'm sure many of us have heard the saying "all dressed up and nowhere to go." And if that vagina is already dressing the part, you'd might as well take full advantage of it and take that sexy bitch out on the town. There are many things that help keep the sexy vibe in a relationship. And the one thing that I have stressed in many previous discussions is that the best way to preserve the greatness in a relationship is to maintain all the variables and elements that this greatness was built on. Think about all the chemistry and excitement that comes with a new relationship, and during the courting stage of "dating and getting to know" one another. This stage is filled with fun dates, and all the new adventures that we want to experience with this new man in our lives. It's a time of discovering and exploring, embarking on many "firsts" together as a couple, and creating memories that leave a lasting impression in our minds and in our hearts.

I know that many of us think that it's only natural to have such chemistry and excitement when something is new, but that it naturally fades over time. And yes, the newness factor alone can easily create that intensity and insane chemistry. However, it's not just about the simple 'newness" factor, it's about the role our brain plays in how we perceive these experiences. The perfect fit of whatever brings us together in the first place is what excites the brain. If new were the only exciting factor, then no one would ever really have a bad dating experience. If it was solely based on the newness factor, you could pluck an asshole off the street, and have a romantic dinner with just about any prick. It's all in what is created in our brain, and when the brain is highly stimulated by one source, it heightens everything encompassed in that source and the overall relationship.

So, the penis picture that I'm painting here is pretty straight forward...unlike an actual penis that for some reason is never really straight. When you really think about it a penis is often either a "righty" or a "lefty" and pretty much every guy is pitching a curve ball…weird, right? Okay, sorry…back to the penile point… It's important for a couple to try and preserve this greatness, and keep the excitement that bonded you together alive. In my relationship, the most notable element that brought my husband and I together was our sense of humor. From the day we met, we would try to top one another's jokes and spend hours laughing about the same silly things. Our humor is so in sync that we will often just glance at one another and without a single spoken word we will burst out laughing. These are the things you want to maintain and nurture throughout the years.

I know that the common perception is that once that newness fades and the years pass, the dynamic changes in the relationship. Yes, things do change, but shouldn't change in the way that many couples often find in their relationships. The dynamic can and will change, and the relationship will evolve and a couple will grow together. These changes can be good for the relationship, especially with the comfort and security that commitment brings. Throughout this entire journey, it is very possible for a couple to still have great chemistry and feel a sense of excitement for one another. The reason why couples find themselves in a state where the chemistry has diminished is because their sense of comfort often evolves into a state of complacency. When people begin to develop a sense of dependency in their expectation for relying on such comforts, they become complacent and less motivated to continue investing in the relationship with great efforts. Even long after the newness stage has long passed, it is very possible for a couple to preserve the chemistry and excitement that they share for one another. And as long as they continue to invest in all the same efforts and practices that their chemistry was built on, then this energy will remain a constant in the union.

I know this may seem easier said than done. Especially when real relationships involve real life with very real responsibilities that grow along with the relationship itself. There's no denying that when a couple is newly dating, this era comes with little worries and responsibilities. Fast forward in the real world, where responsibilities grow, families grow, and playing house and dress up in real life comes with many added stressors and obstacles. I, for one, can totally vouch to this real life challenge. Daily schedules can bring work commitments, parenting, school-shuttle service, sporting events and activities for the kiddies, errands, grocery, laundry, scrubbing toilets, feeding dogs, cats, birds, and even goldfish.... Oh and a stupid ant farm that seemed like a good idea at first, until all those little buggers broke free and began infiltrating your bed and ass while you tried to sleep. I get it, you get it, and we all get it. But just because it's understandable, doesn't mean it's not still detrimental to your relationship. If your bond doesn't get the nurturing that it needs in order to thrive and survive, the relationship will no longer function in the way it once did.

So, the long-penis, short-penis of it all is this... A couple should never stop dating one another. Even after marriage, even after ten or twenty- year anniversary celebrations, a couple should make the effort to preserve the dating element in their union. If a couple loses that sense of excitement, the ten or twenty-year anniversary can begin to feel a lot less celebratory and a lot more like an indefinite prison term. Now, when I say that you should never stop dating your mate, keep in mind that "dating" comes in many forms and can be enjoyed in many wonderful ways. The obvious type of date that comes to mind, and one that every couple should make the time for...is dressing up, heading out and having a date night. There is no replacing this one, and for good reason.

The majority of our time is often spent in the environments that require something from us. Whether our work is defined as a fulfilling career, or a daily mundane job, it is still a commitment and it's taxing. When we're not working, we are back at our home base, and spend the remainder of our time in the home that also requires work. Many of our daily environments are symbolic of all the responsibilities we have in our lives, and quite often all the stressors that come along with it. It's not to say that having a date night at home isn't beneficial, and we'll get to that in a moment. Right now we are talking about the benefits and importance of removing ourselves from such environments....and by doing so, we also remove ourselves from all the stressors and distractions that are tied into these environments. Think about it, how appealing is the thought of a date night at your office?

A couple needs to make the effort to not only remove themselves from their daily physical environment, but to also remove these things from their minds and simply enjoy each other's company. When we place ourselves in a new setting, it's easier to focus on each other and leave our other responsibilities behind. A date night should be an escape from the ordinary, a fun light-hearted experience filled with laughter and good times. Such an experience recreates the excitement when a couple first met.

And let us not forget about the brain. When our brain re-encounters an experience that reminds it of a past memory and era, it automatically stimulates the brain into reproducing all the same sensations and feelings that come along with this memory and era. Think about when you smell something familiar, hear an old song, or see something symbolic that triggers a happy memory from childhood or past experiences. You automatically get this comforting sensation as you are reminded of all the happiness that's tied into this memory. Good times, right? You see, when the brain can pull from past memory data, and an experience is one that replicates a past experience, the brain doesn't bother forming new perceptions and it naturally relies on what has already been formed.

When a couple makes the effort to enjoy nights out and do the things they used to do back when things were new, it mentally takes them back to a time when they were just dating and simply just boyfriend and girlfriend. Keeping date nights a constant in the relationship, helps keep a couple connected and it also helps keep the spark alive. This is a great opportunity to get dressed up and feel sexy and for your partner to dote on your sexiness and express his affections. When a couple removes themselves from their normal environment, it puts them in a better happier state of mind, and a better mood. This makes us feel more at liberty to act fun, have fun and just be funny. Making date nights a constant in the relationship replenishes the bond that a couple shares, each and every time they are out. All the happy little neurons in our brain renews our emotions and reinforces our happiness.

From the early stages in our relationship, my husband and I have always been committed to making the time for weekly date nights. This may sound like a lot, but you can't put a price or limitation on the things that preserve greatness in the relationship. As parents to young children, we often feel guilty to take such time for ourselves. I am one of those mothers always motivated by guilt, and despite my greatest efforts, I always feel that I could have done more. While we do invest great efforts into shared family time and make it a point to do things as a family, it's also important for us to have couple time. At some point those little love bugs need to go to sleep. My husband and I often head out on date nights at a time where our son is headed to bed, and the sitter's only job is to ensure that he's okay and the house doesn't burn down. Through the years we have relied on both family and trustworthy babysitters to help make this happen. This dynamic allows me to enjoy our date night guilt free, as I know that my son is in good hands, and I'm of no added value while he sleeps. He can't miss me while he's sleeping, and although there's no greater pastime in the world than watching your child sleep (heart melts!) I recognize the value in nurturing the bond I share with my husband that is of equal importance to my overall happiness. This is also fundamental to strengthening the overall family bond, and nurturing the entire family unit as a whole.

Truth be told, we are doing our children a service by nurturing ourselves and the relationship. By maintaining all the practices and rituals that feed our heart and happy brain, it makes us not only a better spouse but also a better parent. This is something that many couples stop taking advantage of, and they don't realize the value in keeping up such elements in their relationships. On this point, I'm reminded of a couple I know, who have allowed for such dating practices to fade. Throughout the years have grown into a family of three young children, a dog, a cat, a minivan to pack them all into, not to mention a trunk-load of responsibilities and stressors that come with real life. This couple has been together for almost twenty years, and in the ten years that I have known them, they have never had a date night. Actually, their only alone time is when they are lying in bed at night.

Most of their days are spent to home, and at any given time when they are all under one roof, there's always some sort of chaos. Sure they have fun times, but there is also a ton of pent-up 'cabin fever," which is often a side effect of the brain never having the chance to escape and recharge. At their house, kids bounce nonstop, dogs leap across the house, the mom shouts, and the father runs after the kids. In speaking to this couple, they both admittedly confess that by the time they hit that mattress at night, they are mentally drained. Even when they do have the physical energy to partake in sexual intimacy, their distracted state of mind lends little excitement or flare to the experience. Their only way of mentally coping with their day-to-day lives is to laugh it off when they jokingly say, "Yup, we haven't had a date night in over twelve years!" or "Date night what's that?" They may be joking and chuckling when they say it, but the reality is that it has drastically affected their union and the bond that they once shared. They have become co-parents, and their strongest bond is the titles that they hold as husband and wife. A title in itself is of little value when the role they play in each other's lives is so diminished. Neither one is truly happy, and it's evident that they are happy as a family, but not as a couple.

Weekly date nights may not be a doable reality for everyone, but it's important to at the very least make the effort and the time for date nights and on a consistent basis. As long as these dates are often enough to provide couples with an escape from the everyday, then that's all that matters. I have worked with couples who echo the sentiments of many others out there, when they say, "we just don't have the time for date nights." But, when there is a will, there is a way. And where there is lack of time, there is often a lack of effort. Sure, sometimes there really isn't anytime to be found, spared or rationed out. There are weeks, sometimes two or three in a row, where my husband and I have so many other family commitments that date nights are placed on hold. However, we have invested enough great effort throughout the years that in times like these, it has no effects on our overall union and it sees us through. The problem is that people often don't recognize the importance of such efforts, and they see a date night as an extracurricular activity, and not a necessity. Well, if we waited for these days to come, they never will. Extra time never falls in our laps. It's no different than the idea of expecting a pay check and not putting in the hours at work. We make the effort to show up at work because we get paid. Making the time to connect as a couple and nurturing the relationship is just as important, and it should be viewed as an effort no different than any other one in our lives. Not putting in the work in a relationship, and expecting a paycheck automatically, is never going to happen. When the efforts decline, the relationship will one day stop paying out.

On the topic of paychecks… a common challenge for many couples is money. They may have the time to give, but finances don't allow for extravagant date nights. Understand that there is no set standard for what defines a great date night. Whether it's a fancy dinner at some chic steakhouse, or a stroll in the park and stopping for an ice cream cone. It's not always about the money, and more so about the time spent together and the benefits that these efforts have on the relationship. My husband and I rotate all sorts of date nights. Some nights we will go to a coffee house and have a tea or coffee, take a stroll in the city or by the lake. And sometimes we go all out, get dressed up and head out for a night of dinner and dancing.

During times when it's not feasible to actually leave the house, like when there is no sitter available, impromptu date nights in are just as fun. As long as you shut out all the distractions, and time is spent together uninterrupted, it still has its benefits. My husband and I have these nights often. We will pour some wine, sit in front of the fireplace, have a movie night, or even sit out on our back deck and under the stars listening to music. The wonderful thing about staying connected and keeping the fun element alive is that it has a way of truly connecting a couple in a best friend sort of way. A couple sees one another as their "fun time" partner and as the person that they can have fun with in any setting anytime. You could literally put my husband and me in any place, and in any setting, and we will find a way to make the most of it and just have fun. One of our most favorite pastimes is people watching, as we sit on a bench in a populated area. We sip coffee and watch people interact.

It's like watching reality TV live, with colorful characters that all tell a story as they pass us by. We have the ability to make the most out of the smallest opportunity, and even at night there are times before bed where we lay and giggle in the dark. One of us will start with something comical and before we know it we are laughing our asses off in bed. Sometimes it gets so out of hand, and in an effort to control my breathing from my uncontrollable laughter, I lose control of my bladder and end up peeing myself. True story! And I am not ashamed to admit it, because these are the things that we love about our relationship. The fact that my husband can make me piss my pants laughing while we are in our PJs, in our bed and right at home. You see, we may be in our home, the environment that I cautioned about earlier and the one to escape from. However, it's only because of the mental effects that such environments have, and sometimes if staying at home is the only option, the only requirement is that you have the ability to mentally escape from the reality of the everyday world. Mentally taking yourself to that place and having fun is enough to recreate all the fun that was once had back when things were new.

It's all about making the effort and the time, and recreating that fun vibe. A couple should never stop dating one another, and when we recreate the times, we recreate the new boyfriend/girlfriend roles, and also recreate the happiness and intense chemistry. Placing this effort on infinite repeat will continue to provide the same great benefits over and over and until the end of time.

8. The Unpredictable Vagina: Maintaining a Good Poker Hand

I'm sure by now we have a good understanding of the role that the brain plays in our relationship and satisfaction. As we talked about before, the brain has a hyper-sensitive responsiveness any time it is exposed to new stimuli. If the stimulation remains the same over a prolonged period of time, the brain starts to become immune to this unchanged variable. In vagina terms, the same old thing day in and day out starts to become boring. It loses its appeal, and that's because the brain likes to cash in big and reproduce those enjoyable high levels that also come with all the added elated happy vibes. This is exactly why eating the exact same peanut butter sandwich for lunch every day, and for a year straight is enough to make any vagina upchuck. That is unless it's a penis sandwich, and as long as it's being garnished in new and excited ways no vagina ever bores of a good penis hoagie! When you change the variable, you change the stimuli, and by rotating a variety of variables in an unpredictable manner, you consistently deliver a high level of stimuli to the brain and the brain remains highly responsive. In simple terms, the best way to keep a man on his toes and highly responsive is to be an unpredictable vagina. This is the exact reason why men gravitate to the idea of sexual variety. It helps keep the mental stimuli on high and keeps the sex from becoming that same ol'boring and predictable peanut butter sandwich.

This not only applies to sex, but to the overall relationship. And what's good for the bedroom is good for every other room and every other aspect of the union. I'm sure we can all agree that one of the most desirable elements of a committed relationship is the security and consistency it brings to our lives. It's not so much that the dynamic stays consistent, and more so that it brings a reliable sense of comfort and the predictability in knowing that what is here today, is here to stay and will be here tomorrow. Granted, such predictability only comes when we ourselves are continually investing in the efforts to keep it that way. The most stupendous part about finally having commitment in our lives, means that we can finally stop playing games! Maybe the vagina didn't play a part in initiating the games, but dating sure has a way of sending losers our way. And even the nature of dating itself, the madness of not knowing "when is he going to call?" and then "why didn't he call?" and then, of course, "that small dick mother fucker didn't call!" Vagina fury always has a way of shrinking a man's penis size. It's amazing how there's never a shortage of words in the dick-tionary when the vagina is on a penis smothering campaign.

Okay, so where were we? Ah yes, finding reliable consistency in commitment, and no longer having to endure the dating game. To an extent, this does hold true. However, consistency and predictability should not mean we go on autopilot. Even though our days of playing penis head games are over, a certain level of unpredictability is something that the penis brain finds quite appealing. Men actually see this as a desirable quality in a woman. They are drawn to a woman who brings a sense of unpredictability to their lives, and a mysterious element for the unknown. The only time a guy is not drawn to such a quality is when it involves a woman's mood, or an unpredictable vagina that swings from happy and sappy to hell on heels in the wink of an eye....because one thing men would like to predict is how and when shit will hit the fan, and where the nearest Emergency Penis Exit is.

Vagina mood swings aside, a certain unpredictable and mysterious element in the relationship is what creates excitement, and anticipation for the unknown. Men see this as an adventurous quality, and as one that plays out quite well in the bedroom. This doesn't mean that in order for things to remain in high gear, it has to be something completely new each and every time. There's no need to constantly be pulling new Houdini tricks out of that vagina, and it's the simple idea of finding new and exciting ways to serve up all the "goodies" you and he already know and love in a random rotation.

It's what I like to call "a good poker hand" and a vagina that's successful in always holding a good poker hand, is one who's also successful in holding a man's attention. Now obviously, commitment in itself naturally comes with such attentiveness in the union. However, when a woman has a good poker hand it creates an exciting element of cat and mouse pursuit. It has a way keeping a man on his penis toes and clipping at her heels. He's lured in by the unpredictable nature of her offerings, and never quite knowing what will come next. This is exactly why the new honeymoon phase of a relationship is so exciting, and it's because of all the unknowns and new discoveries have yet to be explored. Having a good poker hand is what recreates that sense of newness and a fun dating element. Inherent to their male nature, men are natural hunters. The male brain likes being on the prowl for new conquests, and is highly stimulated by the thrill of the chase.

This especially holds true for the male sex brain, and when it comes to sex it's in a man's nature to constantly be in a mental exploration mode. This theory is commonly misperceived as a man's need to constantly pursue new women, but the reality is that it has nothing to do with a man's desire to rotate a bevy of new beauties in order to satisfy their needs. What the male brain looks for is any way in which it can produce and keep reproducing a high level of intense stimuli. This quotient can easily be scored from just one source, and a man is truly and fully content when his relationship provides him with this sense of fulfillment. In my years of canvassing men on this very theory, most men have said that the appeal is in finding one woman that brings comfort and excitement, and the simple idea of variety in partners was less appealing. You hear that? Straight from the penis' mouth and right from the source, men prefer an unpredictable vagina. Thankfully, an epic vagina has just what the penis is looking for, and this is exactly where we come in. Same holds true for a woman, and it is human nature for our brain to seek ways in which it can constantly recycle those happy little neurons that provide us with an elated sense of happiness and fulfillment.

The importance of a good poker hand in the sexual relationship is to ensure that sex never becomes a predictable routine for the same ol' thing all the time, or even always at the same ol' time. It's important to switch things up both in frequency and in variety, as this is what helps keep sex from becoming stagnant and unfulfilling. I have a friend who once upon a time, found herself in this very penis pickle predicament. She and her husband had been married for ten years, they had two young children and both worked outside of the home. With both of them sharing a pretty loaded schedule, they found themselves in an ongoing and endless regimented cycle of the same old thing day in and day out. This carried over to the sexual relationship and for one reason or another they found themselves having sex only once a week. When it comes to sex, there's no real standard for what defines greatness. Like honestly, think about it…If the sex sucks then it sucks, and having more of it doesn't make it any less sucky. Sex once a week may not seem like it's often enough, but if a couple sees it as being stupendous sex and they both gain mutual fulfillment then this in itself is what defines for the relationship.

Unfortunately, in my friend's sucky circumstance, both the quality and quantity took a nose dive. For one reason or another, she and her husband found themselves in a lack luster ritual of not only having sex once a week, but on the same exact day, in the same exact way week in and week out. She herself had no idea how this came to be, as it was never really spoken about. Somehow it just became an assumed weekly sex ritual, that took place every Sunday night after they had put the kids down to sleep. They would each get ready for bed, turn out the lights and engage in a ten- minute round of very predictable, very mechanical missionary sex. No foreplay, no talking. And no fulfillment, even if and when either one of them achieved of an orgasm. Such physical gratifications were short-lived and left them both feeling unfulfilled.

This dynamic in their sex life remained unchanged for a really long time, and it eventually affected the rest of the relationship. Mind you, predictable sex alone is not what damages relationships.

What damages relationships is when couples stop investing in different ways to keep the relationship exciting, and allow themselves to fall into a mundane repetitive cycle that remains unchanged. It's not lack of excitement that kills the chemistry, and the unchanged repetitive variables are what no longer continue to provide the mental stimulation that this chemistry relies on in order to thrive. Eventually, this dynamic ceases to appeal to the brain's need for stimuli, and because we rely on mental stimulation as the source that fuels our sense of enjoyment and happiness it eventually affects our overall sense of fulfillment.

There's actually a shitload of science behind the concept of "boredom" in a relationship. And even though it's often viewed as a superficial ailment and immature outlook for people to have in their relationships…The fact of the matter is that the brain plays the biggest role of all, and requires a lot more nurturing than the heart, the penis and even the vagina. Remember, the brain is mission control centre, and without the ability for us to mentally decipher and translate everything for the heart, penis and vagina… they are merely blobs…There is no love, no emotions and no feel good vagina sensations if the brain is not around to process those chemicals, to turn them into perceptions and to form realizations and feelings. Knowing that the brain is the one to make shit happen, a smart vagina goes straight to the source…appealing to a man's mind and getting shit done. The brain will take care of the rest, and see to it that all messages are delivered to the heart and penis. Trust me, this operation never sleeps and his brain is his most efficient worker who never takes days off.

The idea of having a good poker hand is that at any given time, you can unexpectedly pull a wild card out of that vagina, put an unexpected twist on things and VOILA! Being a card shark and hustler is not all that hard, you just gotta know when to hold 'em and know when to fold 'em…and in a way where he'll never be able to read your vagina poker face. So what exactly is required of an unpredictable vagina, and what does this card game entail? Well, it basically involves everything that the relationship relies on now, and simply changing certain variables. For me, I simply look to tap into what makes my husband tick, and the things that makes his brain most responsive. One of the easiest things to tap into is something that's readily available to you at all times…and that's you! Go with you—all the wonderful characteristics of your personality, and your female persona. Confused yet? Okay, I'll stop beating around the vagina bush and get straight to the penis point…

The Three Ladies in His Life

I'm sure that any penis reading the above captioned title is ready to spontaneously combust by the overly stimulating idea that there's about to be an orgy starring none other than his over-zealous erection and three scantily-clad vaginas of his choosing. Actually, this is not what we're talking at all. I know, I know, I can hear all the booing penises now…As if the vagina is to blame, and it has nothing to do with the five- inch slice of birthday cake that the penis is trying to ration out in three ways. Anyway, before anyone gets their vagina flaps in a bunch over the idea that that this story involves three other bitches, let me explain by saying that there's only one bitch...and that bitch is you! There's only one woman in his life, but she represents three female personas that bring a man the most happiness. And when is a man most happy? It's when he has excitement in his life, when he can rely on emotional security and when his sexual needs are met with great fulfillment. So, who are these three vagina characters?

'The Ex-Girlfriend':

No, I'm not talking about the woman he dated before you, so put the stiletto down and don't worry because that bitch is not making a come-back. I'm actually talking about you. Once upon a time, long before commitment, you were the new girlfriend in his life. And as relationships progress so do our female roles...We are no longer the new girl on the scene, and we eventually trade our girlfriend title in for that of a wife or a committed long term partner. My husband actually coined the term "ex-girlfriend" and he's always jokingly said that once I became his wife I was no longer his girlfriend. Well, being that I no longer was his "current" girlfriend, I became his "ex-girlfriend." And that's because even though the title was retired, the girlfriend persona never has been. Of the three, this is the persona that brings the overall excitement element to the relationship. Anytime we find ourselves being carefree and simply having mindless fun, my husband always says, "I love my ex-girlfriend." My husband is appreciative of such fun experiences and he's reminded of a time when we first started dating, and all the adventures that came along with it. It's important to preserve the fun dating element in a relationship, and when we resurrect such girlfriend like behaviors it also stimulates the same happy memories and chemistry.

Every woman should maintain an "ex-girlfriend" persona, and spice things up by throwing that bitch into rotation once in a while. What better time to tap into that fun girlfriend mindset, than when you're out on a date night. You can create a care-free fun vibe through a little playful flirting, and acting just like you did back on those first few dates. There are times when I like to tap into my ex-girlfriend persona, and plan something fun to go along with it. I will send my husband a text saying, "Where's my ex-boyfriend? When is he coming home?"...Obviously, he, too, is my "ex," and the contagious energy I create prompts him to also resurrect the same behaviors and reactions from this dating era. It's like role playing, and we refer to one another as if they are different people and characters other than ourselves. By placing ourselves in a certain place in time, not only does it recreate the memories, but it also has a powerful way of influencing how we act and interact with one another. There are times when my husband and I are engaging in some playful frisky banter and time alone. I will say, "Your ex-girlfriend is feeling naughty tonight. Wanna hang out with her for a while?" And of course, he jumps right on, board by saying "Yes, I do, and yes, she is! What does my ex-girlfriend have in mind?"

Now, I know that this may sound corny, but trust me, the penis loves corny and he eats it up! It's the power of persuasiveness, and the suggestive nature of tapping into this persona is what recreates that chemistry in the relationship environment. It creates such a sense of believability, that it can influence your mindset as well. Just by acting the part, you start to feel the part. I sometimes find myself almost possessed by the "ex" mentality, because of how it makes me feel and how it makes my husband respond to this persona. It really has a way of making a woman feel sexier.

'The Good Wife':
The second persona is an easy one, and encompasses the element of comfort and security. It's the wonderful role that you hold as a female spouse in the committed relationship, and she represents all things loving and secure, and is the stability in his life. Now, don't think that the "Good" reference simply means a well-behaved 1950s wife. It simply means all the goodness you bring to the overall daily relationship and your nurturing alter ego (Trust me, when we get to the next role you'll see why this persona is a good super hero). This persona loves to dote on her partner, and she celebrates him in all his manhood glory. She is committed to investing great efforts into fulfilling his needs and bringing happiness to his life. This basically taps into the ideas that we have discussed throughout the book. It's about a woman becoming the ultimate caretaker of a man's emotional needs and placing him as a priority in the relationship.

Remember, that ALL energy is contagious, and such efforts motivate a man to reciprocate in the same way towards your needs and happiness. You can tap into this persona by investing in daily efforts to show your affections and spend intimate time connecting one on one. This persona is the rock in the relationship, and she is her partner's best friend. Trust me when I say that it's an important role, and no different than a chess board where the Queen acts as the most powerful pawn in the game. The "good wife" stands by her partner through good times and through challenging times. Teaming up as a unified force, a couple acts as each other's support system and each other's biggest fan club. I have found this role to be the most fulfilling and empowering in my relationship, and because I invest great efforts as a wife my husband truly celebrates my greatness and treats me like a Queen. It's this very role that provides me with great comfort and security. And this is what fuels my ability to unleash all my other persona's and explore my sexuality. It's the security in itself that feeds my comfort to be wild and crazy, and push my sexual boundaries to unimaginable heights in our sexual relationship. Who knew that the symbolic security of wedding rings leads to the comfort of exploring cock rings? So, keep in mind that this role may seem pretty standard, but it actually acts as the glue that fortifies the rest of the relationship.

'The Mistress Wife':

Once again, let me clarify that this title is not reflective of a "once-was" mistress who eventually marries her lover. Now I know that when we hear the term "mistress" we automatically associate it with infidelity. However, for the purpose of what this role represents, it has nothing to do with the common social perceptions. This term is simply a play on the social stigma of a mistress and of being a little bit naughty, which the penis loves. In the world of sexual erotica, a mistress is the embodiment of female sexuality and the epitome of a man's sexual desires. She exudes sexual confidence, has no inhibitions and she's like the ultimate sex super hero.

The Mistress Wife is a woman who not only holds the role of a committed spouse, but also as the woman who makes all of her partner's sexual dreams and fantasies come true and is the ultimate caretaker of his sexual happiness. She may be a good super hero, but she has the ability to be a villainess and naughty sex vixen. So don't mess with her! Okay I'm kidding, because this is one bitch that the penis can't wait to mess with. The mistress persona leaves the job of love-making to the good wife. The wife persona can handle all the "making love" aspects of the sexual relationship, and nurturing the emotional connection that is shared in the union. Things like listening to Lionel Ritchie love songs, rose petals, staring into each other's eyes and all that lovey dovey jazz. This mistress persona, and badass bitch brings a world of sensual erotica, sexploration and uninhibited wild sexcapades.

Tapping into this persona is a great way to explore in sexual fantasy and sexual role play. She unleashes all things naughty and kinky, and turns his world on its ass! When it comes to sex, the mistress persona may be a show stopper, but the show never stops when she's on stage. She is a genie in a bottle, and has the ability to make any of his sexual fantasies a reality, and all of his penis wishes come true. She is so powerful and sexually uninhibited, that this bitch will be bringing home the Oscar every year with her Academy Award winning performances.

You see, being the wife and mistress persona in one, we have the upper hand. We know our fella inside and out, and know all his little inner secrets of what makes him tick. We use the information that the relationship feeds us, and we deliver it back through this persona and clobber him over the head with it. The reality is that the majority of the overall relationship usually hosts to a couple nurturing the emotional aspects of their daily union. This mistress persona may not be one that is tapped into every single day, but having the ability to switch things up and turn up the heat every once in a while is a talent that every vagina should exercise. I tap into my mistress persona when my husband least expects it. I will go from loving wife mode to a wild sex vixen, and hit him with a sexy surprise. I will host to a night of all things sex, and even take requests.

My husband loves the idea that he never knows when this Mistress Wife will come out to visit, or when she will strike next. Sometimes, I will even play up the idea that this persona is someone other than his wife, and in the midst of a hot sexual encounter I will say to my husband, "Man, your wife will NOT be happy if she finds out about this." My husband often giggles with excitement and says, "NO, she totally won't be happy…Maybe we shouldn't tell her?" In the beginning he was a little apprehensive and nervous to play into all the 'having an affair' banter, thinking it was a trap. I'm sure any guy would think to himself that he'd better play it safe, because after she snaps out of her role she'll snap on his ass and beat him to a pulp with her stiletto, or even worse her 9 inch dildo. Talk about embarrassing, having to explain to your buddies that your black eye and limp were caused by a rubber cock beat down from your wife...because she caught you with your other wife, who are both one in the same. All jokes aside, this not only adds a sense of excitement, but it tricks the brain into believing that we're being naughty and breaking the rules. Only difference is that it's a good type of naughty...And you're never breaking any rules when your wife knows about your mistress and your mistress is your wife.

An Epic Vagina is a Triple Threat Diva

The idea of tapping into these three personas is that it not only creates variety and excitement in the relationship, but it preserves all the best qualities in a woman. You end up hitting him from every angle. The fresh new feeling of dating, the doting security of a life-long partner, and the wild uninhibited sexual fantasies come true. Who could ask for anything more? Not his penis that's for sure, he'll be too busy trying to keep up with these three bitches and all their wonderful antics. How excited is a man when he can proudly proclaim that he's dating the most amazing woman in the world, who also happens to be his wife...who also happens to be his mistress? It's enough to make any man pinch himself... make him wanna smack his own ass from excitement, and make him run out to the nearest tattoo parlor so he can get his wife's/ girlfriends/mistress's name tattooed all over his penis! Lucky for him (and his penis) that all these women are one and it's only one name...because let's be real here...there may always be room for many characters in the relationship, but there's only so many characters that actually fit on a six- inch penis.

See? You always have his back! That is unless you have a really long name, because if so he may have to sacrifice some extra space on his left testicle. That's okay, he's so high on love he won't feel it. Regardless, the idea is that you want to take full advantage of rocking his world by placing these three personas on constant rotation and always maintaining a great poker hand. You happen to be your own greatest asset in the relationship, and it's because men are drawn to a woman who is multi-faceted, someone who has the ability to transform herself into many different versions of one dynamic woman. She creates an illusion of fantasy, and she is many women yet she is still the one and only woman in his life.

Split Personalities on Vagina Rotation

This is one time that a man has no complaints with a woman who brings unpredictable split personalities to the relationship. The great thing is that you can tap into any one of these personas at any time, and you can host many wonderful adventures. It's important to keep the excitement in the relationship, and to find new ways to keep this a constant. And sometimes, new ways simply means tapping into some of the wonderful practices that were in place back in the days of newly dating. It's like an amusement park experience for the penis, a place with new rides and adventures every time he visits. The wonderful thing about rotating these personas in your poker hand is that there's never a dull moment when you're around. The reality is that not every moment of every day affords us the freedom to rotate all these personas on instant replay mode and to keep belting out endless vagina tricks. And this is good, because this isn't what we want. You don't want it to be a constant state of over stimulation and unrealistic events and efforts. There will be normal days of being in down low mode, unpredictable heightened days in intense mode, and a mix of little sprinkles of excitement in between. We actually want the variety and the ups and downs because this is what creates a roller coaster experience of mental stimuli for the brain and it is the very thing that creates the unpredictable nature in the relationship.

My husband is the first to say, that as much as he loves my mistress wife persona, if this was my only mode and the only vibe in our relationship he wouldn't appreciate her as much. Sometimes he simply wants to kick back with his ex-girlfriend, have some light hearted laughs and be silly. Other times, he wants to simply enjoy some quite intimate time with his 'Good Wife', cuddle up by the fire and listen to some relaxing music. My husband loves the qualities that each persona brings, and he loves the fact that I can bring such variety to the relationship. My husband often tells me that since the day we met, there's never been a dull moment. Even at times of rest and when we're in easy mode, he says I somehow always deliver exactly what he needs in his life. And that's the thing, it's about being in tune with your mate and knowing how and when to shift the tide and keep the chemistry on high. I've become quite in tune with my husband's queues, and know exactly how and when to assert any one of my personas. If he's had a long day at work and comes home exhausted, his 'good wife', will offer up a foot rub, or full body massage and then tuck him into bed.

When it's been a couple of days and I can sense that his sex cycle is peaking and he's a tad backed up, the "mistress wife" comes out in me and I'll give him some light foreplay and just enough to tease him. Keeping it unpredictable I don't always fully deliver, and sometimes I'll tell him that he will get his "treat" the next day after our date night. Come the next night, he's peaking with anticipation on our date, and I will simply bring out my "ex-girlfriend" persona and flirt the night away as I play into it. It's that simple. And some may see the idea of "tease and denial" and engaging in foreplay without having sex, as cruel punishment for the penis...but it's the good kind. The reality is that this is what creates sexual tension and anticipation and the male sex brain loves the enjoyable torture.

Trust me, no penis ever died from being teased and not getting it, and being a "cock tease" is quite impactful if a woman knows how to play it right. Another great way to deliver something like this is by having your partner sit back and take in a vagina solo show, while you and your trusty vibrator go at it. Perhaps this night he gets to partake in the sex festivities, or perhaps he stays benched and gets called into the game tomorrow. This is what a good poker hand is all about, and such unpredictable deliveries help create sexual tension, lust and attraction and intense chemistry in the relationship.

Rest assured, that the contagious nature of such efforts and the perception of happiness it creates in his mind, prompts him to partake in having his own little penis poker hand. My husband invests in an equal amount of efforts, and often brings his own surprises to the relationship. The great thing is that a man truly becomes appreciative of the woman that nurtures his heart, that makes him laugh and that rocks his world. She recreates that chemistry every time she resurrects that girlfriend persona. Keep in mind, that this is the woman he fell in love with and for every time she pops back on the scene, he falls in love with her all over again. These efforts and experiences have lasting power and they continue to play on in our minds. So even on those days and in times where there's no elaborate shows and events, the bond and chemistry remains a constant and the relationship is still riding high.

When you put in the work, it pays itself forward. And even when we have simple and predictable days, he knows that without a moment's notice all of that can change. He may be able to predict that something may come, somewhere and at some point…and his anticipation for what's to come is what he enjoys most. A good poker hand will have him not knowing what the hell he's looking forward to, but whatever it is he knows it will be damn good! How can he be so certain? It's because he feels that he lucked out with a damn good woman in his life…no scratch that…He knows that he landed a fucking epic and great woman, one that makes him feel as though he's the luckiest man alive.

9. Penis & Vagina: Best Friends for Life

There is no greater feeling in the world than having a best friend in a mate and knowing that the person you share your life with is not only your spouse but also your best friend. We all know that when it comes to friendships, a "best friend" is someone who totally understands you and who is there for you no matter what. This type of friendship combines both a sense of security and support, and also a fun element filled with laughter and good times. The funny thing is that commitment and a 'best friend" friendship isn't always a package deal in relationships. Men and women alike, often share a friendship with their spouse, yet they still rely on their "best girlfriend" or closest guy friend outside of the relationship. There are really no rules when it comes to committed relationships and the friendships that we share with a partner or with those outside of the relationship. However, there's something to be said about two people who are not only lovers, but also best friends. It's the ultimate connection in a relationship.

It's truly a privilege to be able to say that "he's not only my husband, but he's also my best friend." Think about it, we share our entire lives with this one person. We expose our vulnerabilities, our insecurities, and we seek shelter in the comforting arms of love and commitment. We intimately connect and we ultimately want to feel as though this one person will protect us and make us feel safe. It's nice to know that we are not only supported emotionally, but that the relationship supports our interests and simply brings laughter and good times to our lives. What often distinguishes successful relationships from others, is this very dynamic and a couple being best friends. Like anything else in the relationship, it's just as important to build and nurture the friendship. The importance of good communication in the relationship is not only to help a couple express their feelings but also sort through their issues. Sharing and talking about our daily lives, seeking advice, giving advice, and supporting one another helps a couple connect as friends. There's no substitute for knowing that this is the one person you can confide in, and he's someone you can trust with your deepest secrets and know that they will always have your best interest at heart.

Think of the friendships that we as women share with our female peers and all the greatness such friendships bring to our lives. Men too share such a dynamic with their guy friends. The best friend dynamic in the relationship should be no different, and despite the fact that two people are of the opposite sex, the friendship should bring that same greatness. Quite often people rely on the emotional aspects of the relationship as what defines their friendship, and couples don't always recognize the importance and benefits of all the other elements found in a best friend relationship. In a committed relationship people sometimes struggle with the idea of assuming a neutral friend role, because of their emotional investments. It requires a great deal of emotional maturity for us to not place our own needs for security when we are trying to be a supportive friend to our spouse. This is why many couples never truly achieve that best friend dynamic. It's not to say that unless there is such a friendship that a relationship will fail. Again, the bond of a friendship is what defines in committed relationships, and this is exactly what an epic vagina is after.

One of the most valuable offerings of friendship is the fun element that it brings to our lives. Sometimes people become consumed with the need to feel grown up and act grown up, that they lose sight of that fun, lighthearted element. They say that laughter is the best medicine, and it's quite true that when a couple laughs together and has fun together it connects them in a unique way. It goes without saying that the relationships we as women share with our female peers are quite different than the friendships that men share with their male counterparts. And there's no denying that we as women will never quite understand the friendships that men share, and in the same way that men too will never quite appreciate our female friendships. In a man's eyes, women like to congregate and cackle like hens while gossiping about shopping and tampons. And in a woman's eyes, male rituals involve grown men acting like kids, talking about sports and flexing their penis's muscles. The reality is that sometimes there's no replacing that same sex dynamic, and the idea of pedicures and football doesn't always make for a mutually gratifying experience. And this is okay, because like we discussed earlier, it's important for both men and women to maintain friendships outside of the relationship. Having the ability to connect with our own kind and partake in rituals that nurture our unique identity in the relationship.

With that being said, it's important for a couple to support one another's interests, and for each partner to have an interest in what the other identifies with and enjoys doing. Part of the reason why couples don't always share a best friend dynamic is because they don't entirely identify with the interests of their partner. Sometimes people feel as though the relationship is not entirely supportive of their interests, or the practices and rituals that are unique to their male/female identity. Now, this is not exclusive to men, but being that we are focusing on men and their needs, we'll discuss this end of it. Men actually appreciate the idea of being able to spend time with their male friends and partake in male like rituals. Sometimes, there's no replacing the pastime of watching a sports game with the guys, heading out for a round of golf, or simply hanging out in a testosterone infused environment and doing dude like things. Sometimes men want to be in a male only 'No vaginas allowed' environment. I know that I'm referencing many stigmas here, and it's not to say that art galleries and food expos are not equally embraced by the male following as is scratching balls and football.

The idea is that even though men appreciate this all male friendship dynamic, they equally appreciate a partner who is embracing of all the same things. A man likes to feel as though the friendship in the relationship allows him to be himself, and that he can hang out with his female spouse in the same way he does with his guy friends. He may not have a need for her to golf with him and the guys every weekend, or sit on the couch and catch a game with the boys…but he likes to know that it's a doable reality in the relationship and that she likes to be around him and his friends. A man also wants to feel that he can be himself and be the same person, whether he's with his guy friends alone and even when he's with his spouse and friends all at the same time. This is why it's truly important for women to make the effort to not only embrace in his "maleness," but to invest in partaking in these interests and supporting the friendship.

This is common area in the relationship where couples often find themselves becoming disconnected. Once upon a time, they both shared similar interests in many of the same things, and for one reason or another one partner eventually loses interest in partaking in these activities or engaging in many of the pastimes that they used to connect on. This can create a disconnection in the relationship, and cause a spouse to feel as though they no longer share a strong bond with the partner that deserted the good times. Eventually, a couple slowly grows apart and they lose that friendship bond. This is why it's important to nurture the friendship and maintain all the interests you two have always shared in the relationship and that has always brought you two together. And it's not to say that if you two always golfed together, that you have to tee up until your tits fall off and retire. Sometimes couples discover newfound interests and hobbies they both enjoy, and the important thing is to make the effort to maintain the connection and keep the friendship alive.

My husband and I have always shared this dynamic in our relationship, and all of the friendships in our lives are ones that are mutually shared in the relationship. My husband will be the first to say that the one thing he loves the most in our relationship is that we are truly best friends. He loves the fact that he can hang with his friends and his wife at the same time, and that the dynamic is no different than if it was just the guys. I have always made it a point to truly embrace his interests and even his male behaviors and rituals. My husband truly appreciates the ability to act himself around his friends, even when I'm in the mix. I mean sure, hanging with his friends may be a totally different experience than when I'm with the girls. However, because we connect as best friends, I truly enjoy being a part of every aspect of his life. It's almost as though I transition into my best friend persona, and simply put myself into a lighthearted fun state of mind. It's times like these where we simply remove ourselves from all of life's serious factors, all the emotionally complex factors and we simply have fun.

The funny thing is that my husband prefers to have me be a part of hanging with the guys, and he finds it less fun when I'm not around. I actually feel the same way, and because we are best friends the most fun is had when we are together. I sometimes have to urge him to make it a night with just the boys, and he is reluctant to go unless I tag along. I always say to him "Don't you want it to be just the guys?" and he always says, "No way, it's more fun when you come! You're funny and it's fun to see you torture my friends." By this I think he means that his friends are enamored by what I do, and the conversation often leads to women, dating and sex. And also often involves my sarcastic delivery of bursting their male ego bubbles with reality facts of fake female orgasms and average penis size. By the time these guys go home, they may have had a reality check but they appreciate the ability to be themselves and simply be real. What is it about guys poking fun at one another, being competitive and tearing each other down, and enjoying the shit out of it in the process? The funny thing is that when we as women are amongst our peers, we build each other up in saying things like "I love that sweater….You look amazing! That's so cool that you've taken up yoga." Guys are the exact opposite and will say things like "You've had that gut since high school… You totally couldn't keep up today, and we only ran three miles. Hopefully you have better stamina in bed with the wife, because with that huffing and puffing you're not taking care of business buddy."

Like I said, even though we may never understand men and their ways, the simple fact is that a couple should connect in every way and have a best friend dynamic that supports each partner's version of "fun." And being best friends doesn't have to mean that your guy is tagging along for mani's and pedi's at the spa, or joining you and the girls for a hot yoga session. I mean, it could be fun, but there's no need to partake in every female festivity just to say that you two are best friends. Especially if hot yoga is not his thing, or he's sensitive to heat and not all that flexible….because it's all fun and games until his sweaty testicles become strangulated in a downward dog pretzel and he ends up passing out. The last thing you need is to show up in the ER at the hospital, with his nuts in a sweaty knot and his toe nails painted red…Remember, the pedi's at the spa? When he was trying to impress your friends and make them laugh? Yeah, well his male ego definitely won't be laughing now.

The good news for you is that you too won't have to endure a day of playing tackle football with all of his friends and their sweaty balls. That is unless you want to, and if so, then throw your vagina in the game and go crush some skulls and some sweaty balls! The best friend dynamic in the relationship can simply be a merging of both worlds and interests, and creating your own unique friendship that supports having fun and staying connected. The funny thing is that my husband loves getting an insider view on what women like to do when they're together. He will happily sit through a girl's lunch and take it all in. He finds it amusing and quickly volunteers to partake in such girl activities. He's the guy that will come to the spa with me, get a "man pedi" and enjoy all the spa banter that he encounters. He's the guy that you can put in a room full of women, and within ten minutes become engaged in all sorts of female discussions. The funny thing is that ladies love him, and it's because he's a mix of charming and comical.

Taking the time to nurture a best friend dynamic in the relationship fortifies the bond that a couple shares. It connects two people not only as mates, but also as sidekicks for life. It creates an ongoing unified journey that's filled with fun adventures and good times. Sometimes what we really need in life is an escape from it all, and even the actual relationship. I know this may sound odd, the idea of wanting to escape from the relationship. It's not so much that we are escaping the relationship, it's more so that we are simply taking a break from all the serious stuff that often involves emotional nurturing and that requires us to tap into our emotional mindset. It truly takes an epic vagina to be able to put our emotional mindset aside, and simply be a fun and light-hearted supportive friend to our mate. Many moments in a relationship involve discussing emotions, discussing roles and discussing deep feelings. This in itself is great! The overall relationship should have this dynamic too, and such conversations should take place often. However, sometimes the mode calls for nothing more than mindless fun. Opting to discuss nothing important at all, and simply laugh, be silly and just let go.

My husband and I have a solid friendship, and it's the level we connected on when we first met and before commitment ever came around. We're each other's 'go to' person and the first person we turn to when either of us has big news to share, gossip to tell, or just need someone to listen to us bitch. One of us will call the other up and say "OMG! Guess what?! You're gonna shit when I tell you this! Are you ready?" And of course either one of our smart asses normally responds, "Well, hold on now, let me prepare for this and go sit on the toilet before you tell me." We truly have an amazing friendship and we have invested a lot of great efforts throughout our relationship to build it and keep it this way. We have the ability to lose ourselves in a world of just two best friends hanging, be it sitting outside of Starbucks and people watching, driving around aimlessly with the windows rolled down and music blaring, or lying in bed and in the dark pissing our pants laughing over some mindless joke. I said it before, and we often end up laughing so hard that it hurts and one of us ultimately peeing our pants. Okay, fine, I'm that one, because I'm the one who always ends up peeing and since I have a stupid urinating funny bone. Hey, it may not be a desirable quality to the penis and his erection...but it's a quality that my husband loves and a part of our friendship that he wouldn't trade for the world.

When a couple has the ability to connect in every way possible, it enriches the quality of the relationship and it strengthens the bond that they share. This ties into the one-stop-shop theory I spoke about earlier, and the idea of having one source that encompasses it all and provides us with ultimate fulfillment and happiness. There is no greater feeling in the world than sharing a life with someone who makes you feel loved, makes you feel beautiful, makes you laugh and makes you happy. Ultimate happiness for a man is when he can say that he has a "beautiful wife, and a best friend for life."

10. The Evolution of Love: Happily Ever After on Infinite Repeat

In this world there are so many unknowns. The laws of the universe provide us with little justification for the unexplainable forces that are sent our way. The reality is that in this lifetime, there will always be variables that we cannot control and despite our greatest efforts we will face circumstances we did not expect. As humans, any time we face something in life we have this need to rationalize things in our head in order to place comfort around it and regain order in our minds. This is exactly why we created this little thing called "fate" and this other little thing called "destiny." Anytime we face something that we can't justify in our minds, we simply say that it's left to fate and it's out of our hands. When we end up with outcomes we did not expect, we simply say that it was written by a higher power and our chosen destiny. To an extent, when it involves things in this world that we cannot control there's nothing wrong with having this belief and finding comfort in such a theory. However, this only applies to things that we truly cannot control, like a car accident, or a hereditary illness. On the other hand, neglecting to put gas in your car and stalling on the side of the road with an empty gas tank is a controllable circumstance that could have been avoided had we stopped at the gas station when that little light came on. And illness that is often brought on by poor lifestyle choices and that could have been prevented had we taken better care of ourselves. This is where many people confuse "uncontrollable" forces with that of failing to recognize the "controllable" factors that often influence outcomes. They say that ignorance is bliss, but when it comes to relationships, such an outlook will deliver anything but blissful happiness.

This is the exact reason why I say that it's important to be a realist when it comes to relationships. Yes, things can be magical and dreamy, but only when we recognize the reality of what it takes to make it this way. "Happily ever after" is a fairy tale illusion that lives in our minds and for what we dream of achieving. We have the ability to create this perception of our reality, but only when we have a true understanding towards the controllable factors that go into building such a fairy tale like relationship. When it comes to relationships, dreams can come true, but not for those who simply dream about it becoming a reality. In this world, dreams are what inspire us, and it's this inspiration that should become our motivation to action on the efforts that will influence our reality. They always say that there are no guarantees in life, and although we may not have the ability to predict our outcomes with great certainty, we do have the ability to guarantee ourselves a much more probable outcome when we take advantage of all the controllable factors available to us.

When it comes to relationships, we always go in with only the best intentions and the highest hopes for ever-lasting love and this is what acts as our inspiration. Relationships fail for many reasons, and even when two people invest great efforts to make love last a lifetime, it doesn't always pan out that way. However, relationships are built on great investments and the storybook of love is written through the tireless efforts of two people. At the onset of a relationship, a fairy tale ending is yet to be determined…and ultimately is determined by each and every interaction, action, reaction, effort and investment that each partner puts forth and into the union that they share. Most often relationships fail because people don't think that it will fail, or that failure is a potential reality. They are blinded by their perceptions of reality. Quite often when people find true love, they feel as though they have unlocked the code and tapped into that pot of gold. With tunnel-like vision they fast track towards that finish line with only one thing in mind.

Much of this is human nature, and people often don't realize the importance of being a realist when it involves all the touchy feely emotions of love. We endure years of dating all the wrong dick heads, and when we finally land a great dick with a good head on his shoulders, we sometimes have this sense of entitlement. We feel we've put in our time and have earned ever-lasting love. Everlasting love is never earned, and it's something that we must always continue to strive towards. It's this very sense of entitlement that causes people to become unaccepting of failure. We equate stages in courtship with successes of securing our keep and reaching the ultimate destination and stage of commitment and marriage.

Once this ultimate goal is achieved, people often feel a sense of accomplishment, and think they can rest.

I always say that security and comfort should rightfully be enjoyed, but never taken for granted. There's no denying that it feels good to enjoy the fruits of our labor, but it's important to remain humble and of the mindset that a relationship is a privilege. The reason why many people have a hard time seeing a relationship in this way is because of that sense of entitlement. Marriage is no different than the privilege of having a driver's license, and when we stop obeying the rules of the road and simply do as we please, we risk losing our license. There may be no such thing as having a marriage certificate suspended, but it does become invalid when people stop investing in their relationships. The best way to ensure that a relationship lasts is to recognize the reality of how delicate it is and how easily it can be lost. Marriage is not an entitlement earned through rite of passage. It's a privilege, one that we are humbly honored to be granted each and every day.

A marriage certificate is not a free pass and passport that we pull out anytime we need to exercise our rights and certify our security. How should a relationship be viewed by two people? Each and every day two people make a conscious choice to stay in their union for one another day. Signing up for one more day of love and celebration, happiness and commitment. A marriage should not be viewed as a whole, or an infinite period of time. A successful relationship is one where two people see it as one day at a time. Every day they will each invest their greatest efforts to secure one more tomorrow. Keeping with this mindset is what allows days to turn to weeks, weeks to months and years, and ultimately a lifetime of happily ever after. Our relationship motto should always be: ***"Success never sleeps and greatness never takes a break."***

The picture that I paint in the pages of this book is based on the idea that a woman should invest her greatest efforts into learning all there is to know about a male partner and investing great efforts to fulfill his needs and grant him happiness. Now, without analyzing the entire theory and process of how this pays itself forward for a woman, many women may quickly raise a vagina brow at such a concept. The thought of "why should a man be placed as such a priority in the relationship? How about a woman's needs? It should be about a woman not a man." Actually, it's both! Neither a man nor a woman should take precedence in a relationship. It should be equally about a man and a woman. However, when a woman makes the man a priority, and a man makes the woman a priority, they share equal importance at the highest level possible.

There is a reason why we walked into this relationship with this man. We have identified him as someone who can fulfill our unique needs, ones that we cannot fill for ourselves. This is why we're here right? If we were a self-service being with the ability to provide ourselves with ultimate fulfillment, we wouldn't seek out companionship. Why the hell would a self-sufficient vagina even bother putting herself out there, and enduring all the tireless efforts of doing the tango with that often puzzling penile character if we didn't have to? It's because we have a need for him and his unique offerings that only he can supply us with. We can't do it for ourselves, so we should let him do his job. His job is to fulfill our needs, and our job is to fulfill his. A woman shouldn't interfere with that process or try to manage the penis on how to do his job. If two people are busy working on one project, who's manning the other station? The vagina needs to stay at her penis post! Everyone serves a purpose in a relationship, and when we focus on doing our part and doing it right we can proudly say that we had a hand in the finished product. If a woman doesn't have faith in the penis executing his job properly, then she picked herself a poor candidate for the job.

Assuming that our vaginas are good pickers, a woman must have faith in her partner's ability to bring the goods. Let him do his part, and she can focus on hers. A smart vagina recognizes a good opportunity when she sees one, and it's in the theory that such efforts and energy is contagious. When a partner feels as though he is a priority in the relationship and he's provided with a great sense of happiness, he is motivated to reciprocate and partake in all the positive energy and efforts. This is based on the simple principles and psychology of a positive rewards system. Good behavior is rewarded, and this prompts us to continue the behaviors that keep providing us with positive rewards. When we are most happy, we are most attentive and the most motivated. If this is built successfully in a relationship, one where a woman invests all her efforts into a man, and he does the same, it will set the positive cycle into motion. As I mentioned earlier, a man knows himself best and nothing replaces the value of going straight to the source. Just the same, a woman knows herself best and it's her job to teach a partner about her unique needs and what she requires to achieve fulfillment and happiness. The vagina is never at a loss for words when it comes to voicing her needs, and all you have to do is give him the tools to help make this happen. The only requirement at that point is to continue in all the very same efforts that set it in motion, as these are the things that will keep the relationship propelling forward in the same reliable fashion.

Keeping the momentum in a successful relationship requires a realist mindset at all times. It's about recognizing the realities, looking beyond the immediate moment and understanding how we can pay it forward in our favor in the long run. Understanding the realities and risks of what could happen should we not continue to invest in the same manner, and always using this as a marker and reminder to maintain such efforts. They say that fear is the best motivator, and where there is fear of losing something there is great motivation to keep us from losing it. Does this mean that a woman should live in constant fear that she can lose her relationship at any time? No, of course not. The whole wonderful purpose of commitment is the comfort and security it brings. However, being mindful of the delicacy of the relationship and recognizing the risks of losing it should our good efforts cease. People enter into relationships for fulfillment and happiness, and people are motivated to stay in relationships that continue to provide them with such fulfillment and happiness. What's the motivation if there's little fulfillment and little happiness? Not much motivation at all, and the notion that a commitment was made is a foolish one. Commitment is based on two people committing to sign on for what is in place at the time they sign on. When we sign on with a cell phone carrier, we agree to pay monthly dues in exchange for promised service. If the phone company cuts off service, would you keep paying your monthly bill?

Okay, I know that this conversation is starting to sound like it's headed in the opposite direction of success. However, it's important to give those vaginas a reality check once in a while, and remain equally mindful of where we want to see ourselves and where we never want to find ourselves. With eyes wide open, we can happily move forward with a good mindset and go on to enjoy love and happiness. Smart and prudent business people know to look at all the risks prior to making investments. They know how to make sound business decisions and they know what it takes to make a business succeed. You and I are those vagina CEOs in our relationships. We are smart enough to know how to keep a level head, look ahead to all the benefits and risks and place ourselves on a trajectory towards success and happiness. It really comes down to our mindset and our outlook towards the relationship and what we are trying to achieve.

This is the very mindset that I took on many years ago. My sole inspiration and motivation is not based on "what I want" but what I don't want. I know, it sounds like I have my vagina on ass- backwards… but hear me out for a moment. For years, I did what many others do, and I chased all the things I wanted in a relationship. I did what I felt were all the right things, but what I lacked was the right mindset. Until one day I found myself divorced and deeply discouraged. It wasn't until I met a guy, who I now call my wonderful husband, that I began to see things much differently. He had all the magical makings of what I wanted in a man, and I really wanted it to work. I told myself, "self…," (yes I talk to my vagina often…you should try it, it's therapeutic)…I said, "Self, you know where you have come from. You have seen failure and you have seen many attempts at happiness with what you thought were the right investments, but came to learn from those mistakes. Knowing where you've been, and the things that got you there… You will learn from those mistakes and you will not make the same ones again." My motivation was in the idea that I knew where I wanted to be, and where I didn't want to be…which was back in the same failing cycle that I had always found myself in. For once I was going to stop listening to society for how things ought to be and how everyone else is doing it. I was so done with those idiots and all their 'society says' nonsense and I was ready to try things my own way.

Now, I know this may be a bad analogy, but stay with me… when you're cheating on a test and you're cheating off of someone who's only pulling a 50% average in that class, you can't expect to Ace that class. If the odds already suck, then it would make sense to study on your own and achieve a way better grade. Knowing that I never wanted to fail at love ever again, I vowed that each and every day I would invest in buying myself one more tomorrow with this great man. The efforts that I put forth today will afford me security for tomorrow and tomorrow I will work on securing the day that follows and so forth. From the very first day, and up to today, I wake each morning and I ask myself "Self, what can I do today to show my husband my appreciation for him being in my life? How can I celebrate him today?" And at the very least, I vow to do one thing each day that honors my husband and the commitment he has made to me and this relationship. Quite honestly, some days it's a simple text message professing my love, other days it may be something more elaborate like giving him a foot rub or massage. And some days I pull out all the stops, suiting up in those sexy heels, throwing down those vagina magic tricks and reminding him of all the reasons why his ass signed on to this relationship and all the greatness I bring to it and to his life. And just to make sure that all my efforts are up to date and meeting his current needs, I will often ask my husband if there's anything he needs and if there's anything more I could do for his happiness. It's almost like a software update and making sure you have the latest version for optimal performance.

And just as predicted by such a happiness and positive reward cycle, my husband equally jumped on board with all the same investments from day one. Each and every day we both make the effort to show our appreciation for one another. To express our gratitude in how lucky we are to have earned the love of such a wonderful person. Our efforts and our hearts say "Thank you for picking me as the person to spend the rest of your life with, to share your happiness with and to experience all that life has to give… together and as one." I know, it sounds corny, and kind of like one of those chick flick movies, but what woman hasn't dreamt about finding a love like in *The Notebook* movie? And quite honestly thus far this is exactly what the relationship has felt like.

Actually, our relationship is more like *The Notebook* meets *Dumb and Dumber* and with some XXX flicks sprinkled in between. Hey, we gotta keep it spicy and unpredictable right? This is all a girl could ever ask for, the sort of love that you only see in movies, and yet somehow, and some way we were able to make it become our reality. You want to hear the real shit kicker in this story? Based on statistics and the failure rate for a second marriage, we once willingly took this relationship on knowing that our odds were pretty much 75% not in our favor. Crazy right? Second marriages are even at a higher rate for divorce and really only have about a 25% chance of succeeding. Based on those odds, it makes me feel like I won the penis lottery, or like I won an Academy Award. Seriously, it's moments like this that make all the years of dating Mr. Wrongs, all worthwhile. And in Academy Awards fashion, it almost makes a vagina want to give an acceptance speech: "I'd like to first and foremost thank my parents, because without them I wouldn't be here today. Thanks for forgoing the use of a condom in that moment of lust, and for not opting on a quickie blow job on the day I was conceived. I'd like to thank my ex-boyfriend Mark, who broke up with me in 10th grade. And I'm sorry for flushing your goldfish down the toilet, after we broke up. That was pretty immature of me. Oh and sorry for setting up that profile of you on that Gay Dating website after you dumped me….but hey, look at the bright side, who knew that I would help you come out of the closet in the years that followed and that both of us would find husbands?!. Funny how life works out…"

'Happily Ever After is not about the destination or ending… it's about the story and the journey in itself'

Okay, jokes aside… I always tell couples, that when it comes to their efforts and investments, the quotient to maintaining a successful relationship is found in the exact same variables and formulation that went into building that union. When a relationship is new, people are always motivated to invest their greatest efforts and to celebrate the new love they have found. It's no different than baking a pie and if you keep to the recipe and put in the exact same ingredients, you'll always end up with an award winning pie. That's assuming that you don't bake it for too long, because you could burn that shit and then it won't be the same. You get the idea. As women we often miss out on a valuable opportunity to truly fulfill a partner's needs because we see our emotional needs as having precedence over a man's. Men are often seen as self-sufficient and masculine, and as not having big emotional needs or vulnerabilities. Earlier we discussed the idea of the "emotional penis" and how men rely on their sexuality and sex to gain emotional fulfillment. This is where many women miss out on this opportunity because they don't recognize this need. The reality is that a man needs all the same things that a woman needs, it's just that he achieves fulfillment in his own unique way and expresses himself differently than a woman. Finding success means changing our approach and recognizing all of a man's unique needs and what it takes for him to achieve happiness. He doesn't want vagina style lovings and he needs unique customized penis lovings in order to be truly happy. Again, much of the emotional fulfillment is similar to a woman and it's simply expressed and achieved differently. A woman needs to recognize a man's needs as being equal to hers.

All the offerings we expect to receive from a man, we must be prepared to invest back into him. The vagina wants love and respect? He too wants to be loved and respected. The vagina wants to be fussed over and doted on and for the penis to make her feel sexy and pretty, the penis also wants the same fussing and to feel pretty…okay, maybe not that last one. It's important to view your partner's needs in the exact same way you view yours. A man is no different and sometimes he too feels vulnerable, or misunderstood. When a woman nurtures a man's emotional needs, it makes him feel accepted by the relationship. With good communication a couple is able to identify what each partner views as being most important to their happiness. You want to tap into this and invest your efforts into what makes him happy. Remember it's contagious and the energy will carry through to all areas of the relationship and provide for mutual happiness. The important thing is that you don't allow your efforts to ever fade, because when the investments fade so does the quality in the union. You must always make the time to nurture the relationship and find time to connect one on one.

The reality is that we're only human and not every day is going to be perfect, and we will fuck up and we will make vagina mistakes. The important thing is that we do our best and make every effort to invest in all the right stuff. And as I mentioned earlier, not every day is going to be an opportune one for rotating it all, work, kids, laundry, blow jobs, blah, blah, blah… When you take the time to build it right and keep it good, it gives us the comfort in knowing that each day doesn't have to be filled with magic tricks, jumping through hoops, and breathing fire balls out of your vagina. Actually, that's probably a good thing, because a fire breathing vagina is something that any guy's balls really has no interest in. I mean, he may be kinky and all, but toasting his left testicle is nothing like toasting marshmallows…. and trust me when I say that it taste nothing like it either. Not that I would know, I'm just making an educated vagina guess….

On a serious note, even when we see our relationship as being a great one, there's always an opportunity to make it even greater. Take the time to really improve your communication in the relationship and make it even better. Evaluate and re-evaluate often and never stop talking about the relationship. The goal is to achieve a balanced relationship that also meet our needs, and since we are already pretty well versed in our vagina knowledge, our focus has been on a man and his unique male needs. I seriously can't stress this enough, about the benefits to a woman taking the time to customize her approach in the relationship and to love a man in the way in which he needs to be loved. All a man could ever ask for is to find a relationship that is accepting of his unique male identity and one that allows him to simply be himself. When a man finds this in a woman, this is what becomes her greatest security.

The penis is no fool, and when he finds one source that brings it all, he locks in and remains loyal to the hand (and vagina) that feeds him. His ass isn't going anywhere, and you couldn't shake his penis if you tried. Okay, well you can actually shake his penis, and he'd probably really like that…but you know what I'm trying to say…. When a man finds anything and everything he could ever ask for, all in one woman he has found heaven on earth and locks in for life. That fucker ain't going anywhere! Okay, that's a bit cocky… let's tone it down a notch…

Remember, we are humble vaginas. I always try to keep a humble vagina mindset because it helps keep me on my toes and at the top of my vagina game. I like to think of the relationship like a boat out in the ocean. And I must rely on this boat to last me for many years to come. If I take care of my boat, then we stay afloat, safe and dry. If I don't take care of it, the boat may corrode, giving way to a hole. The penis may like holes but this is not that type of hole and not a good thing because the boat will start to fill with water. This is representative of the relationship falling apart and in mayday mode. Eventually the boat will sink and we will be swimming in deep shark infested waters, trying to stay together, and stay alive. I'm no fool, and there ain't no way I'm losing this big ass fish I caught and man I landed…one that I invested so much time in training and molding to my vagina liking. When we take good care of our penis boat, we have the comfort in knowing that there's never any risk of a shark (aka bitch) coming along and eating our penis… No way! I'm the only bitch who gets to eat this penis! Wait, that came out wrong…okay maybe it didn't. Anyways, I keep a tight ship, and I've worked too hard to come to this place in my life. My husband brings so much greatness to my life, and loves me more than any other person has ever loved me. There is no way that I am willing to let my ship sink…and with my vagina as captain and at the stern of this ship, I will ensure that it keeps on sailing right on into the sunset. Okay, enough penis fishing tales, I'm sure you get the idea.

It's about keeping the magic by keeping it unpredictable, and when he least expects it hit him with an epic vagina dose and rock his penis socks off (yes, they all wear socks and some of them don't take those damn things off during sex) An epic vagina makes that shit happen and puts it on infinite repeat! Thankfully, we have just what it takes, especially since we just concluded our journey in this book and we are now officially full pledged epic vaginas! There's no time waste. Remember, success never sleeps…so grab those super capes and someone pass us a penis STAT! Okay, maybe now's not a good time, especially if you're at work. It's kind of awkward if you ask to borrow your boss' penis for our pep rally. So put that thing on ice and wait until you can get your hand on your own penis…I mean the one in your relationship.

Make sure that you and your partner take the time to complete the exercise in the next chapter. It's a great way to delve into some candid conversations about sex and the relationship. Hey, you never know and you may find out new things about one another and embark on new sexplorations. Just be sure to thoroughly discuss new ideas before you try them out, because you don't want to risk any misfires or injuries. Remember, it's all fun and games until someone loses a banana in their vagina, or loses a testicle (after he already lost the other one in last week's mishap) I mean, the banana may eventually come out, but I know for certain that balls don't just screw back on so he'd be screwed. Okay, I'm done talking about penis and vagina.

Well, it's been fun my fellow epic vagina sister, I hope you have found some inspiration to take back to your relationship. And before my vagina finally shuts up, I'll leave you with this... Happily ever after is not destination but a journey. A great relationship and love story is a never-ending tale of "once upon a times" and "happily ever afters" on infinite repeat. And also an endless amount of stupendous blow jobs...sorry, my husband made me add that in there. All of a sudden he's an expert on men.

THE END...Wait...

Penis.

Okay, *THE END*.

Appendix

Toolbox: Penis Pliers and Vagina Vice Grips

<u>The Golden Rules of Epic Vagina Sisterhood:</u>

I always strive to be the hostess with the mostess, and I like to send my fellow epic vagina sisters off with a little parting gift. The best way to preserve your epic aura is to refresh your positive mindset on a regular basis. Use this as your daily affirmations and any time you need a little vagina lift.

1. Maintain a positive outlook: Remember, the laws of attraction: we attract circumstances that mirror our outlook. Place positive words in your sentences, and banish any negative vocabulary.
2. Nurture yourself: become the primary caregiver of your feelings, and don't rely on others.

3. Be real and be true. Speak your truth, find your voice and don't feel apologetic for doing so.
4. Make yourself accountable. Own up to commitments you make for yourself and don't flake on "you."
5. Enhance your self-perception: perception is everything, and you must believe in your worth.
6. Do a social detox: surround yourself with only positive people who raise you up, and distance yourself from those who bring toxins into your life. Keep your inner circle tight and right!
7. Forgive yourself: don't be hard on yourself, and allow yourself forgiveness. No one is perfect, so don't always expect perfection from yourself.
8. Embrace your imperfections: find beauty in even your flaws because they make you unique.
9. Celebrate yourself: find frequent opportunities to recognize your greatness and pat that vagina on the back daily.
10. Start working towards how and what you want to be: take small steps in achieving even the biggest dreams. When you start to believe, it will start to happen.
11. Stop making excuses: stop finding reasons to place blame elsewhere and stop procrastinating. Replace excuses with actions.
12. Stop expecting the world from yourself. You are only human, and only one person.
13. Accept your successes and your failures: don't mourn your failures and instead celebrate your successes.
14. Stop measuring your worth by comparing yourself to others: no two people are the same and there is no set standard for what defines greatness.
15. Don't beat yourself up over the things you cannot control, instead place your efforts towards the things you can control.

16. Stop looking back: don't harp on what has passed, focus on today and what tomorrow will bring.
17. Become your biggest fan: when we believe in ourselves and celebrate our greatness, those around us too will believe and join in the celebration.
18. Learn how to say no and don't over extend yourself: saying yes all the time and failing to keep up only creates stress.
19. Learn to let go: don't hold on to resentment or ill feelings, it will only eat away at your happiness.
20. Do something each day that feeds your mind, body and soul: take a walk, write a journal, drink a healthy shake, or simply sit on the couch with some popcorn and watch trashy reality shows while flipping through gossip magazines (Hey, sometimes guilty pleasures are the best therapy for a gal!)
21. End each day with a recap of your awesomeness: each night before bed, have a talk with yourself and remind yourself what made you so awesome today.

Remember, in a world of many, you may be only one woman...but you're the one dynamic woman who encompasses it all, and that makes all the difference in his world.

Prioritizing Love Between the Sheets: Sex Assessment for Couples

Each partner should answer the following questions individually. Once completed, a couple can compare and discuss their answers together. This assessment should be completed in an environment that's free of distractions and during a time when each partner is in a good frame of mind. Taking this survey right after your coveted penis forgot to put the toilet seat down and replace the cap on the toothpaste tub may have an affect on your perception towards that forgetful wanker. So mental clarity is important, as is the need to be completely honest in your answers. This provides the most benefits and it helps ensure that your assessments are an accurate reflection of how you view the overall sexual relationship. This is only meant to be used as a guide and to help initiate candid discussions on sex. After collectively reviewing your assessments, the responsibility is on you and your partner to keep the lines of communication open and the sex dialogue constantly flowing.

Using the scale below, score each of the following statements as it pertains to how you view your sexual relationship (**"5"** being a consistently true statement and an accurate reflection of your relationship and **"1"** being least true and unreflective of your relationship):

5	4	3	2	1
Strongly Agree	Agree	Somewhat Agree	Somewhat Disagree	Disagree

- I'm happy with the communication on sex in our relationship. ___
- I feel as though I can tell my partner anything. ___
- My partner is supportive of my sexual needs. ___
- My partner makes me feel comfortable to speak candidly about sex. ___
- Kissing during sex is important to me. ___

- Foreplay is important to me. ___
- I feel comfortable in the overall sexual relationship. ___
- My partner makes me feel comfortable during sex. ___
- I am happy and content with my current sex life. ___
- I'm content with how often my partner and I have sex. ___
- I'm content with the amount/type of
- foreplay we have during sex. ___
- I'm happy with the amount of orgasms I experience from sex. ___
- I'm happy with the variety in our sex life. ___
- I'm content with my partner's efforts in initiating sex. ___
- My partner makes me feel sexy. ___
- My partner makes me feel desirable. ___
- I have a healthy sex drive and a frequent desire to have sex ___
- My partner has a healthy sex drive and a frequent desire to have sex ___
- My partner expresses an interest to have sex with me. ___
- My sexual relationship is supportive of my sexual interests. ___
- Sometimes I wish my partner's penis was bigger… Okay fine, I'm just kidding. Don't answer this for real, especially if you're the partner with the penis…where were we?

Choose the answer that best describes you:

The thought of my partner and I engaging in a threesome with someone else:

a. Infuriates me
b. Excites me
c. Sounds cool, but some things are better left to fantasy

If you had to choose only one of the following types of sex play:

a. Rose petals, kissing and a romantic, Lionel Ritchie love-making session
b. Sensual and carnal kissing and two sweaty bodies having erotic lust-filled sex
c. Lights on, unleashed and uninhibited kinky sex topped with dirty talk

Choose a theme that you find most appealing:

a. No frills: nothing but birthday suits and just two naked bodies
b. Simple and sexy, a little lace lingerie goes a long way
c. Dress up all the way: naughty nurse, naughtier school girl and misbehaved masseuse

When it comes to dirty talk between the sheets, do you prefer:

a. Less talk and more walk (like a penis/vagina walk-a-thon)
b. Moans and groans mixed with a few kinky verbal exchanges
c. The dirtier the better! Naughty sex narration is hot!

Answer the following questions with a writen statement/explanation:

1. What's your ultimate sexual fantasy of all time? (This can be something that you've yet to experience, or have experienced, even if it was in a past relationship):

2. What is one aspect of your current sexual relationship that you're not willing to part with? (this can be frequency, oral sex, role play, cuddling, etc):

3. What is one aspect of your sexual relationship that you could do without (something that you may not be crazy about and have

never voiced your feelings. You don't have to have an answer for this if you're happy with it all!):

4. Name the most memorable sexual experience you and your partner have ever shared (why was it so memorable and what is it that you enjoyed so much?):

Finish the following statements as it pertains to sex:

I love when my partner (this can involve a type of play, talking dirty, etc):

I wish my partner would:

The best part of our sex life is:

Some thing(s) I'm curious to try in the bedroom is:

The sexiest body part on my partner is:

Remember: The purpose of this test is to compare notes and see how you two measure up in these various areas. A similar ranking between the two of you does show good compatibility, but it doesn't imply the opposite if there are differences in your answers. It may simply be an indication that the relationship can benefit from a more open and candid communication style. Having frequent talks about sex allows a couple to stay engaged in the sexual relationship and it helps strengthen the bond that they share. The goal is to promote conversation and talk about your individual comforts, your curiosities and your overall sexual needs. This guide will also help ensure that the sexual relationship remains in good standing, and that each partner maintains their happiness in the sexual relationship. It's important to do these assessments often and as a way to keep up with each partner's changing needs.

Sextionnaire: Sexual Compatibility Quiz for Couples

The following is a quiz that you and your partner can each take individually and once completed you two can compare and discuss your answers. You'll want to take this quiz when you're relaxed and in a non-sexual environment, as this ensures accurate and organic answers (because in a sex-infused state of mind, your overzealous vagina may write a check that you have no interest in cashing come morning.) Your answers should be based not only on your current relationship, but also past sexual experiences/partners. It's important to be completely honest when filling this out. Remember even if individual interests and comforts don't coincide with one another, there are no right or wrong answers and achieving the right results comes from being supportive. The goal is to identify shared interests, to develop a comprehensive understanding for a partner's sexuality, gain insight into what makes them tick and how their sex brain works. You can access a printable version of this quiz on my website (www.marieisabelle.com).

For each of the following items, check either **"Yes"** or **"No"** based on if you have or haven't already experienced it. Also, check **"Willing to do/try"** if it's something that you tried and you liked, or have yet to try, but are open to exploring it further. Alternatively, you should leave this third column blank if you feel that it's totally not your cup of tea. Once you've completed the quiz, you can tally up your score based on the following point(s) value: Give yourself **(1) One point for each "Yes," (1) point for each "Willing to Do/Try" and (0) Zero points for each "No."**

Sex Act	YES	NO	Willing to Do/Try
1. Morning sex	_____	_____	_____
2. Nooners	_____	_____	_____
3. Biting	_____	_____	_____
4. Sensual massage	_____	_____	_____
5. Sex with the lights on	_____	_____	_____
6. Candles	_____	_____	_____
7. Lingerie	_____	_____	_____
8. High heels	_____	_____	_____
9. Giving oral sex	_____	_____	_____
10. Receiving oral sex	_____	_____	_____
11. Whipped cream	_____	_____	_____
12. Handcuffs	_____	_____	_____
13. Blindfolds	_____	_____	_____
14. Anal sex	_____	_____	_____
15. Anal stimulation/play	_____	_____	_____
16. Spanking	_____	_____	_____
17. Sex in shower	_____	_____	_____
18. Watching porn	_____	_____	_____
19. Making home movies	_____	_____	_____
20. Taking naughty pics	_____	_____	_____
21. Phone sex	_____	_____	_____
22. Sexting	_____	_____	_____
23. Bondage	_____	_____	_____
24. Watching partner masturbate	_____	_____	_____
25. Masturbating for partner	_____	_____	_____
26. BDSM activities	_____	_____	_____
27. Hot candle wax	_____	_____	_____
28. Exhibitionism	_____	_____	_____
29. Voyeurism	_____	_____	_____
30. Feet/Toes	_____	_____	_____
31. Hair pulling	_____	_____	_____
32. Rough sex	_____	_____	_____

33. Light pain _____ _____ _____
34. Moderate pain _____ _____ _____
35. Fantasy roleplay _____ _____ _____
36. Dirty talk during sex _____ _____ _____
37. Sex toys _____ _____ _____
38. Exotic striptease dance _____ _____ _____
39. Sex props/Sex swing _____ _____ _____
40. Stripper pole in bedroom _____ _____ _____
41. Sex during menstrual period _____ _____ _____
42. Dominant role during sex _____ _____ _____
43. Submissive role during sex _____ _____ _____
44. Strip clubs / lap dances _____ _____ _____
45. Sex in front of mirrors _____ _____ _____

Coming Together and Comparing Notes

The highest possible score is 90 points, but this is irrelevant to the overall picture and there are no bonus points for scoring the highest. The importance is in how well your individual results match up, and the spread between the two scores. The closeness in numbers is reflective of good compatibility in sexual interests and comforts. If the difference between your individual scores is:

Less Than a 10 Point Spread:

A pretty solid sexual match. You two have a high level of sexual compatibility and share a similar mindset towards the same interests and your sexual comforts. Sexploration comes with ease and skies the limit for where you two take this sex-ship.

Within a 20 point Spread:

You and your partner have good sexual compatibility and like-minded sexual comforts allow for sexual exploration in the relationship. Take full advantage of this by comparing the areas where you two share similar interests and discuss all the endless possibilities of exploring one another's fantasies.

A Spread Within the 30-40 Point Range:
This may seem like a big differential, but remember to always focus on the positive. You and your partner do have sexual compatibility in many areas and these are the things that you should look to explore. Candid discussions will allow you to compare each item and identify your strengths and areas of opportunity. Keep in mind, that perhaps one of you is simply lacking that little added comfort that will give you that extra push to step out and embark on sexual explorations together. Communication is key, and it's important to always come out and ask for what you need, because the quality of your sexual relationship depends on your comforts.

A Spread of 50 Points or More:
All is not lost! The reality is that, yes, this is an indication that the sexual compatibility is low in the sexual relationship. However, this alone isn't an accurate form of assessing compatibility. This could be an indication of a lack of communication in the sexual relationship. Couples who lack open and candid communication on sex end up missing out on truly getting to know one another. Sometimes when you improve the quality of discussions on sex, you start to discover many things about your partner you never knew. Talking about sex is a great way to build compatibility and to develop an intimate bond that helps nurture comforts. There's great value in the chapters where we thoroughly covered sex communication and that will help a couple develop the skills required to help get them on track. Remaining positive is key and you can start by exploring the few things you two do share in common, as one exploration often leads to another new discovery.

Again, keep in mind that this is only meant to be used as a guide and to initiate candid discussions on sex. There's never any shame in recognizing an opportunity to work on the relationship, even if it means reaching out for professional help and therapy. Sometimes a neutral party allows for organization and provides assistance in building the best possible version of yourself and your relationship. The list above is only a small general sample of potential sexual interests. It's definitely not gospel and you're never limited to any one set of ideas. Feel free to come up with your own sexy list for you and your partner to quiz one another with your own kinky variations.

Remember: Sexual tastes and curiosities are constantly evolving and placing this type of activity on rotation ensures that you never miss out on an opportunity to enhance the sexual relationship. And this is uber important because… a couple that plays together, stays together! Trust me, when it involves sex, this is one time that the penis is not complaining about all the extra homework. And to help keep things in check, revisit this "Penis Pliers and Vagina Vice Grips" chapter often and continue all the stupendous possibilities and ways in which the penis and vagina can do naked yoga together. Just be sure to always play smart and stay safe…because the last thing you need is to find out that handcuffs don't always make the best ball/cock ring and that you require a real pair of pliers to free his strangulated left testicle. ***Remember, it's all fun and games until someone loses a testicle, or someone pulls their vagina.***

Made in the USA
Columbia, SC
07 August 2024

39719764R00176